South Dakota

South Dakota

T. D. Griffith
Photography by Paul Horsted

COMPASS AMERICAN GUIDES
An imprint of Fodor's Travel Publications

Compass American Guides: South Dakota

Editor: Sarah Felchlin
Compass Editorial Director: Daniel Mangin
Compass Creative Director: Fabrizio La Rocca
Compass Senior Editor: Kristin Moehlmann
Photo Editor and Archival Researcher: Melanie Marin
Map Design: Mark Stroud, Moon Street Cartography
Production House: Twin Age Ltd., Hong Kong
Editorial Production: David Downing

Cover photo (Mount Rushmore): Paul Horsted

Third Edition

ISBN: 1–4000–1243–0
ISSN: 1542–3298

The details in this book are based on information supplied to us at press time, but changes occur all the time, and the publisher cannot accept responsibility for facts that become outdated or for inadvertent errors or omissions.

Compass American Guides, 1745 Broadway, New York, NY 10019

PRINTED IN CHINA
10 9 8 7 6 5 4 3 2 1

For Charles and Patricia, who taught me
that any road is negotiable at the proper speed.

C O N T E N T S

Literary Extracts

Topical Essays

Maps

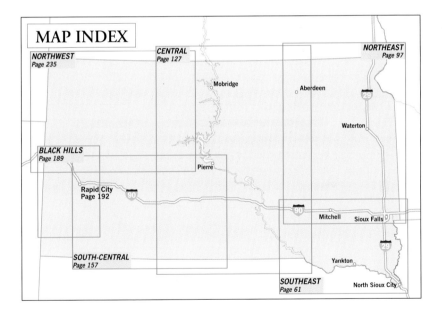

Facts About South Dakota

The Mount Rushmore State

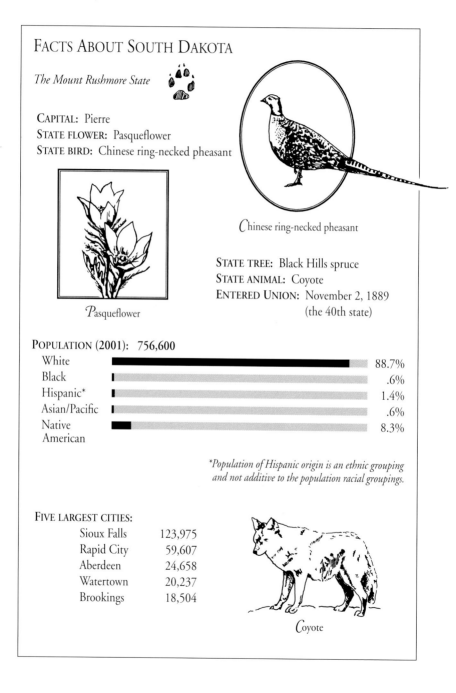

CAPITAL: Pierre
STATE FLOWER: Pasqueflower
STATE BIRD: Chinese ring-necked pheasant

Chinese ring-necked pheasant

Pasqueflower

STATE TREE: Black Hills spruce
STATE ANIMAL: Coyote
ENTERED UNION: November 2, 1889
(the 40th state)

POPULATION (2001): 756,600

White	88.7%
Black	.6%
Hispanic*	1.4%
Asian/Pacific	.6%
Native American	8.3%

Population of Hispanic origin is an ethnic grouping and not additive to the population racial groupings.

FIVE LARGEST CITIES:
Sioux Falls	123,975
Rapid City	59,607
Aberdeen	24,658
Watertown	20,237
Brookings	18,504

Coyote

*B*lack Hills spruce

ECONOMY:
Principal industries:
agriculture, tourism, manufacturing, services
Principal manufactured goods:
food and kindred products, machinery,
electric and electronic equipment
Chief crops (2002):
corn, oats, wheat, sunflowers, soybeans,
sorghum
Per capita income (1999): $17,562
Tourism: Travelers' impact $1.66 billion

GEOGRAPHY:
Size: 77,121 square miles
Highest point: 7,242 feet at Harney Peak, Pennington County
Lowest point: 962 feet at Big Stone Lake, Roberts County

CLIMATE:
Highest temperature recorded: 120°F (49°C) at Gann Valley on
                                  July 3, 1936
Lowest temperature recorded: -58°F (-50°C) at McIntosh on
                                  February 17, 1936

Wettest place:
29.99" annual rainfall at
Deadwood in Lawrence County

Driest place:
12.29" annual rainfall at
Ludlow in Harding County

FAMOUS SOUTH DAKOTANS:
Sparky Anderson ◆ Tom Brokaw ◆ "Calamity Jane" ◆ Crazy Horse
Oscar Howe ◆ Cheryl Ladd ◆ Dr. Ernest O. Lawrence
George McGovern ◆ Billy Mills ◆ Al Neuharth ◆ Sitting Bull

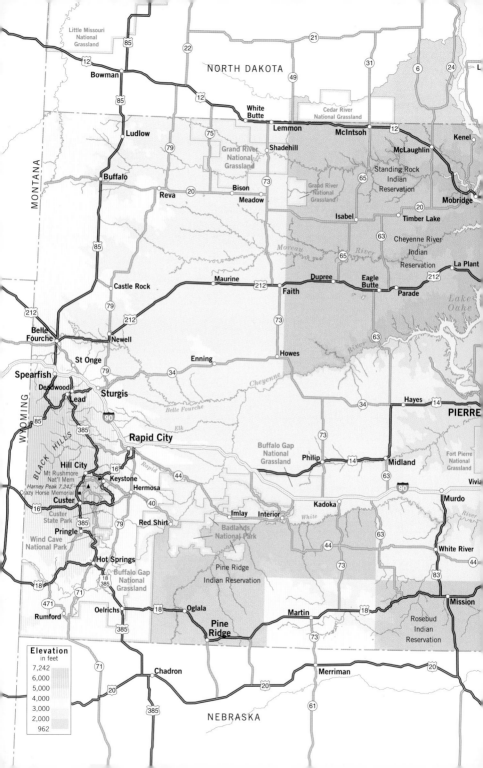

SOUTH DAKOTA

0   25   50 Miles
0   25   50   75 Kilometers

NORTH DAKOTA

MINNESOTA

NEBRASKA

IOWA

Ashley
Ellendale
Leola
Eureka
Mound City
Bowdle
Gettysburg
Faulkton
Ipswich
Aberdeen
Groton
Britton
Sisseton
Lake Traverse Indian Reservation
Big Stone City
Milbank
Webster
Watertown
Clear Lake
Doland
Clark
Redfield
Bonilla
Miller
Highmore
Blunt
Washington
Wolsey
Huron
De Smet
Arlington
Brookings
Crow Creek Indian Reservation
Stephan
Fort Thompson
Lake Sharpe
Lower Brule Indian Reservation
Kennebec
Wessington Springs
Woonsocket
Howard
Madison
Chamberlain
Dell Rapids
Garretson
Mitchell
Salem
Sioux Falls
Brandon
Bridgewater
Parkston
Lennox
Canton
Freeman
Dixon
Platte
Winner
Gregory
Armour
Lake Andes
Maxwell
Viborg
Midway
Yankton Indian Reservation
Avon
Tyndall
Yankton
Vermillion
Santee Indian Reservation
North Sioux City
Sioux City
Elk Point

Lake Traverse
Big Stone Lake (ele 962)
Missouri River
Lake Francis Case
Lewis and Clark Lake
Big Sioux River
James River

■ AUTHOR'S ACKNOWLEDGMENTS

THERE IS NOT ROOM ENOUGH on these pages to thank the South Dakotans—friends and strangers—who lent me support, and sometimes directions, during the months of traveling and writing. In a state where you're a newcomer unless your grandparents are buried in the local cemetery, I was welcomed and assisted time and again. Of my many helpers, several stand out: Jim Kuehn, former editor of the *Rapid City Journal;* Rex Alan Smith, a wonderful writer and friend; Sheri Sponder, a research librarian with her finger on the pulse of South Dakota; historians Keith and Bonita Cochran; and Larry Atkinson, whose good nature is cherished and admired. Others helped as well, whether in tracking down leads or pointing me in the direction of the next great South Dakota vignette: Bonnie Krueger, Deb Fowler, Paul Putz, Gordon Garnos, Jerry Olson, Terry Reetz, Susan Edwards, Dee Dee Rapp, Kristen Brost, Robb DeWall, Jim Popovich, Bill Honerkamp, and the entire staffs of the South Dakota Department of Tourism, the Rapid City Public Library, the South Dakota Cultural Heritage Center, and the Adams Museum of Deadwood. Commendations are due the editors of the original edition of this book, Kit Duane and Julia Dillon, and my original publishers, Chris Burt and Tobias Steed. It is also certain that this book would not have been fit for public consumption without the support of friends David and Nancy Bertocchi, Louie Lalonde, and photographer Paul Horsted, whose brilliant eye and camera have focused on the heart of this great state. And finally, my loving wife Nyla, whose gentle nudging is reflected in the copyright date, as well as in every page.

National Park Service workers inspecting cracks at Mount Rushmore descend the face of Thomas Jefferson.

INTRODUCTION

Wander through South Dakota today and you'll explore a land that has been home to great Indian warriors, French fur traders, prairie settlers, and gold prospectors. Today, vast regions of the state remain sparsely settled, its towns often no more than meeting places for farmhands or cowpokes. Buffalo are rare now, the once-wild rivers have been tamed, and much of the state's native grassland has been replaced by crops, yet quiet South Dakota still sheepishly claims the title "America's Outback."

Driving across their state, South Dakotans can see almost too much sky, more than a hundred miles to the horizon. This landscape offers some lovely surprises—millions of acres of rugged badlands, river breaks, fertile farmland, and an emerald oasis known as the Black Hills. To truly see South Dakota, travelers must get off the interstates—the well-worn ribbons of concrete known as I-90, the 380-mile-long roadway bisecting the state east to west, and I-29, which stretches 245 miles north to south in extreme eastern South Dakota—and wander through small towns and visit numerous parklands and lakes.

The people who live here are proud of their heritage and of the livings they carve from the prairies and plains. If South Dakota has hosted some of the most colorful characters of the Old West—Sitting Bull, Calamity Jane, and Wild Bill Hickok—the state has also been home to some of the nation's most industrious and generous people. More South Dakotans are employed in agriculture than any other occupation. Nearly half of South Dakota's residents live on its 35,000 farms, and farms and ranches cover about nine-tenths of the state. Most farmers and ranchers are hospitable to a fault. On the back roads, they'll wave at you from their battered pickup trucks—and will know you're from out of town if you don't wave back. Each fall, rural South Dakotans welcome urban neighbors and tourists at fairs and festivals celebrating the state's heritage. At colorful powwows and buffalo roundups, South Dakotans recall their ancestors—the Sioux warriors, sodbusters, and frontiersmen whose pride and tenacity are trademarks of the folks you'll meet there today.

(opposite) Custer State Park flora: the prairie in full spring bloom.

(following pages) Custer State Park fauna: wild burros begging for treats. (Robert Holmes)

H   I   S   T   O   R   Y

South Dakota was, of course, for millions of years undefined by the rectangle that marks it off as the fortieth state of the Union. Its prehistory witnessed shifting climatic zones, changes in the course of the Missouri River that divides it, and the evolution of its flora and fauna. To the east of the Missouri were lowland prairies, to the west the arid sweep of the continent's dry, high plains region. Within and above the prairies evolved a complex natural life that we're only now beginning to appreciate, but most evident were its great herds of buffalo and millions of migratory birds that nested in lakes and waterways as they flew south from Alaska and north from the warm Caribbean.

Into this vast sweep of land came gradually the first humans, those prehistoric people we now define rather academically as "Paleo-Indians"—hunters whose ancestors had followed game across the land bridge of the Bering Sea from Asia and eventually, over centuries, migrated south into the American continent. By the time European explorers arrived in the area, South Dakota was peopled by the Arikara (or Ree), Cheyenne, and Sioux Indians, whose descendants inhabit South Dakota still. Magnificent horsemen and fearless warriors, they were the proud possessors of an independent life and a world they found abundant.

After the early 1600s, history as we know it began to accelerate. Explorers sent by the great European powers came to claim territory and look for commercial opportunities. Twenty-seven years after he wrote the Declaration of Independence, Thomas Jefferson, as president of the fledgling United States of America, sent American explorers Lewis and Clark to map this region in 1803. By the end of the nineteenth century, thousands of Europe's poor and America's pioneers were moving into the region, with perspectives and dreams of their own, and their ambitions clashed with those of the Sioux, Cheyenne, and Arikara. As immigrants built fences, settled towns, and often prospered, both Indian culture and the great herds of buffalo were confined and crushed.

In the twentieth century, South Dakota's history moved on with the rest of the nation's, as its citizens watched the end of the Gilded Age, suffered through the Dust Bowl, the Depression, and two world wars. In the volatile 1960s and 1970s, the Sioux, now living on reservations, began to gather strength and fight

A photograph of an unidentified Sioux tribal leader from the extensive archives at the Center for Western Studies at Augustana College in Sioux Falls.

for cultural renewal, and today they remain one of the most powerful and well-known of all America's tribes. In the late twentieth century South Dakota has emerged as a place holding fast to many of the best values embedded in the American psyche yet also adding its spark to the nation's entrepreneurial energy.

■ EARLY INDIAN ERA

Anthropologists now estimate that up to four great migrations of four very different groups of people crossed the land bridge from Asia over a period of 30,000 years and covered the North American continent. The first clear indications we have of a human presence in South Dakota are the remains of a "Paleo-Indian" who hunted in the prairies more than 9,000 years ago and was found buried with skinning knives and finely crafted spear points. This 5-foot 5-inch-tall hunter probably led buffalo "surrounds," in which the animals were prodded to stampede, then steered over the edge of a butte. That Indians were using buffalo hide to make tepees 2,500 years ago is evident from carbon-dated tepee rings from that era that can still be seen in Custer State Park. More recent Plains Villager sites dating back 1,000 years have been discovered along the Missouri and other South Dakota rivers. These people were both hunters and gardeners—planting maize, crafting earthenware ceramics, and constructing large earth-lodge towns surrounded by ditches and dirt walls to fend off enemies. Those inhabiting the fertile land near the Missouri River used bison scapulae hoes to plant maize and other plants; those farther west relied more heavily on bison hunting. Artifacts that belonged to the seminomadic Mound Builders and date about A.D. 500–800 have been uncovered in the northeastern part of the state. These people took great care in burying their dead: the body was often wrapped, and the departed's most precious possessions—fine spears, flints, tools, and hide pouches—were buried alongside in large earthen mounds.

During the millennia, Indian tribal groups ebbed and flowed across and up and down the North American continent. In most cases, tribes settled their conflicts peacefully. When warfare could not be avoided, most Plains Indians fought in ritualized battles and small ambushes, killing few people. But in A.D. 1325, near present-day Crow Creek, 500 Arikara men, women, and children were massacred in one of the most ruthless examples of pre-Columbian tribal violence in the archaeological record. Most likely feeling the pinch of increasing population and the concomitant depletion of natural resources, the attackers stormed the village, burning it and mutilating the dead. The remains were discovered and excavated on an archaeological dig by the University of South Dakota in 1978.

By 1500, the Arikara (or Ree) Indians were inhabiting the state. The Sioux (or Lakota) Indians began migrating from the Mille Lacs region of Minnesota into South Dakota in the 1700s, in turn driving the Arikara north and west. For a good 150 years the Sioux reigned supreme in the Dakotas. Organized into three major tribes (Teton, Yankton, and Santee), smaller bands, and clans or "tiyospayes," they followed strict rules of behavior that provided for the well-being of the community and the care of children. As horsemen and hunters they were unparalleled, as warriors fearless and ruthless.

Though fighting for land among themselves, by the seventeenth century many tribes were also being pressured from the east by European settlers. The British who came to Jamestown in 1607, some 250 years before pioneers moved in force

Prairie Meadows Burning *(1832), by frontier artist George Catlin.*
(Smithsonian American Art Museum)

(following pages) A stunning photograph by John Grabill of a
Brule Indian village in 1891. (Library of Congress)

into South Dakota, recorded seeing the Sioux and buffalo in the Shenandoah Valley. During those centuries, the Sioux and many other groups forged their way west, battling for living and hunting space. They would eventually be pushed aside, defeated by the superior numbers and arms of white settlers. With their demise a wild, uncompromising culture—marked by buffalo hunts and trance-inducing Sun Dances—began to fade.

■ EXPLORERS AND TRADERS

In the seventeenth and eighteenth centuries, the French sent explorers and Jesuits to plant their feet firmly on bleak bits of land and, surrounded by curious Indians who didn't understand French, to claim territory in the name of their king. It was in this spirit that, in 1743, Francois and Joseph La Verendrye claimed the region near present-day Fort Pierre in central South Dakota for Louis XV, a monarch almost 5,000 miles away who wore white wigs and satin pants and was as famous for his indolence as for his mistresses. The La Verendryes left behind a metal plate attesting to their claim, which presumably everyone else ignored.

Thirty-two years later, in 1775, Pierre Dorion, a French Canadian mountain man, came up the Missouri River from St. Louis, stopped near Yankton, and married

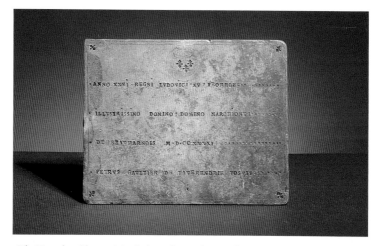

The Verendrye Plate, originally buried in 1743, was discovered by children playing on a hillside outside of Pierre in 1913. (South Dakota State Historical Society, Pierre)

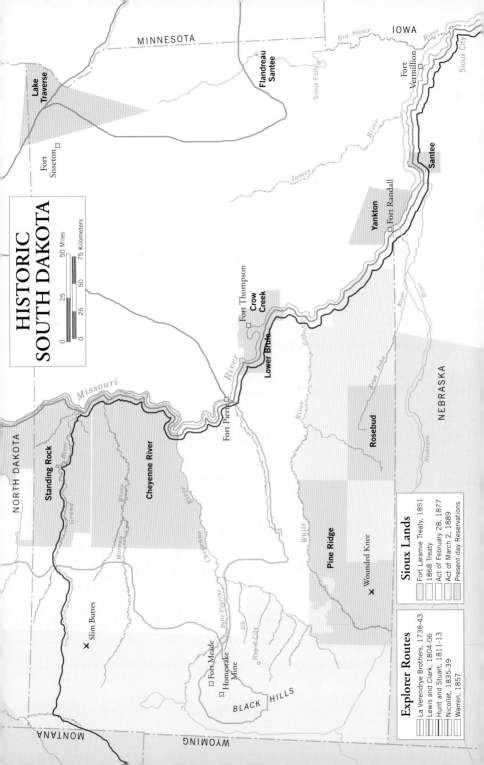

HISTORIC SOUTH DAKOTA

Scale: 0 — 25 — 50 Miles; 0 — 25 — 50 — 75 Kilometers

Sioux Lands

- Fort Laramie Treaty, 1851
- 1868 Treaty
- Act of February 28, 1877
- Act of March 2, 1889
- Present-day Reservations

Explorer Routes

- La Verendrye Brothers, 1738-43
- Lewis and Clark, 1804-06
- Hunt and Stuart, 1811-13
- Nicollet, 1835-39
- Warren, 1857

MINNESOTA

IOWA

Big Sioux River

Flandreau Santee

Sioux Falls

Sioux City

Fort Vermillion

Lake Traverse

Santee

Fort Sisseton

James River

Fort Randall

Yankton

Fort Thompson

Crow Creek

Lower Brulé

Rosebud

NEBRASKA

Niobrara River

Keya Paha River

NORTH DAKOTA

Missouri River

Fort Pierre

Standing Rock

Grand River

Moreau River

Cheyenne River

Cheyenne River

White River

Pine Ridge

× Wounded Knee

× Slim Butes

Belle Fourche

Elk

Rapid City

× Fort Meade

□ Homestake Mine

BLACK HILLS

MONTANA

WYOMING

SIOUX NATION

Sioux Indians comprise the second most populous language family north of Mexico (the largest being the Algonquian) and take their name from the largest and best-known confederacy of that group, the Sioux (or Lakota). Their name is an abbreviation of *Nadowessioux,* a French corruption of *Nadowe-is-iw*—Ojibwa for "snake," or "enemy." The Sioux in western South Dakota refer to themselves as "Lakota," or "an alliance of friends"; those in the east call themselves "Dakota."

Before their contact with non-Indians, the Sioux occupied much of the land extending west from the Mississippi and north from the Arkansas River almost to the Rocky Mountains. Those in Arkansas were first encountered by Spanish explorer Hernando de Soto in 1541. The Dakota—the Sioux tribe now in eastern South Dakota—lived on the east side of the Mississippi between the Wisconsin River and Mille Lacs; the Winnebago and other northern Sioux tribes lived in Canada, toward Lake Winnipeg, and accounts of their lives were recorded by Jesuit missionaries in the 1640s and 1650s. Another group of Sioux lived in the South, occupying parts of Virginia, Mississippi, and the Carolinas; colonial Virginians noted Sioux living in the Shenandoah Valley early in the seventeenth century.

In the first half of the eighteenth century, the Ojibwa Indians, who'd been supplied with guns by the French, forced the Dakota Sioux out of present-day Minnesota, pushing them onto the South Dakota plains. They weren't the only group that was forced to move: the Chiwere Sioux tribes split from the Winnebago and also moved toward the Missouri River; and the Siouan Mandan and Hidatsa tribes were pushed from the upper Missouri by the migrating Dakota. Yet by the end of the eighteenth century, the Sioux were at the height of their power, living on a vast tract of land covering about 80 million acres, the center of which lies in present-day South Dakota.

These many interrelated Sioux tribes did have some things in common. They were divided into bands, then into still smaller groups called "tiyospayes," extended families whose members lived together. Children, elders, and the sick were cared for by the entire tiyospaye, and decisions were left to the older, respected members. Most of the southern tribes of the western Sioux and almost all of the eastern tribes raised corn, but the Lakota and the Crow—those inhabiting the Great Plains—depended on buffalo and other game. Eastern tribes inhabited bark and mat wigwams; those on the Great Plains built earth lodges and buffalo hide tepees. The Sioux kept dogs for food and to carry babies and tepees as the tribe moved. Through their trade with the tribes of the Southwest, they acquired horses, and rode them in pursuit of buffalo and in warfare. Until a Jesuit priest, Father Eugene Buechel, compiled a grammar and dictionary in the early twentieth century, the Sioux tribes had no written language. However, among the western tribes, history and heritage were preserved through story-tellers and "winter counts"—drawings arranged in a spiral on an animal hide, one drawing for each winter. A single hide might have drawings covering 50 years or more.

More than 70,000 Sioux live in South Dakota today. The three major tribes are the **Teton,** including the Oglala, Minneconjou, Brule ("Burned Thigh"), Hunkpapa, Sihasapa, Oohenonpa (or "Two Kettle"), and Itazipcho; the **Yankton,** comprising the Yankton and Yanktonai; and the **Santee,** made up of the Sisseton, Wahpeton, Wahpekute, and Mdewakanton. There are nine Sioux tribal governments in the state, six with reservation boundaries and three without. The six with reservation boundaries are the Cheyenne River, Crow Creek, Lower Brule, Pine Ridge, Rosebud, and Standing Rock; the three without are the Flandreau Santee, Sisseton-Wahpeton, and the Yankton. Indians on these reservations hold public ceremonies or powwows, offering non-Indians a glimpse into their lives. (See the "PRACTICAL INFORMATION" CHAPTER for a listing of powwows and festivals.)

—Julia Dillon

An unidentified Sioux woman poses in full costume. (Center for Western Studies)

into the Yankton Sioux tribe. In the 1790s Jacques d'Eglise and Joseph Garreau, French Canadians in the employ of the Spanish (who were established in the Southwest and California, and off and on in Louisiana), went into Dakota territory to trade furs. Their insolence offended both the Arikara and the Sioux, and in 1794 the Spanish Missouri Company sent out an expedition, under the leadership of Jean Baptiste Truteau, a former schoolteacher, with orders to stop d'Eglise and Garreau from representing them in the territory. Truteau safely entered Indian territory, spending the winter of 1795 near the future site of Fort Randall. The company passed a year with the Arikara until the Sioux attacked the tribe in May 1796. The white men, not yet considered a threat to Indians, were let go.

By 1803, South Dakota was part of an area claimed by the French that Americans referred to as the Louisiana Territory. Thomas Jefferson, in order to protect America's western flank and its trade on the Missouri and Mississippi Rivers, offered to buy the vast wilderness from France for three cents an acre. Napoleon, needing money to finance his campaigns in Europe, agreed, and the United States was soon the owner of an 828,000-square-mile swath west of the Mississippi extending from New Orleans in the south to the Rocky Mountains and Canada. To map this new land and open it up to Americans, Jefferson asked Congress to authorize an expedition headed by Lewis and Clark. Before they undertook this journey Jefferson sent them the diary of Truteau's experience nearly 10 years prior.

■ LEWIS AND CLARK

In 1804, Meriwether Lewis, personal secretary to President Jefferson, set out to explore and map a route through the western wilderness to the Pacific Ocean. Together with his longtime friend, William Clark, he was directed to follow the Missouri River to its headwaters, hop the supposedly short divide to the Columbia River, and observe the growing British presence in the Pacific Northwest. The pair was also charged with introducing native people west of St. Louis to the concept of American government. The Corps of Discovery included 29 additional men, all of whom could contribute to the success of the expedition. Some were excellent hunters, and one played the fiddle. Another was Clark's personal servant, York,

MEETING THE SIOUX

30th of August, 1804

The fog was so thick that we could not see the Indian camp on the opposite side, but it cleared off about eight o'clock. We prepared a speech, and some presents, and then sent for the chiefs and warriors, whom we received, at twelve o'clock, under a large oak tree, near to which the flag of the United States was flying. Captain Lewis delivered a speech, with the usual advice and counsel for their future conduct. We then acknowledged their chiefs, by giving to the grand chief a flag, a medal, a certificate, with a string of wampum; to which we added a chief's coat; that is, a richly laced uniform of the United States artillery corps, and a cocked hat and red feather. One second chief and three inferior ones were made or recognized by medals, and a suitable present of tobacco, and articles of clothing. We then smoked the pipe of peace, and the chiefs retired to a bower, formed of bushes, by their young men, where they divided among each other the presents, and smoked and ate, and held a council on the answer which they were to make us tomorrow. The young people exercised their bows and arrows in shooting at marks for beads, which we distributed to the best marksmen; and in the evening the whole party danced until a late hour, and in the course of their amusement we threw among them some knives, tobacco, bells, tape, and binding, with which they were much pleased. Their musical instruments were the drum, and a sort of little bag made of buffalo hide, dressed white, with small shot or pebbles in it, and a bunch of hair tied to it. This produces a sort of rattling music, with which the party was annoyed by four musicians during the council this morning.

—The Journals of the Expedition
   of Lewis and Clark, 1804

*From the collection of the Cultural
Heritage Center, South Dakota
State Historical Society, Pierre.*

whose physical bulk, great strength, and black skin unfailingly impressed those who saw him.

Between Vermillion and Yankton, the explorers met their first Sioux and gained a Sioux interpreter—Pierre Dorion, the same French Canadian who'd come to the area more than 30 years earlier and married into the Yankton tribe.

Lewis and Clark passed fairly peaceably through South Dakota. There was one stand-off with the Teton Sioux, a belligerent tribe that by this time had pushed most of the Arikara into western South Dakota. Warned that the Tetons were known to rob traders, Lewis and Clark ordered the corps to be armed and ready to fight. The explorers and the tribe entered into negotiations lasting a few days. With the help of whiskey and a show of bluster—the explorers ordered their men to draw their swords when a besotted Teton got rowdy—Lewis and Clark managed to pass on through without violent incident.

Farther up the Missouri, the party was joined by French trader Toussaint Charbonneau and his 15-year-old wife Sacagawea, a Shoshone who'd been captured by the Blackfeet, sold as a slave to the Hidatsa Sioux, and won by the Frenchman in a gambling match. Sacagawea accompanied the expedition all the way to the Pacific.

When Lewis and Clark returned east in 1806, their journals were avidly read. Lewis had a knack for recording elegant, detailed observations. William Clark's passages were more earthy. Both were rife with misspellings. Their personalities were as different as their writing styles. Lewis, scholarly and refined, was prone to depression. During the trip, whenever he fell under a dark cloud, he stopped writing and his partner continued. Clark was personable, having a good rapport with the Indians and a knack for doctoring. When Lewis was feeling good, Clark was a slack diarist, usually just copying Lewis's meticulous notes.

Spanish explorer and entrepreneur Manuel Lisa paid close attention to Lewis and Clark's reports before leaving in 1807 for the upper Missouri valley to trade with the Indians. By 1809, Lisa had organized the fur trade between the St. Louis Fur Company and the Indians along the entire length of the Missouri River, thereby opening the way for frontier forts, pioneer settlements, and inevitable confrontations between Indians and whites. Eventually, from 1814 to 1817, Lisa served the U.S. government as sub-agent to the upper Missouri Indians—under William Clark, then superintendent of Indian Affairs in St. Louis.

■ MOUNTAIN MEN AND ARTISTS

Another fur company to make its mark on trade in South Dakota was the Rocky Mountain Fur Company, which organized trading parties in 1822 and 1823. The core of that group contains many of South Dakota's—and the Wild West's—most familiar names: James Clyman, Jedediah Smith, Thomas Fitzpatrick, Jim Bridger, Hugh Glass, Edward Rose, David Jackson, and William Sublette. Thanks to their discovery, exploration, and publicizing of Yellowstone, Jackson Hole, Salt Lake, and more, these men encouraged travel to the West—with South Dakota and the Missouri River en route.

By the early 1830s, most of the mountain men had gone west of the Dakota region, and steamboats were paddling up and down the region's rivers. In 1831, the *Yellowstone*—the first steamboat on the Missouri River—reached Fort Tecumseh (later known as Fort Pierre). Years earlier, men such as Henry Brackenridge, who published a journal of his 1811 journey with Manuel Lisa, traveled on the Missouri by keelboat. In his journal he commented, "The beauty of the scenery, this evening, exceeds any thing I ever beheld—The sky as clear as in a Chinese painting, the country delightful. . . ."

The steamboat made river travel faster and easier, and the territory began attracting more settlers, as well as other temporary visitors who came to paint, write, or study rather than fight or trap. Among these visitors was George Catlin, who spent his days on the *Yellowstone* taking notes and making somewhat romanticized sketches of the Indians and landscapes he encountered. Catlin's appreciation for the beauty of the West and his admiration for the Indians were reflected in his writing and art. He described his sorrow at the tragedy of the lives he saw disappearing before him—one entire Dakota-area tribe, the Mandans, was wiped out by smallpox contracted from fur traders.

Another traveling artist was the Swiss Karl Bodmer, who accompanied Maximilian, prince of Wied, and illustrated Maximilian's thorough and informative book *Travels in the Interior of North America*. Maximilian had served as a general in the Prussian army in the Napoleonic Wars; both he and Duke Paul Wilhelm, who recorded his travels in the Dakota region in the late 1820s, numbered among the Europeans who sought a New World tour to broaden their education, much as their counterparts in the eastern United States took the grand tour of Europe to further theirs.

Little Bear, A Hunkpapa Brave *(1832), by George Catlin, perhaps the frontier's preeminent artist. (Smithsonian American Art Museum)*

In 1843, one of America's quintessential nineteenth-century "characters," John James Audubon, journeyed up the Missouri River. Born in Haiti to a slave trader, Audubon was brought up in France, and smuggled himself into the United States to avoid being drafted into Napoleon's army. Once in the United States he set about failing at most things he undertook, but he did like to wander, and became skilled at drawing pictures of the many birds he shot and stuffed on his travels. When he arrived in South Dakota, he described a bleaker landscape than had his earlier fellow travelers. In responding to Brackenridge's descriptions of natural beauty, Audubon wrote that he saw "no 'carpeted prairies,' no 'velvety distant landscape.'" And of Catlin Audubon commented that the earlier artist must have seen different natives entirely to paint such ideal scenes.

In the same year that the *Yellowstone* paddled to Fort Tecumseh, the first permanent white settlement in South Dakota was established at Fort Pierre Chouteau in central South Dakota, near present-day Pierre. By then, an increasing number of trading and military posts were providing security and comfort to whites. In the years that followed, conflict with the Sioux escalated, and most fur trading posts were turned over to the military.

Fort Pierre, mouth of the Teton River, 1200 miles above St. Louis. *Mr. Catlin overestimated the distance between Fort Pierre and St. Louis when he titled this view near the fort in 1832. (Smithsonian American Art Museum)*

■ SODBUSTERS AND PIONEERS

Like a wave on a prairie ocean, immigrants to the American frontier kept pushing westward in search of unbroken ground and a lease on the future. Most of those who arrived in South Dakota in the mid-nineteenth century followed the route of trappers and traders, heading west out of St. Louis and north through Nebraska via the Missouri River. They settled first in the southeastern corner of the state, in Vermillion, Yankton, and Sioux Falls, fanning out and building their homesteads along waterways: the Big Sioux, Vermillion, James, and Choteau Rivers. Their vision for a new life included farms and houses, and to their eyes the land they first encountered was empty.

In 1862, the U.S. Congress passed the Homestead Act and sold 160 acres of unsettled land (for about 18 dollars in parts of the Dakota Territory) to men and women willing to meet a few government requirements. Once a pioneer had paced off 160 acres as his claim, the government compelled him to complete several steps to "prove up"—or hold onto—his claim. The first order of business was to

Mrs. Gustav Hanson of Hartford, just north of Sioux Falls, poses with children and neighbors before a typical prairie sod house. The lack of timber and extreme winter cold made it necessary to use sod strips like bricks for construction and insulation.
(South Dakota State Historical Society, Pierre)

construct a dwelling. Due to a lack of building materials, early dwellings were most often tarpaper shacks, dugouts carved from swells in the land, or sod shanties. "Sodbusters" cut long strips of 3-inch-deep sod with a spade and then sliced the strips into manageable lengths. These were stacked like bricks into four walls, with openings for a window and a door. If the settler was lucky, trees growing on banks of a nearby stream or creek would provide enough wood to construct a crudely framed roof strong enough to support more sod. The completed sod shanty was windproof, fireproof, and structurally sound, but it often failed to keep out the rain.

Though few of these original structures can be found today, they once littered the landscape. The large number that were built, only to be summarily abandoned, provided mute testimony to the struggles of trying to make a life on a vast, treeless prairie, broiling hot in the summer, freezing cold in the winter, and for the most part, arid.

The deep, impacted prairie grasses rendered planting the first crops extremely difficult. No matter how sharp their blades, plows could rarely churn up earth so entangled with tough roots. After chopping at the earth with an ax, many settlers simply dropped seeds into the crevices, then waited in their little "soddies" for the grain to grow. If the first crop was spared by drought, hail, grasshoppers, and fire, a homesteader might have enough money by the end of the summer to buy seed to plant a few additional acres. With luck, the cultivated acreage would increase each year, allowing the family to grow a vegetable garden, buy a milk cow, purchase lumber for a real house, and get shoes for the children. The success of these pioneer families often relied as much on their own ability to endure in the face of solitude and misfortune as it did on the weather.

■ BROKEN TREATIES

Like other hunter-gatherer cultures, the Great Plains Sioux needed to control a wide swath of territory to sustain the animals they hunted. Their traditions, legends, art, and folklore revolved around a roaming and hunting life, and when they observed whites on their lands, the last thing they wanted was to emulate them by settling down and growing corn. Rather, they fought off settlers as they would an encroaching Indian tribe, and they considered a farming or ranching life to be one

(following pages) Eagle Dance *(circa 1845–1848), by George Catlin.*
(Smithsonian American Art Museum)

without spirit or soul. These differences engendered an endless series of skirmishes, massacres, and battles, as whites and Indians fought, and made treaties, broke them, and fought again. Control of either side by a central authority proved difficult. Whites, individualistic, intrepid, and hungry for land, kept pouring into any "empty" space they could find, indifferent to treaty boundaries. And although one Indian chief might sign a treaty, the tribes themselves were divided into fiercely independent groups that more or less did what they pleased. When these small self-directing groups were out hunting on the prairie and found yet another group of whites trying to plant crops in Indian hunting grounds, they saw blood.

The Laramie Treaty of 1851 attempted to deal with the problem by allotting the Sioux 60 million acres and establishing tribal borders. The U.S. government recognized the sovereignty of the Indian tribes and, in recognition of the fact that their hunting grounds were being infringed upon, promised an annuity to each tribe. In return the Indians agreed to allow the government to construct roads and military posts within their territory, and they guaranteed restitution should any U.S. citizen be wronged. They also promised to keep the peace among themselves— a futile gesture, since the Sioux tribes were not centrally governed, rendering such self-policing impossible. In addition, the U.S. Senate did not approve the annuity terms of the treaty, committing themselves only to compensate the Indians for losses of property and buffalo for the next 10 years. By 1856, the U.S. government had sent the topographical engineer Lt. G. K. Warren through Nebraska into Sioux territory to explore land near the Black Hills.

During the late 1850s, the first land speculators arrived. One large group from St. Paul, Minnesota, settled in the Sioux Falls area, while another large group, hailing from Iowa (usually Sioux City), settled in Yankton. Although much of the land just west of these towns belonged to Indians, the speculators envisioned settlers— perhaps even a railroad—on that land. In 1858, the organizer of Sioux City's Upper Missouri Land Company, Capt. J. B. S. Todd, a cousin of Mary Todd Lincoln, took part in the negotiation of a treaty with the Yankton Sioux for the purchase of 14 million acres between the Big Sioux and Missouri Rivers for 12 cents an acre.

Following the Yankton Treaty of 1858, Norwegians began to establish claims near the Vermillion and James Rivers, forerunners of thousands of Norwegians who would eventually settle in the state. Irish immigrants began arriving in 1860, and by 1861 the region had attracted enough residents for Congress to organize it under U.S. law. Part of the Dakota Territory, it was administered along with present-day North Dakota, Wyoming, and Montana. Yankton, a small settlement in extreme southeastern South Dakota, was designated the territorial capital. With the passing of the Homestead Act of 1862, by which settlers could purchase 160-acre parcels of land for $18 each, the territory's population continued to grow.

Following the Minnesota Uprising in 1862—when Sioux tribes in that state violently protested a government order confining them to small reservations—and a series of skirmishes and raids that left hundreds of settlers and Dakota Indians (the Sioux tribe in Minnesota and eastern Dakota Territory) dead, the government made a last attempt to pacify the Indians while continuing to allow westward expansion.

The 1868 Fort Laramie Treaty established the Great Sioux Reservation, which included the Black Hills, as permanent home of the Sioux Nation and preserved Powder River and Bighorn Country as "unceded Indian territory." It granted the tribes rights to all land in Dakota Territory west of the Missouri River to the Bighorns of western Wyoming. The treaty nonetheless limited the amount of land the Sioux held that they were entitled to roam and inhabit, and the American officials were hard-pressed to coax Oglala Sioux chief Red Cloud—one of the most powerful Sioux leaders—into signing. Finally, treaty negotiator Major Dye persuaded Red Cloud to sign by informing him that the U.S. government would withhold ammunition from the Sioux if he didn't.

Chief Red Cloud of the Oglala Sioux.
(Center for Western Studies)

In addition to establishing the reservation, the treaty of 1868 assigned the Sioux tribes to a number of reservation agencies that would distribute yearly allotments of food, clothing, and money to them. (These agencies would later become instruments of U.S. governmental control over the tribes.) Also, under the terms of the treaty, the American army was to defend the Great Sioux Reservation against white settlement. But continued reports of gold in the Black Hills and unrelenting pressure from a flood of immigrants helped changed the government's collective mind and soon compromised its honor.

■ GOLD RUSH

Back in 1848, when Father Pierre-Jean (Peter John) De Smet visited the Black Hills on South Dakota's southwestern border, an Indian chief presented the priest with a bag of glimmering powder. Recognizing it as gold and already fearing for Indian rights in the area, De Smet quickly responded, "Put it away and show it to nobody." Unfortunately, during the two decades following the Homestead Act,

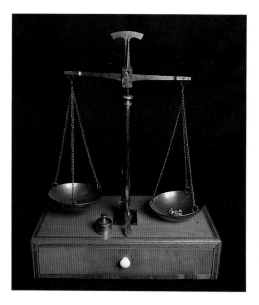

A gold scale used in the Black Hills during the late nineteenth century. (South Dakota State Historical Society, Pierre)

Indian scout helmet. (South Dakota State Historical Society, Pierre. Photo by Paul Jones)

the secret got out of the bag. Hordes of whites came to the sacred Paha Sapa (Black Hills), a beautiful wilderness of pine-clad cliffs and mountain meadows.

In the early 1870s, the Northern Pacific Railroad began laying track through the Powder River country west of the Black Hills. Though angered by the obvious violation of their treaty, the Sioux did not go to war. In 1873, the Dakota Territory legislature asked Congress for soldiers to rid the Black Hills of "hostile" Indians—those who rebelled against reservation confinement. On July 2, 1874, a charismatic leader with flowing yellow hair, Lt. Col. George Armstrong Custer, was sent with ten cavalry and two infantry companies on the first white expedition into the Black Hills. Although ostensibly sent to gather information about the region, Custer broadened his mandate to look for the gold he'd heard rumors about. Much to his surprise, Custer met with few Indians, and so he had plenty of time to admire the landscape and write dispatches to his commanding officers in Bismarck. Then, in one such dispatch, Custer casually mentioned that gold seemed to be everywhere in the Black Hills. A Chicago newspaper picked up the word that the "Custer Expedition" had confirmed the presence of gold in the sacred land of the Sioux. The paper ran the news, and the gold rush was on.

Meanwhile, the War Department, attempting to protect the Black Hills, called a meeting with all of the region's major tribes—the 10 Sioux tribes plus the Arapaho and the Northern Cheyenne—at which government negotiators encouraged the tribes to sell off their land for money that would be needed when the buffalo died off. No decision could be reached. In late 1875, the Commissioner of Indian Affairs issued an order to the Sioux that all bands not already reporting to the reservation agencies to which they had been assigned must do so by January 31, 1876. Those Indians who didn't return would be considered "hostile" and would be sent back to their agencies by force if necessary.

The commissioner's order, intended to quell attacks on settlers, soldiers, and peaceful Indian tribes, was ill conceived and poorly timed. It made no allowance for smaller groups absent from their tribe: even a few dozen hunters attempting to supplement the government's meager rations with wild game were considered hostile. The order reached some agencies only days before the deadline and it failed to take into account the realities of travel in the middle of winter on the northern Great Plains. Indeed, due to severe weather, the army had stopped its operations on the Plains in late November. Yet Indian warriors, women, and children—not nearly as well clothed or well fed—were expected to travel many miles across wind-swept plains during the coldest month of the year.

In March, Gen. George Crook took the field against the hostiles, and Lt. Col. George A. Custer commanded one of the forces sent. The Indian response was led by the Hunkpapa Sioux leader Sitting Bull, who summoned Sioux, Cheyenne, and even some Arapaho warriors to his camp in Montana Territory. Crook's troops were forced to retreat in a battle on June 17, and the Indian chiefs moved their encampment into the valley of the Little Bighorn River in what is now southeastern Montana. There Sitting Bull performed the Sun Dance, entering into a trance and receiving a vision in which soldiers fell from the sky like grasshoppers. Custer and his men spotted the Indian camp on June 25, 1876, and he elected to divide his forces and attack. One group was assigned to Capt. Frederick Benteen and the other to Maj. Marcus Reno. Custer took his own troops and led the charge onto the battlefield of Little Bighorn. Custer and his command, however, had severely underestimated the strength of their adversary. After being pinned down by some of the 4,000 warriors in the camp, Benteen and Reno could only watch as smoke filtering over the plains signaled the annihilation of Custer and over 200 soldiers.

The Indian victory was short-lived. After scattering to the winds, homesickness, starvation, and cavalry pursuit eventually led most of the Lakota back to the agencies of the Great Sioux Reservation. By August 1876, Congress even began punishing the peaceful agency Sioux for the acts of their hostile brethren by cutting off their food and rations until they agreed to cede the Black Hills and allow passage through the rest of their land.

President Ulysses S. Grant appointed the Manypenny Commission—with its "sell or starve" agenda—to meet with the Sioux. Ironically, the commission was made up of prominent friends of the Indians, who believed that if the Sioux relinquished their land, the Indian nation might thrive, perhaps joining white civilization or forging a more "modern" way of life. In despair, some leaders of the tribe signed an agreement that fall and the Black Hills were lost to the Lakota. Congress moved quickly and ratified the agreement February 28, 1877, unleashing another great gold rush.

Soldiers marching across the state during the Indian campaigns of the 1880s.
(Center for Western Studies)

■ SIOUX RESISTANCE

As miners and "mule skinners" (muleteers, or mule drivers) flocked to the Black Hills and established gold mining camps in the summer of 1876, three bands of the Lakota remained at large. The bands of Sitting Bull and Gall had fled to the Canadian wilderness, while Crazy Horse and his people remained in the Bighorn Mountains. After pressure from other Indian leaders, Crazy Horse and his band of about 1,100 men, women, and children surrendered to authorities at the Red Cloud Agency—near Fort Robinson in present-day Nebraska—on May 6, 1877.

■ CRAZY HORSE

Later that summer, knowing that the Sitting Bull and Gall bands roamed free, Crazy Horse became restless and began planning to escape the agency. When his mood became known, army officials decided to arrest him rather than allow the Dakota leader to influence others and lead a mass exodus. In early September, troops were sent to the village of Crazy Horse and found it had broken up the previous night. Most of the band was quickly returned to the agency, but Crazy Horse had fled on his own. However, he too was soon in the custody of the military, which escorted him to Fort Robinson. When Crazy Horse was taken to a guardhouse and learned he would be confined, a struggle ensued and the great Sioux leader received a fatal wound from a soldier's bayonet. He died at midnight on September 5, 1877.

Sioux horse effigy. (South Dakota State Historical Society, Pierre. Photo by Paul Jones)

■ SITTING BULL

Sitting Bull, whose strong "medicine" foretold of falling bluecoats and Custer's Last Stand, would also die at the hands of authorities, albeit after spending years in the presence of whites and even traveling to Europe in Buffalo Bill's Wild West Show.

Five years after the Indian victory over Custer's Seventh Cavalry at Little Bighorn, Sitting Bull remained in Canada with a remnant of his people. After numerous visits by commissions from the United States, the Canadian government finally wearied of its uninvited guests and ordered Sitting Bull to leave. The great medicine man of the Hunkpapa Sioux surrendered and was escorted to Fort Buford (on the Missouri in present-day western North Dakota) and finally to Fort Randall in the same territory. After two years of confinement, Sitting Bull was sent to the Standing Rock Agency near Fort Yates, North Dakota.

Nine years later, in the fall of 1890, warriors in Sitting Bull's camp became swept up in a form of spiritual fervor spreading through America's Indian tribes—in a sense the only recourse left to them in an increasingly bitter and impoverished life—and began to participate in Ghost Dance rites. These were taught by Wovoka, a Paiute holy man known as Jack Wilson to the Nevada family that

Indian chief bonnet. A feather was added for each successful coup. (South Dakota State Historical Society, Pierre. Photo by Paul Jones)

had adopted him. According to Wovoka, if the Indians prayed and danced long and sincerely enough, all dead Indian warriors would return and the white men would disappear. Although Sitting Bull himself did not believe in the teachings, he did nothing to discourage his people from participating. Nearby whites, who found the dances mysterious and threatening, began to advocate military action.

On the morning of December 15, 1890, 39 Indian policemen and four special agents under the command of Shave Head and Bull Head appeared in Sitting Bull's camp and pulled him from his bed. As he was being led from his home, his son taunted him for being taken captive so easily. Two shots were fired from a crowd of Indians who had gathered to watch the arrest. In the melee that followed, Shave Head, Bull Head, three other policemen and eight Indians were killed, as was Sitting Bull.

■ GALL

A war chief of the Hunkpapa Sioux, Gall led the third band of renegades who refused to subject themselves to reservation living. But, in the fall of 1880 and after staying with Sitting Bull in Canada for nearly five years, Gall chastised

A rare photo of a Ghost Dance performed by Sioux on the Rosebud Reservation in the fall of 1890. In the next few months, the Ghost Dance frightened American settlers and officials enough to provoke further violent repression of the Sioux. (Center for Western Studies)

Sitting Bull, labeled him a coward and a fraud for not openly confronting the U.S. government, and returned to the United States. Scarcely into the new year, he too surrendered with some 300 of his followers. Gall settled on a farm on the Standing Rock Reservation, ultimately became a friend of the whites, and was influential in inducing the Indians to accept the government's plans to educate their children. Gall died several years later at his home on Oak Creek in South Dakota.

The great chief Sitting Bull in 1884. (Library of Congress)

MASSACRE AT WOUNDED KNEE

Meanwhile, the tension in the square became something larger—a feeling of peril that was ominous and growing. The Indians felt it. They remembered that this was the Seventh Cavalry. At the Battle on the Greasy Grass (Little Big Horn) it had suffered the bloodiest defeat ever given white soldiers by Indians. It had lost Long Hair Custer and two hundred sixty-four men, whereas the Indians had lost only a handful. There were some who claimed that the Seventh had been thirsting for revenge every since. Their sense of danger was quickened even more by Yellow Bird as he continued to dance among them chanting, "Don't be frightened—let your hearts be strong to meet what is before you—the Great Holy is with you—your ghost shirts will keep the bullets from you." Nerves tightened like drying bowstrings, and there was a feeling in the air like the cold wind that runs ahead of a thunderstorm.

The young troopers were as nervous as the Indians. They were green and unseasoned, and the greatest military danger most of them had experienced so far was learning to ride a horse. Now, suddenly, they were facing the Sioux. They knew from their dime novels that the Sioux were treacherous, butchering savages. On top of that there was a fierce-looking old man wearing a painted and feathered nightshirt hopping around out there, chanting and blowing a whistle and throwing dirt at them. Their palms moistened and their fingers curled around the triggers of their old Remingtons.

The officers smelled danger, too. Lieutenant Mann recalled, "I had a peculiar feeling come over me—some presentiment of trouble." He passed the word quietly through K Troop, "Be ready. There is going to be trouble."

Colonel Forsyth called to Philip Wells, who was trying to persuade the influential Horned Cloud to quiet the medicine man and the young Indians, "You'd better get out of here. It's looking dangerous."

"Just a minute, Colonel," replied Wells, "I'm trying to get this fellow to quiet them." Even as he spoke, however, Wells saw a powerful young warrior stalking toward him from behind. Turning, Wells cautiously began to back out of the square.

Meanwhile, Black Coyote (or Hosi Yanka) had torn a strip of paper from an old brown bag and had moved off to the side. Holding his beloved rifle in the crook of his arm, he was trying to roll a big cigarette in the paper. As he did so, two sergeants who were after his gun slipped up from behind and seized him. There was a quick, fierce scuffle. The gun pointed skyward and fired. Then all in the same instant Yellow Bird threw a cloud of dust into the air, and half a dozen young Indians threw off their blankets and aimed their Winchesters at K Troop.

Lieutenant Robinson yelled, "Look out! They are going to fire!"

Varnum looked up from the search line and cried, "By God! They have broken!"

Philip Wells whirled around to find his Indian stalker lunging at him with a knife.

Lieutenant Mann remembered thinking, "The pity of it! What can they be thinking of!"

A split second later the Indian volley ripped into K troop, and Mann heard himself screaming, "Fire! Fire on them!"

Instantly, both B and K Troops fired volleys into the Indians, and the square exploded into a roar of gunfire and disappeared under swirling clouds of yellow-gray powder smoke.

"There was an awful roar." (Dog Chief)

"It sounded much like the tearing of canvas." (Rough Feather)

"Everything was smoking from then on." (Peter Stand)

"The smoke was so dense I couldn't see anything." (White Lance)

"People were lying all about where formerly they were all sitting or standing." (Richard Afraid-of-Hawk)

Philip Wells partially deflected his attacker's knife—it sliced through the end of his nose, which dangled over his mouth, held on by only two strips of skin.

Captain Wallace was running to rejoin K Troop when the second Indian volley tore away the top of his skull.

Big Foot struggled to sit up, caught a bullet in his head, and fell back beside the body of Horned Cloud. Seeing her father fall, Big Foot's daughter ran screaming toward him, was shot in the back, and fell dead across him.

—Rex Alan Smith, *Moon of Popping Trees*, 1975

Chief Big Foot lies mortally wounded on the battlefield at Wounded Knee. (Center for Western Studies)

■ SETTLERS MOVE ONTO RESERVATIONS

The 1880s saw the beginning of the reservation period in earnest. The bison were on the brink of extinction because of the many settlers and soldiers who hunted them and the ranchers who used the grassland for cattle-grazing, and with them was eradicated the way of life of the Plains Indian. The original inhabitants of this changing environment were forced to rely on the political whims of the federal government for rations of food and clothing.

From 1882 to 1889, several government commissions attempted to persuade the Dakota to give up more of the tribal lands. The "Great Dakota Boom" and its accompanying influx of Bohemians, Germans, Swedes, Finns, Poles, and Swiss made land scarce and confrontation likely. Finally, on March 2, 1889, the Sioux relented, gave up nearly half of the Great Sioux Reservation, and agreed to allow it to be divided into six smaller ones. In later years the reservations would be reduced even further in size. Through the Dawes General Allotment Act, land not allotted to the Indians was designated as surplus and open for white settlement. South Dakota entered its first year of statehood in 1889 with open ground, settlers sweeping the state, hammers pounding, and white civilization closing the door on the Sioux.

In addition, with no buffalo to hunt, drought stalking their attempts at farming, and rations of flour, corn, and beans reduced below treaty obligations, the late 1880s were a time of considerable hunger for the Sioux. As with other Indian tribes throughout the West, the Lakota sought solace in the Ghost Dance teachings of Wovoka. To the whites who feared an Indian uprising and further bloodshed, the Ghost Dance movement was known as the Messiah Craze, alarming Indian agents and army troops. After first contributing to the death of Sitting Bull, the Ghost Dance religion resulted in a far more terrible experience at a place called Wounded Knee, where 200 Indians were massacred by the Seventh Cavalry. (See the "SOUTH-CENTRAL AND BADLANDS" chapter.)

■ DAKOTA FEVER

Despite feeble attempts by the federal government to enforce provisions of its treaty with the Lakota and keep whites from entering the Black Hills, settlers by the hundreds stormed the Paha Sapa. In their steep canyons and lush meadows, placer miners began building sluices and shacks, gambling for gold against defensive Indian attack and an army scolding. Deadwood, known as one of the wildest and wickedest mining camps in the American West, sprang to life after Custer's confirmation of the existence of gold. Seven months after the news was out, the population of the gulch swelled from a few ramshackle huts to more than 7,000 uninvited residents.

The settlement of the Black Hills led to a stampede on the remaining frontier in the Dakota Territory. As western South Dakota grew, so did the needs of miners and businessmen: supplies, equipment, food, and an efficient way of delivering them. Until 1878, farming settlements were generally restricted to extreme south-eastern South Dakota. Only a few settlers had drifted into the rich river valleys of the James, Vermillion, and Big Sioux, leaving the vast expanse of prairie in central and northern South Dakota virtually uninhabited.

But in that unbroken prairie, immigrants, Civil War veterans, and the sons and daughters of earlier homesteaders caught "Dakota fever." Railroad officials saw dollar signs—not only did settlers need transportation to their plots, but with plots so isolated, they would certainly require a means of shipping crops and livestock to market or to their fellow settlers in the Black Hills. Together, railroad tycoons,

The rough-and-tumble main street of Deadwood circa 1880s. (Adams Museum, Deadwood)

An allotment crew ready to divide land on Pine Ridge Reservation. (Center for Western Studies)

riverboat captains, and real estate agents promoted the Dakota Territory's rich river valleys and open plains to eager immigrants.

As fears of Indian uprisings diminished, and farming and commerce swept the state, railroads extended their lines west from Minnesota. Residents of Vermillion and Yankton took advantage of an increasing number of steamboats plying the Missouri River, laden with supplies for settlers and miners. Cattle ranchers drove their herds from Texas, eastern Colorado, western Nebraska, and Wyoming onto the virgin grasslands west of the Missouri River and north of the Black Hills. Early settlers lobbied for county seats and railroad stops. When railroaders ignored some requests, whole communities packed up and rebuilt their settlements next to the line. Today, southeastern South Dakota, indeed the entire state, is dotted with townsites abandoned as soon as the settlers saw that access to transportation would be limited.

The "Great Dakota Boom," one of the last massive land rushes in the United States, witnessed thousands of immigrants pouring into the Dakota Territory. From 1870 to 1880, the population of the southeastern area of the state rose from about 10,000 to 82,000. By 1885, a quarter of a million inhabitants were engaged in farming, trades, and business, or vying for the marginal tracts of land that remained open under the Homestead Act.

But the region's population increase by no means indicates that life in the Dakota Territory was easy. Major blizzards occurred in 1873, 1880–1881, and 1888. Plagues of grasshoppers destroyed crops in 1864–1865, 1873–1874, 1876, and 1936. Drought fried the fields in 1889, 1894, 1910–1911, and during the dust storms of 1933 and 1934. As if that weren't enough, disease was never far away: in 1869–1870, the early years of the Dakota Boom, settlers had to be concerned with consumption, freezing, fever, and pneumonia, the most common causes of death at that time. Other frequently cited causes of death included croup, dropsy, acute diarrhea, cancer, diphtheria, gunshot wounds, cholera, lung fever, bronchitis, and fits. Ten years later, the causes of death were even more varied: gravel, worms, alcoholism, heart disease, sunstroke, and teething; and getting struck by lightning, kicked by a horse, murdered, gored, scalded, struck by a falling body, killed by Indians, and "shot sparking another man's wife." And then there were the economic depressions, the worst being the Great Depression of the 1930s, which left thousands of farms and small-town merchants destitute.

Despite the dangers of disease and violence, and the setbacks borne by insects, drought, blizzards, and depressions, the settlers who stuck it out left behind descendants who were strong, healthy, and determined, qualities that have become

Wind erosion in the mid-1930s virtually blew away South Dakota's topsoil, ruining most farmers in the state. (Library of Congress)

The State Capitol building in Pierre.

time-honored in South Dakota. This was not a world in which laboring from dawn to dark was found remarkable, or the activities of leisure time (with the exception of hunting and fishing) a major topic of discussion. Residents continued to toil in grasshopper-infested fields and on parched prairie; leaders continued to extend rail lines and commerce, dam rivers, and make even its most inhospitable places habitable.

■ STATEHOOD

As the territory's population rose despite hardship, so did its residents' voices clamoring for statehood. The voices were most numerous in the south, where the population was almost twice that of the north. The settlers of southern Dakota wanted admission of separate southern and northern Dakotas as much as they desired statehood itself, for they believed that the southern region, with its greater resources and higher population, should benefit from its own wealth. Those in the north, fearing that Congress might not think the northern territory's numbers high enough, believed that a "one-state" drive was their only hope.

In 1885, Dakota governor Gilbert Pierce, a two-state advocate, called a second constitutional convention (the first one, called in 1883, had failed to achieve statehood). In the 1885 southern Dakota election to approve the constitution, voters elected a state government, approved the constitution, and named Huron the new state capital. That same week, Indiana senator Benjamin Harrison introduced the bill admitting North and South Dakota to statehood. The two-state proposal met with much political debate, as both the Democratic Congress and President Grover Cleveland realized that admission of the largely Republican territory as two states would mean four Republican senators, rather than two. After a few years of obstacles—rejection of the Harrison bill by the House Committee on Territories, the appointment of a new one-state territorial governor, Congressional endorsement of a northern Dakota one-state plan, and the Northern Pacific Railroad preference for any one-state plan—the constitutional convention met again.

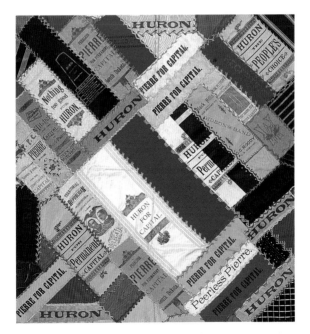

*A political ribbon crazy quilt illustrates various
cities' efforts to be chosen state capital.
(South Dakota State Historical Society, Pierre)*

By 1889, the tide had turned, perhaps because it became clear to the politicians that public sentiment favored the admission of the Dakota Territory as two states; it also favored the admission of Montana and Washington. Benjamin Harrison was even elected to the presidency, though Cleveland himself signed the bill before leaving office. The boundary with North Dakota was drawn, and on November 2, 1889, South Dakota became the nation's fortieth state. The city of Pierre was nominated as "temporary" capital because it was the most central town in the state, and it defeated five other contenders, largely because competition among the others—Mitchell, Huron, Chamberlain, Watertown, and Sioux Falls—was so heated that the tiny central South Dakota town slipped through unnoticed.

■ SOUTH DAKOTA TODAY

Since World War II, hydroelectric projects, control of the Missouri River, farm mechanization, industrial expansion, and massive memorials carved from the ageless granite of its mountains have initiated a new prosperity for South Dakota. Today's powerlines, interstates, and convenience stores represent vast changes in lifestyle from those endured by South Dakota's early pioneers. But the landscape has changed little since Crazy Horse, Sitting Bull, and other Sioux leaders traversed it with their nomadic bands centuries ago.

It took a mountain carving known as Mount Rushmore, built from 1927 to 1941 in the Black Hills, to attract international attention to South Dakota. More than six million tourists visit the state each year, generating well over a billion dollars worth of economic activity and employing one out of every dozen workers in South Dakota.

With more than 32,500 farms and three quarters of a million people, South Dakota is nevertheless smaller in population than the cities of Minneapolis, Minnesota, and Denver, Colorado. Its largest city, Sioux Falls, has a population of 124,000, and the next largest, Rapid City, only half that. South Dakota is a place where the state bird, the imported Chinese ring-necked pheasant, still outnumbers the taller, two-legged residents who attempt to shoot it out of the sky each fall. For the record, people also are outnumbered by deer, walleye, trout, corncobs, cattle, and ponderosa pine.

First National Bank of Brookings, ca. 1920s. On Roosevelt's "Bank Holiday" in 1933, the Nystrom Bank in Wall was the only U.S. bank not to close: no one had notified the owner about the order. (Underwood Photo Archives)

THE SOUTHEAST

A few years ago, a South Dakota newspaper editor was visiting Los Angeles when, feeling a bit weary of city life, he sought the comforting confines of a taxi-cab. As his tension lessened, the editor struck up the obligatory banter with the cabbie who, with a firm grasp of the obvious, guessed that his passenger was from out of state.

"Where ya from?" the cabbie asked.

"South Dakota," the editor answered, then waited for some form of recognition. Following a lengthy pause, and a couple of nervous glances in the rearview mirror, the cabbie said, "Isn't that one of those square states?"

Well, not quite square. But *almost* as square as nearby North Dakota, Wyoming, Colorado, and perhaps Kansas. What throws South Dakota off the list of straight-line states are a few rivers on which surveyors conveniently relied to draw the state's borders. The location of Lake Traverse and Big Stone Lake in extreme northeastern South Dakota allowed Minnesota to take a geographical bite out of that region, but the path of the Missouri River along the state's southeasterly edge recouped some land from Nebraska.

As the Missouri reaches its confluence with the Big Sioux River, it forms a "toe" that extends to the southeast from South Dakota's lower right border. Surrounded by Nebraska on the west and Iowa on the east is a mini-peninsula. A legion of North Sioux City and other I-29 residents here can enter three states in a matter of minutes, but because they are cradled in the arms of two rivers and between the lines on a map, they call South Dakota home.

■ HISTORY

Long before steam engines, asphalt roadways, and concrete runways, wild rivers were the major means of transportation in the southeastern corner of South Dakota. On these rivers—the Big Sioux, Vermillion, James, and Choteau—Arikara and later Sioux Indians fished and gathered food. In 1804, explorers Lewis and Clark traveled through the area, and commented in their journals on the treachery of the Missouri River, as well as its beauty. Most of South Dakota's first adventurers and fur trappers followed the Missouri up into the state, as did the pioneers who

THE SOUTHEAST

Elevation in feet

7,242
6,000
5,000
4,000
3,000
2,000
962

0   15   30 Miles

0   15   30   45 Kilometers

arrived after 1862 when the Dakota Territory was opened to homesteaders. In the early 1860s, the only part of the state settled was a strip along the Missouri extending from present-day Sioux City, Iowa (just over today's South Dakota border), up into Yankton. By 1870 the region had expanded to include the area extending from the mouth of the James east to the Big Sioux River as far north as Sioux Falls. On this treeless prairie, sodbusters built their homes with sod strips and chopped at the grass-clogged earth with an ax before planting seeds.

Today, the fertile soil of South Dakota's eastern half is home to the majority of the state's farms. In the southeast, the towns of Yankton, Vermillion, and Sioux Falls are the anchors of economic and cultural life. Outside these areas you encounter rambling farmsteads, feedlots, vast cornfields, and river valleys. Dust clouds and plumes of diesel smoke rising from tractors and combines working the flat fields announce spring planting and fall harvest. In winter, the landscape is a barren, snow-packed tundra. From early November until mid-March, most rural residents huddle in their houses, hang out at the local café, attend 4-H Club meetings, or root for a basketball team in a packed high-school gymnasium.

In most years, when an adequate but not excessive amount of sun shines and rain falls, it's a comfortable existence. At other times, when dark clouds cover the plains like a wet blanket for weeks at a time, or when the sun bleaches the soil and paints a brown tint all the way to the horizon, it's not as easy. Each of those situations, good times and bad, success and struggle, can be found on the faces of old-time residents of this region, in their determined smiles and the weathered creases around their eyes.

■ VERMILLION   *map page 61, D-3*

Vermillion, a few miles west of I-29 on State Highway 50, is located on a Missouri River bluff and named for the red clay on which it was built. With a population of 10,000, it has an unpretentious small-town atmosphere. It's clean, maybe even scrub-brushed, and because the University of South Dakota is here, Vermillion is pleasantly collegiate.

The earliest settlement in the area was Fort Vermillion, established by the American Fur Company in 1835. The town itself originally was founded on the banks of the Missouri and Vermillion Rivers a mile south, but a major flood hit the valley in 1881 and swept away most of the existing structures. Following the flood, houses were built higher up, on surrounding bluffs that overlooked the original townsite. Today, Neoclassical and Queen Anne influences abound in the residential architecture, and examples of Italianate and Mediterranean styles stand among homely bungalow houses.

The **University of South Dakota** (USD) was founded in 1862, when the territorial legislature selected Vermillion as the site for the Dakota Territory's first university. They failed to provide funding, however, so civic-minded residents, led by Darwin Inman, a pioneer banker and politician, took matters into their own hands and raised the funds to underwrite the institution. Its architecture is dominated by the Neoclassical style of the **Old Main** building and the handsome Georgian Revival style of the **Inman House,** which serves as the alumni center. The state's only medical and law schools are on the well-manicured campus.

Populating the campus and surrounding neighborhoods is the usual mix of academics, athletes, and aesthetes; the student body numbers approximately 8,700. University alumni, all devoted to their mascot, the coyote, like nothing better than to look down their noses at the other South Dakota institutions of higher learning. The "Cow College" (South Dakota State) at Brookings, where the noble

Randolph Street in downtown Vermillion, circa 1870.
(South Dakota State Historical Society, Pierre)

jackrabbit serves as mascot, often is their favorite target. One of the less refined habits of USD students during winter basketball contests between the two schools is to throw dead, frozen jackrabbits on the hardwood floor—a great way to ignite a hometown crowd. Some of the same USD students have recently discovered that if they let the furry critters thaw out under their seats until halftime, they don't bounce. In the early 1980s jackrabbit hurling suffered its greatest setback when some South Dakota State students threw a well-preserved but equally inanimate coyote to the floor of the gym. It didn't bounce either.

Several fine museums are on or near the University campus. The most unusual museum in the community is the **National Music Museum,** on campus. Widely acknowledged as one of the finest institutions of its kind in the world, the museum houses more than 10,000 rare antique musical instruments, which are presented in eight galleries. Its renowned collections include ivory lutes from Elizabethan times, Civil War band instruments, hand-painted Persian drums, and instruments by the Italian masters. Specially featured are a spectacular trumpet mask from the South Pacific, an eighteenth-century Swiss organ, and one of only two Antonio Stradivari guitars known to have survived. *414 East Clark Street; 605-677-5306.*

The National Music Museum in Vermillion contains an eclectic collection of musical instruments.

The **W. H. Over Museum,** beside the campus, contains exhibits of natural history and heritage. Many of the archaeological specimens and other artifacts in the collection were amassed by the museum's namesake, William Henry Over, South Dakota's most distinguished naturalist. A collection donated by the family of David Clark, an Episcopalian minister to the Sioux, includes pre-reservation and early reservation Lakota art and artifacts, as well as pioneer artifacts, firearms, and historic photographs and costumes. *1110 Ratingen Street; 605-677-5228.*

Built in 1882, the **Austin-Whittemore House** rests on a riverside bluff overlooking Vermillion and serves as headquarters for the **Clay County Historical Society Museum.** Filled with Victorian displays and settings, the museum, perhaps the finest example of Italian villa–style architecture in the state, is well worth a visit. *15 Austin Street; 605-624-8266.*

■ SPIRIT MOUND   *map page 61, D-3*

Seven miles north of Vermillion, visible from State Highway 19, Spirit Mound rises above the surrounding prairie—a bald, brown mound interrupting the flat horizon. On a hot and gusty August day in 1804, Meriwether Lewis and his dog Seaman, William Clark, and members of their expedition walked to the mound, which an Oto Indian had told them was inhabited by feisty midget-sized warriors. In their journals, the explorers noted that they observed a flock of swallows feeding on insects on the lee side of the mound and were afforded a splendid view of the surrounding grasslands from the mound's apex. They did not report sightings of pygmy warriors.

■ YANKTON   *map page 61, C-3*

On U.S. 29, less than 30 miles upriver from Vermillion along the tree-lined banks of the Missouri River, Yankton, the Mother City of South Dakota, claims a heritage steeped in riverboat and railroad investment schemes, frontier development, and just a hint of lingering dissatisfaction over not being selected the state capital in 1889. The sleepy burg recalls its days as a riverboat boom town on lazy summer evenings, when residents hear the steady chugging of the *Far West* paddle-wheeler, its deck lined with travelers looking out across the still waters.

A passenger on this scaled-down version of the original *Far West* could easily wonder whether riverboat travel was once more exciting than this. It surely must have been. A century ago, before dams slowed the current and deeper water and dredges virtually eliminated the danger of sandbars, settlers must have questioned the next bend, the security of their worldly possessions, and the coming of tomorrow. But today, riding a paddle-wheeler doesn't differ much from taking a stagecoach or being caught in the left lane of a traffic jam. It's a slow journey and you can't get off. Perfect for the faint of heart.

Named for the Yankton Sioux tribe that once dominated the area, the community has devolved from its heyday as capital of the Dakota Territory in the 1860s, to a college town (Yankton College) with grain elevators. Its central business district gives the appearance of a town somebody started but didn't finish. Stores and service stations accommodate families and fishermen, all stocking up for a weekend of camping, boating, and other out-of-the-office—or more commonly, out-of-the-cornfield—pleasures. Homes are filled with retired farmers and a few young families—the rest are making a living on the farms outside of town. Yankton's a friendly, old-fashioned place with Extension Clubs, clean streets, manicured lawns, and Fourth of July parades. Its replica of the old capitol building and its stately historic homes and museums document a history molded by Indians, explorers, settlers, riverboat captains, and railroad tycoons. Some of the town's 13,500 residents still claim kinship to the well-paid steamboat captains and pioneer passengers who first settled the area.

The most bustling town in the region during the nineteenth century, Yankton was a favorite stop for travelers, traders, and soldiers. When Lt. Col. George Armstrong Custer was headed west in 1873, he camped with his Seventh Cavalry at Yankton. After his visit, according to the *Yankton Daily Press and Dakotan* (founded in 1861 and still published today), the U.S. Army took more than 20 years to settle its debts with local merchants.

■ HISTORIC DISTRICT

Wander around Yankton's historic district, as many of its citizens like to do on humid summer nights, and imagine the time when riverboats were king and Yankton was the commercial center of the Dakota Territory. Roughly laid out along Fifth and Sixth Streets and between Mulberry and Cedar Streets, its 152 buildings, including Queen Anne and Italianate residences and Gothic churches, reflect a variety of styles.

The **Charles Gurney Hotel** (Third and Capital Streets), at one time the courthouse, was the site of the second trial of desperado Jack McCall for the murder of Wild Bill Hickok. McCall had earlier been acquitted by a vigilante court in Deadwood, and left for Nebraska, where he made the mistake of bragging about Hickok's murder. He was caught and turned over to the Yankton authorities, where residents gladly hanged him and buried him in an unmarked grave. (See "BLACK HILLS" chapter for more about Wild Bill Hickok.) The Charles Gurney Hotel was also the scene of perhaps the first murder of a territorial official, when a local banker fatally shot South Dakota's first territorial secretary.

A block away at Fourth and Capital Streets stands the neoclassical **Carnegie Library** (1902), which still has most of its original features, including ornate woodwork and leaded windows. Nearby is the **Cramer-Kenyon Heritage Home** (509 Pine Street) and memorial gardens, an interesting stop for those with a botanical bent or a passion for furnishings from the 1870s and 1880s. The **African Methodist Episcopal Church** (508 Cedar Street), also a worthwhile stop,

Yankton waterfront during a major flood in 1881.
(South Dakota State Historical Society, Pierre)

was built by former slaves in 1885 and is the oldest black church in the Dakota Territory. The **Excelsior Flour Mill** (Second and Capital Streets) was built with soft yellow sandstone and Sioux quartzite in 1872, when milling locally grown wheat was one of Yankton's major industries. The **Yankton College Conservatory** (12th and Douglas Streets) was constructed in 1883 of red Dakota quartzite. The bell and clock in the tower still function. You can't visit this site, however—the campus is now part of a federal prison camp.

The **Dakota Territorial Museum** contains Sioux artifacts, steamboat memorabilia, and period furnishings and clothing. It also exhibits the musical instruments and papers of Felix Vinatieri, an Italian-born musician who immigrated to the Dakota Territory and was asked by George Custer to join the Seventh Cavalry as bandmaster. Vinatieri enlisted, served as chief musician, but missed the fabled Last Stand because Custer ordered the band left behind. *610 Summit Street; 605-665-3898.*

■ B U B B L E   M A C H I N E
In 1928, WNAX Radio went on the air in Yankton and helped jump-start the long career of a middle-American phenomenon. Lawrence Welk, a young accordionist from Strasburg, North Dakota, had just run out of cash in Yankton. A long way from anywhere, and with no dance hall dates in sight, Welk and his band sought to replenish their reserves by coaxing some broadcast time out of WNAX. After the station manager fed the band, he put them on the air. Listener reaction, particularly from Norwegians and Germans in farmhouses scattered through the countryside, was immediate and positive. Despite the low pay, Welk accepted the manager's offer of a regular spot and stayed for nine years. Eventually, Welk and his band became the centerpiece of one of television's most popular family programs.

Today, reruns of the *Lawrence Welk Show* echo the folksy, fox-trotting tone of much of South Dakota. There are still places without cable television where residents are as out of touch with the world of fashion and musical trends as they are in touch with their neighbors, the latest town scandal, and the final score at Friday's high-school basketball game. It's a slow-paced world, and it's not for everyone. Nonetheless, people in this region seem to revel in it. Ask rural South Dakotans why they choose to live here, and they're as inclined to wonder why you asked as they are to answer the question.

■ LEWIS AND CLARK RECREATION AREA   *map page 61, C-3*

What Yankton and its environs lack in sophistication is more than made up for in their natural beauty and waterways, some found in the **Lewis and Clark Recreation Area,** 5 miles west of town on State Highway 52. The 22-mile-long Lewis and Clark Lake can be, in any season, either tranquil or challenging. At times, its silence is interrupted by little more than the occasional call of a meadowlark, while at other times, its tree-lined bluffs resound with the drone of powerboats and are whipped by the same relentless prairie winds that drove hundreds of homesteaders crazy.

Golf courses, campgrounds, cabin sites, beaches, and marinas line the shore of Lewis and Clark Lake. About a million people visit each year, the majority between May and September, when getting near the water for sailing, water-skiing, or reclining in a chaise longue becomes a necessity. The lake isn't known for its fishing. Weekenders with a penchant for flashy speedboats and a pocketbook for 14-foot, benched-seat fishing boats find this an ideal spot to look around for used watercraft, especially in late fall, when arctic blasts and the fiscal realities of winter lead to a run on "For Sale" signs at the local hardware store. For those without a boat, the setting may be a little obnoxious. But for those with the right

Awesome thunderstorms rake South Dakota every spring and summer; in springtime, tornadoes develop in the eastern part of the state.

speedboat, in summer, when the marina slips are packed and beer sales peak, Lewis and Clark Lake is a roaring, wave-crashing vacation spot. *For help in planning a visit, call 605-668-2985; for camping reservations, 800-710-2267; and for accommodations, 605-665-2680.*

■ YANKTON INDIAN RESERVATION *map page 61, A/B-2/3*

About 40 miles west of Yankton on State Highway 50 stands the Yankton Indian Reservation, a 36,561-acre reserve established in 1853. The southern boundary of the reservation is formed by the Missouri River, a portion of which has been impounded by **Fort Randall Dam.** At the base of the massive earthen dam stands the **Fort Randall Historic Site,** which commemorates a military outpost established in 1856 to keep peace between the white settlers and the Sioux. Its roster of visitors included Philip Sheridan, William Tecumseh Sherman, George Custer, and Sioux leader Sitting Bull, who was held prisoner at the fort for two years before being allowed to return to Standing Rock Reservation. The only original structure still extant at the site is the **Fort Randall Chapel,** a white-chalk rock structure constructed in 1875. *Fort Randall Visitors Center; 605-487-7847.*

■ RURAL LIFE ALONG THE HIGHWAYS *map page 61*

A good way to see southeastern South Dakota's countryside is to follow U.S. 81, which extends due north from Yankton, roughly retracing the path of the state's first homesteaders. Three miles out of town, the multi-lane highway becomes a two-lane blacktop that passes cornfields and silos and a small town every 12 to 15 miles.

In each community, the accents of longtime residents announce the lineage of the town's founders. The Germans, Czechs, and Norwegians who first settled southeastern South Dakota tended to band with their own kind to establish towns in the early years. In doing so, most found comfort in facing the trials of everyday life and weather that was alternately colder and hotter than their homelands. More than a century later, the nondescript one- and two-story buildings on each main street belie the locals' enthusiasm for their ancestry. Despite being fourth-generation Americans, most of these folks still spend a weekend every few months celebrating their heritage at a festival or street fair, eating bratwurst or lefse.

HUSBAND AND WIFE ON THE PRAIRIE

That summer Per Hansa was transported, was carried farther and ever farther away on the wings of a wondrous fairy tale—a romance in which he was both prince and king, the sole possessor of countless treasures. . . .

These days he was never at rest, except when fatigue had overcome him and sleep had taken him away from toil and care. But this was seldom, however; he found his tasks too interesting to be a burden; nothing tired him, out here. Ever more beautiful grew the tale; ever more dazzlingly shone the sunlight over the fairy castle.

How could he steal the time to rest, these days? Was he not owner of a hundred and sixty acres of the best land in the world? Wasn't his title to it becoming more firmly established with every day that passed and every new-broken furrow that turned? He gazed at his estate and laughed happily, as if at some pleasant and amusing spectacle . . . . Such soil!

❖　❖　❖

Beret [Hansa] had now formed the habit of constantly watching the prairie; out in the open, she would fix her eyes on one point of the sky line—and then, before she knew it, her gaze would have swung around the whole compass; but it was ever, ever the same . . . . Life it held not; a magic ring lay on the horizon, extending upward into the sky; within this circle no living form could enter; it was like the chain inclosing the king's garden, that prevented it from bearing fruit . . . . How could human beings continue to live here while that magic ring encompassed them? And those who were strong enough to break through were only being enticed still farther to their destruction! . . .

They had been here four months now; to her it seemed like so many generations; in all this time they had seen no strangers except the Indians—nor would they be likely to see any others. . . . People had never dwelt here, people would never come; never could they find home in this vast, wind-swept void . . . . Yes, *they* were the only ones who had been bewitched into straying out here! . . . Thus it was with the erring sons of men; they were lost before they knew it; they went astray without being aware; only others could see them as they were. Some were saved, and returned from their wanderings, changed into different people; others never came back! . . .

At these times, a hopeless depression would take hold of her; she would look around at the circle of the sky line; although it lay so far distant, it seemed threatening to draw in and choke her . . . .

—Ole Edvart Rölvaag, *Giants in the Earth,* 1927

Along the direct route between Sioux City and Sioux Falls on I-29, towns are sometimes few and far between, so pit stops are a necessity. For motorists entering the state at its southeastern edge, where billboards bark orders to stop at every interchange, **Edgar's Old Fashioned Soda Fountain** (107 East Main Street) in the Pioneer Drug at Elk Point—60 miles south of Sioux Falls on I-29 and 26 miles south of Vermillion—is an enchanting stop. The restored early-twentieth century soda fountain, which still has its original wooden booths and counter stools, serves root beer floats, sodas, and banana splits that'll make you forget about checking the gas gauge.

A side trip from I-29 is **Newton Hills State Park.** At the southern tip of the Coteau des Prairies (Hill of the Prairies), 11 miles east of I-29, a little south of Canton on State Highway 11, Newton Hills is arguably the most idyllic park in eastern South Dakota. Its rich soil was rescued from the plow and now supports an abundance of plant and animal life. Grassy knolls and wooded ravines harbor deer, marmots, foxes, wild turkeys, and more than two hundred species of birds. Both

Sioux Falls was recently ranked as one of the three best cities in America in which to raise children.

A cold winter moon looms over a lonely farmstead.

the park's **Woodland Trail** (a National Recreation Trail) and the **Coteau Trail** provide .75-mile-long escapes into unsettled South Dakota. You'll share the park with hikers, campers, horseback riders, skiers, birders, and photographers.

Liberally scattered throughout this landscape are hundreds of ponds and lakes, which range in size from 3 to 15,000 acres. Hidden from major roadways, they are worth seeking out, as anglers can find walleye, bullhead, perch, northern pike, crappie, and largemouth bass, as well as rainbow trout, catfish, and bluegill.

■ HUTTERITE COMMUNITIES *map page 61, C-2*

North of Yankton on U.S. 81 and west on U.S. 18 near Olivet, at the junction of the Wolf Creek and James Rivers, the **Wolf Creek Colony** has maintained a fruitful existence as the second oldest Hutterite community in the state. Wolf Creek Industries, its most recent business venture, now takes orders for furniture and

Quilt-making was an essential home industry in the Hutterite community
of Bon Homme when this photo of a quilting bee was taken in the late 1890s.
(South Dakota State Historical Society, Pierre)

lumber, often supplying newly established colonies with necessary building materials for new churches, schools, and houses. But its staple remains agriculture, and the colony raises milk cows, pigs, beef cattle, chickens, and turkeys.

The Hutterite sect originated in Moravia and the Tyrol in 1533 as a branch of the Anabaptists, taking its name from Jacob Hutter before he was martyred in 1536. Between 1872 and 1879, 100 Hutterite families left Russia to establish new colonies in the Dakota Territory. Persecuted during World War I, most Hutterites fled to Canada. Gradually, in the 85 years since, Hutterites have returned to South Dakota, replenished their stock, expanded the number of colonies, and dramatically increased their land holdings. Once reportedly numbering fewer than 100 worldwide, today more than 38,000 Hutterites live predominantly in South Dakota and Canada. Fifty-two colonies currently exist in the state, while more than 400 can be found elsewhere in the United States and Canada.

Preferring a plain and simple life, with little outside intervention and no exposure to radio or television, Hutterites quietly go about their business of farming and furniture-making. They live a life of worship and hard work centered around family and tradition. Men work the fields and maintain equipment; women wash, cook, and tend the gardens—as if little had changed around them and they lived at the center of a pure and completely understandable world.

In their modest lifestyle, the Hutterites resemble the Amish, the conservative Christian agricultural communities of southeastern Pennsylvania and parts of the Midwest. But unlike the Amish, Hutterites do not reject technology. Their farms feature the latest in agricultural equipment and computers, both used to create greater efficiency and more profit for the colonies. Hutterites are inclined to expand operations, purchase property, and create new colonies as membership increases, and as technology overtakes agriculture in employment prospects, to establish manufacturing businesses to diversify their holdings and provide new jobs. Nonetheless, farming remains the cornerstone of most colonies, particularly those in southeastern South Dakota.

Their success in communal living has provoked the envy of neighboring farmers concerned over the amount of property the Hutterites own. That concern, which flares every decade or so, has even led to proposed legislation to restrict land acquisitions by Hutterites. Fortunately for the Hutterites, South Dakotans have always favored individual liberty over state regulation, and such bills die a quick and meaningfully silent death in legislative committee.

■ SIOUX FALLS *map page 61, D/E-1*

In 1856, the Western Town Site Company claimed a strip of land near the falls of the **Big Sioux River,** began enticing settlers, and started constructing the territory's newest community. In 1862, violence overflowing from the Minnesota Uprising to the east became more tangible when a father and son, haying on the outskirts of town, were killed by Indians. That act sent the entire town scampering for Yankton two days later, and the claim was all but abandoned. Following the Civil War, pioneer homesteaders returned to the area, only to find the deteriorating and charred remnants of their village, which had been destroyed by Santee Indian raiders.

With protection from the U.S. Cavalry, the rebuilding of Sioux Falls began in the late 1860s, and by 1873 the town claimed 573 residents. From a sweat-stained start as a trade center for agricultural products and fur pelts, Sioux Falls slowly evolved into a major trade and distribution hub. With the arrival of the railroad in 1886, the water and power available from the falls of the Big Sioux, and growing stockyard and exchange activities, the city became the leading commercial center of South Dakota by 1890. In the 1890s, South Dakota's relatively lax divorce

(above) Sioux Falls' Main Street, early 1900s. (South Dakota State Historical Society, Pierre)
(opposite) The Old County Courthouse and Museum in downtown Sioux Falls.

laws kept Sioux Falls attorneys, hoteliers, and merchants busy catering to a colorful collection of people sitting out the required six months to obtain their divorces. It wasn't until 1908 that religious leaders were able to rally their forces and have the residency requirement lengthened.

■ SIOUX FALLS TODAY

The only city in the state with more than 100,000 residents, Sioux Falls is located at the junction of Interstates 29 and 90. In addition to industry and commerce, the city can rightly lay claim to being the cultural capital of the state as well. Private and college-affiliated art galleries abound, as do museums, a symphony orchestra, playhouses, and dance companies. Theaters, sporting events, and 62 park areas encompassing 1,600 acres of land—including an exceptional greenway through town—make Sioux Falls the most cosmopolitan community in the state. The mature city also claims pricey boutiques, world-class health-care facilities, five golf courses, amusement parks, a respectable zoo, and more than 150 restaurants, including **Minerva's** (301 South Phillips Avenue; 605-334-0386), which serves probably the finest cuisine in Sioux Falls.

Despite its continued efforts to be the state's cultural capital, Sioux Falls still smacks of its agricultural origins. At church suppers and square dances, rodeos and neighborhood taverns, life goes on much the same as it has for decades. Sioux Falls is still the place that farmers go when they get all slicked up, locate their cleanest baseball cap, and head to town for business or pleasure.

Sioux Falls has accomplished what most ag-based economies have not over the past 20 years by attracting new industry and providing new jobs. Unlike many midsize Midwestern towns, this one is growing at a steady clip. Sioux Falls owes much of its success to a blend of about 5,000 businesses involved in manufacturing, banking, medical services, transportation, communications, and wholesale and retail trade. Citibank and the John Morrell meatpacking company, both with major operations here, are among the state's leading employers.

In 1991, the *New York Times* reported, "With business proliferating as fast and thick as the black-eyed Susans, tiger lilies, and prairie roses in nearby fields, Sioux Falls is becoming equally renowned as a major regional retail center, a rapidly growing medical center . . . and a transportation and wholesale distribution hub." The same year, *Newsweek* magazine said Sioux Falls was the best place to live in the United States because of its exceptionally low crime rate, lack of pollution, low-cost housing, abundance of jobs, and laid-back lifestyle. For South Dakotans, who battled downturns in the agriculture, mining, and timber industries in the 1980s and 1990s, Sioux Falls' success is a matter of pride.

The downside to this development is that the city is suffering some growing pains. Modern office buildings are constructed in the muddy remains of fields that held rows of corn just the year before. Streets are becoming congested, and an increasing number of strip malls, chain restaurants, discount stores, and parking lots have begun to overpower the town's quaintness and intimacy.

■ HISTORIC DISTRICT

In the early days of Sioux Falls, prosperous businessmen constructed grand Queen Anne–style homes, several of which still stand today. The depression of the 1890s stalled further construction on so grand a scale, but families and preservationists continue to maintain several of the classic structures in the **St. Joseph's Cathedral Historic District**, located between Fourth and Tenth Streets and bordered by Prairie and Spring Streets.

One of the most interesting historic homes is that of South Dakota's first full-term U.S. senator—Richard F. Pettigrew. The senator purchased his 1889 Queen Anne–style house in 1911. An avid traveler, he collected artifacts from around the world, and when he died in 1926, the house and its contents were bequeathed to the people of Sioux Falls. Historians speculate that Pettigrew may have made the donation to ensure some measure of immortality, which might not have been assured based on his political career alone. During two six-year terms in the Senate, Pettigrew was a Democrat, a Republican, a Populist, and finally a Socialist before South Dakota voters began to regard him as an eccentric radical and removed him from office. His professional career was equally turbulent. Described early on as a mover and a shaker, Pettigrew amassed a multi-million-dollar fortune and claimed ownership of more than a dozen Sioux Falls area businesses. When the Panic of 1893 hit the financial world, Pettigrew's investments faltered and he was forced to close or sell off the majority of his holdings.

The restored **Pettigrew Home and Museum** offers a glimpse into the senator's political, personal, and business life, as well as an insightful tour of exhibits that explore the natural and cultural history of Sioux Falls and Minnehaha County. The displays feature many Native American objects, and the home's research library contains Pettigrew's personal papers in addition to a 5,000-volume library. *131 North Duluth Avenue; 605-367-7097.*

WIND AND DUST SPELL DISASTER

One November morning in 1933, the weather bureau in Huron, South Dakota, reported "a disturbance moving rapidly southeastward" over Canada. They didn't predict that the next day, a clear, crisp Sunday morning in Sioux Falls, the seemingly harmless air mass of moderate winds would become a huge dust storm.

Midwestern windstorms generally fall into three categories: tornadoes or whirlwind storms; cyclones or shift-wind storms; and—most unusual of the three—straightwind storms. Straightwind storms are formed when a low-pressure point or cyclone meets a high-pressure point or anticyclone, and, as the barometric pressures of the two systems equalize, gale forces erupt. It was the latter sort of storm, coming after years of drought, that was to initiate the disastrous period that came to be known as the Dust Bowl.

That Sunday morning of November 12, as the sun rose, the wind picked up and quickly reached 35 mph. As its speed increased, the wind became a black cloud carrying seeds, sprouts, and topsoil as well as tumbleweed, gravel, and small rocks. Within a few hours the cloud grew to 9,000 feet. As the cyclone moved southeast, so did the windstorm, and by the time the storm reached Sioux Falls, the turbulent mass of dirt and dust—now moving at 60 mph—was 100 miles wide. By 11 A.M., the city, reported the Sioux Falls *Argus Leader,* was "plunged into darkness."

The storm created cacophonous noise, and the wind "howled throughout the day, snapping off telephone poles and trees, smashing windows, and grounding fences." The storm continued on through Iowa, pulling bricks off chimneys. One woman's roof was lifted from her house, then carried and deposited across the street, completely intact. The storm then swept through Minnesota, Nebraska, Missouri, and Illinois.

Around 3 P.M. that Sunday, the wind died down, and as the dust hovering in the air settled, the city of Sioux Falls began to emerge from darkness. On Sunday night the temperature dropped from 50 degrees to 18 degrees F (10° to -8° C). When Midwesterners awoke on Monday morning, their world, inside and out, was covered in dust, gravel, and grime.

If Sioux Falls was badly damaged—caved-in storefronts, destroyed displays—the rural areas suffered much greater losses. The *Argus Leader* stated: "The wind exposed the roots so that winter killing is inevitable even where the grain was not completely blown from the ground. . . . It is estimated that farmers, already hard hit by economic and climatic conditions, will not be able to receive seed back from their fields." The worst news, however, was yet to come. The drought that had already turned the soil to dust continued relentlessly. Broken-down soil took on the consistency of ash, and small gusts swept up clouds of dust. Estimates are that 300 million tons of topsoil blew away from the Great Plains during this era.

The U.S. Soil Conservation Service was established in 1935 to develop techniques to slow soil erosion. Agronomists suggested contour plowing, strip cropping, and other techniques in a near-futile attempt to make the land productive, but not until 1939 did normal amounts of rain fall. By then, 100 million acres of farm land had become desert, and 3.5 million people had lost their livelihoods. Only after years of good rain had fallen and millions of government dollars had been spent did the shifting sands become productive land once again.

—Julia Dillon

A massive dust storm (sometimes called a "black blizzard" in the Dust Bowl)
bears down on the town of Gregory in the spring of 1934.
(South Dakota State Historical Society, Pierre)

The exhibits of the **Old Courthouse Museum,** which occupies part of the restored old courthouse building of 1890, also reflect on local history, and the museum supplements its interpretation by presenting special activities throughout the year. In spring, reenactors at the Almost Forgotten Crafts program revive sheep shearing, tin smithing, weaving, and other pioneer skills. Accompanying the fall buffalo feed are performances of Native American and ethnic dance, and in September the **Northern Plains Tribal Arts Festival** (605-334-4060) attracts native fine artists from around the nation.

Radiating historic grandeur, the building, constructed of Sioux quartzite, is embellished with 16 murals of varying sizes created by Ole Running, a Norwegian-born artist, from 1915 to 1917. Most of the murals depict early Sioux Falls scenes. Between the second and third floors, staircase murals represent scenes of what are believed to be Norway. One dreamlike painting portrays a lush forest with an elk. Above the trees a waterfall flows and above that, high on a mountaintop, sits a lonely castle. The building also houses the Minnehaha County Historical Society and the Sioux Valley Genealogical Society Library. Both the Old Courthouse Museum and the Pettigrew Home continue to collect objects in order to preserve, exhibit, and interpret the history of the "Sioux land" region. *200 West Sixth Street; 605-367-4210.*

The newest attraction in the Sioux Falls historic district is the **Washington Pavilion of Arts and Science**, the region's premier entertainment, cultural, and educational facility. Venues housed within it include the Visual Arts Center, Kirby Science Discovery Center, Wells Fargo CineDome Theater, and Husby Performing Arts Center. *301 South Main Avenue, 605-367-7397.*

■ WESTERN AND INDIAN ART
Before the price of Western and Native American art began to skyrocket in the 1980s, Sioux Falls was already home to a host of galleries exhibiting such work. Today, several of those same galleries and a few more feed the appetites of art collectors and sidewalk gawkers.

Most of this gallery art is for tourists, for the Easterners and West Coasters who will happily pay thousands of dollars for "Indian art" sometimes made by artisans with no Native American blood, and sometimes by residents of Taiwan. Rest assured, though, that even when this art is actually made by a Native American, a white man often makes most of the money from its sale. That's the way it is in South Dakota, and that's the way it's been with few exceptions for a hundred years. On the other hand, discriminating tourists and collectors who browse the galleries will also find the finest examples of authentic Native American art, pieces characterized by the exquisite detail typical of the work done by men and women who often live a lonely existence on one of South Dakota's bleak reservations.

Although it is impossible to provide a comprehensive list of galleries here, there are several in Sioux Falls that distinguish themselves by displaying art depicting early-day South Dakota, along with contemporary pieces by local, state, national, and international artists.

The **Prairie Star,** located downtown amid a number of lesser galleries, shows the best in South Dakota–made art and has one of the state's premier selections of handmade Native American beadwork, drums, star quilts, rattles, quilled and horsehair work, and dance sticks. The jewelry of Lakota silversmith **Reed Haskell** is an additional bonus. Haskell's award-winning work, which includes finely detailed bolo ties and belt buckles, is stunning.

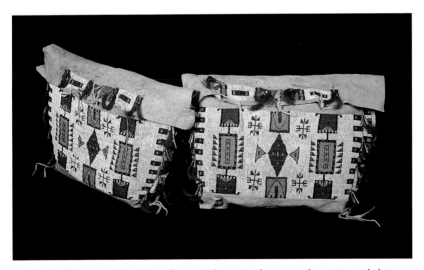

A pair of Sioux tepee-bags. Dogs often carried tepees in these across the prairies and plains.
(South Dakota State Historical Society, Pierre)

■ A U G U S T A N A   C O L L E G E

The **Center for Western Studies** at Augustana College proves its dedication to its mission—preserving and interpreting the history and cultures of the northern prairie and plains—through displays of historic photographs and manuscripts, Sioux Indian artifacts, Norwegian rosemaled furniture, and prairie art. The Center also houses the workshop of the late Jim Savage, a master wood sculptor, and some of his original works. Its gift shop has a fine selection of books, original artwork, jewelry, and bronzes. *2201 South Summit Avenue; 605-274-4007.*

Also at Augustana College is a reminder of Sioux Falls' own ambivalent cultural attitudes—the statue of Moses. In 1976, monumental full-scale bronze castings of Michelangelo's *Moses* and *David* were donated to the city by Thomas Fawick, a wealthy philanthropist, and Sioux Falls civic leaders believed the sculptures would bring a sense of culture, prosperity, and pride to the city.

At the time of the acquisition, judged by many citizens to be among the most significant in their city's cultural history, supporters faced the Midwestern sensibilities of some prim but well-heeled locals. As city fathers debated the final site of the striking but unclothed *David*, residents of a nearby highrise scolded their leaders for forcing tenants to face the nude *David* in all his full-frontal glory on a daily basis. After considerable discussion, a new location was found for *David*, who now gazes over a viaduct and a dreary railroad yard, his back turned meekly toward the highrise and its occupants. Meanwhile, the robed *Moses* continues to stand on the campus of Augustana College.

■ S H E R M A N   P A R K

Along Kiwanis Avenue between 12th and 22nd Streets is Sherman Park, the largest park in Sioux Falls. Within its 205 acres are a memorial to World War II dead, a zoo, and, within that, a natural history museum. Each of these attractions gives residents and visitors a place to go when they tire of fast-food restaurants, dusty roads, and strip malls.

The USS *South Dakota* **Battleship Memorial**, honoring the most highly decorated battleship of World War II and the 42 men who died serving on her, is as far from the ocean as possible on the North American continent, amid a vast sea of prairie. The *South Dakota* fought in every major battle in the Pacific between 1942 and 1945, and earned 13 battle stars and two U.S. Navy unit commendations. The memorial, outdoors in Sherman Park, consists of the ship's outline in concrete, actual size, outfitted with the original mast and anchor, a 94-ton, 16-inch gun barrel, and other parts, plus a museum with historical memorabilia and numerous photographs (open from Memorial Day through Labor Day). *12th Street and Kiwanis Avenue.*

Siberian tigers, black-footed penguins, grizzly bears, and birds of prey stalk visitors at the **Great Plains Zoo,** where exhibits approximate the natural habitat of species from five continents. Modeled after the San Diego Zoo, but smaller by several hundred acres, the facility allows visitors to experience the rugged expanse of a North American plain, the wild recesses of an African veldt, and the serenity of the Australian outback with attractions that include a children's zoo, a penguin pool, a primate building, a birds-of-prey island, and bear dens. *805 South Kiwanis Avenue; 605-367-7003.*

The **Delbridge Museum of Natural History** displays mounted game animals from around the globe. The collection, among the largest known in the world, was assembled by Henry Brockhouse, an unlikely candidate for the task. For years Brockhouse, who hunted big game in many obscure locales, displayed his trophies at the back of the unkempt and dusty hardware store he owned in north Sioux Falls. Each day, curious kids with parents in tow would wind their way through packed aisles, past curtain rods and hammers, power tools and widgets, to view Brockhouse's fearsome assemblage of dead animals. When he died, his collection was purchased by C. J. Delbridge, who donated it to the city with the stipulation that it build an appropriate facility to house it. The museum, which opened in 1985, displays an African elephant, rhinoceros, giraffe, giant panda, and other animals, each in a natural, albeit indoor, setting. The African water hole, Nile riverbank, and "restless Earth" displays are of particular interest. *605-367-7059.*

■ F A L L S   P A R K

The natural wonder in this park gave the city its name. Six viewing areas, walkways, and picnic areas allow sightseers to enjoy its scenic beauty and to survey some of Sioux Falls' earliest buildings, including the foundation of the 1887 Queen Bee Mill and a hydroelectric plant built in 1908. The Falls Park Visitor Information Center has an observation tower and provides information on the park and other Sioux Falls attractions. *309 East Falls Park Drive; 605-367-7430.*

■ MALLS

As the regional retail hub for southeastern South Dakota, southwestern Minnesota, northeastern Nebraska, and northwestern Iowa, Sioux Falls has become a community filled with the same chain stores and asphalt parking pads found throughout the United States. Its more boosterish residents, eager to discount the magnetic appeal of Mount Rushmore in the western part of the state, are quick to note that Sioux Falls' massive **Empire Mall** (I-29, Exit 77 on 41st Street) is visited by four times as many people as the mountain memorial each year. In fact, the mall's only distinguishing characteristic is its size; it's interchangeable with any other mall in the country. Three other malls and myriad specialty shops, bookstores, and galleries make Sioux Falls South Dakota's only true shopping center.

■ NORTH TO GARRETSON   *map page 61, E-1*

The area north of Sioux Falls is part of a region of vast farmlands that extend from Wisconsin through southern Minnesota and onto the seemingly endless prairies of

Despite variations in the national economy, Sioux Falls continues to grow and prosper.

central South Dakota. The eastern half of the state produces 37 billion bushels of corn each year, ranking South Dakota eighth in the United States for corn production. In addition to corn, in 2001 South Dakota produced 7.8 million bushels of oats (fifth in the United States); 76.8 million bushels of wheat (ninth); 0.3 million bushels of flaxseed (second); 0.4 million bushels of rye (third); 8.9 million bushels of sorghum (ninth); 138.6 million bushels of soybeans (eighth); 995.8 million pounds of sunflower seeds (second); and 9.2 million tons of hay (second).

A few miles north of I-90 on State Highway 11 lie the town of Garretson, population 1,165, and nearby **Devil's Gulch, Split Rock Park,** and **Palisades State Park.** The area's unique red quartzite rock formations and creek-carved canyon walls are all accessible to the average hiker. Garretson's fame has something to do with the legend of Jesse James and what transpired at a shaded footbridge over a hidden canyon known as Devil's Gulch. By 1876, Jesse James and his brother, Frank, had led their gang on a 15-year, $300,000 spree of bank heists and strong-arm robberies. But after a decade and a half of losing family fortunes and a few town residents to errant bullets, settlers decided that they didn't have to take it anymore.

Annual balloon rallies take place in towns all over South Dakota. Pictured at this rally in Sioux Falls is a Marine "bulldog" balloon.

In the fall of 1876, the James Gang rode into Northfield, Minnesota, intent on relieving local townsfolk of their stored-up currency. The villagers, heavily armed and deeply irritated, foiled the robbery, killing two gang members in a Main Street shoot-out and then forming a posse to dispose of the rest of the renegades in similar fashion.

With his wounded brother in tow, Jesse split from the rest of the gang to avoid the posse. The two brothers headed for the lawless sanctuary of the Dakota Territory, only to discover that the posse had pursued them, rather than the other outlaws. Just north of Garretson, the James brothers went separate ways and attempted to outrun the law enforcers on horseback. Frank scurried down the west side of Split Rock River and Jesse took the east side, not knowing that a deep, impassable chasm known as Devil's Gulch lay ahead.

As Jesse James reined in his horse and cursed his luck, he stared across a canyon 20 feet across and 50 feet deep. The hoof beats of the posse were getting louder and the shots from carbines were echoing off the canyon walls when Jesse retraced his steps to get a running start. Then, with a whooping battle cry, Jesse dug his spurs into his horse's flanks and together they leaped the ravine, leaving the posse to mill about in disbelief on the other side. After reuniting and holing up in a cave near present-day Palisades State Park for a few days, the James brothers headed into Nebraska. Unable to establish a new gang because of their notoriety from the Northfield fiasco, the brothers attempted the straight life. Jesse was shot and killed by Robert Ford six years

*Jesse James (left) with brother, Frank.
(Denver Public Library, Western History Dept.)*

later for $10,000 in bounty money. Soon after, Frank turned himself in and was found not guilty of assorted crimes by a sympathetic jury. He held a variety of jobs until he died peacefully in 1915.

In August each year, **Jesse James Days** are held at Split Rock Park in Garretson. Activities include a parade, pontoon rides, a heritage fair, a chuck wagon feed, and a theater production commemorating the exploits of one of the most famous outlaws ever to set foot in South Dakota. *605-594-6721.*

■ MITCHELL AND VICINITY *map page 61, B-1*

About an hour west of Sioux Falls on I-90, Mitchell, a quaint Midwestern town of 14,600, has a tradition of attracting the unusual, the notable, and the road-weary. The steeple of its massive brick Catholic church is visible from 20 miles away on the interstate. Its downtown is filled with old-time jewelers, law offices, and bars, all tucked inside three- and four-story storefronts. Most of the major chain stores have relocated to the strip malls on the town's northerly edge, leaving the tourists to roam downtown streets. Nearby residential neighborhoods are quiet and shaded by hundred-year-old cottonwoods. On summer nights, thousands of locusts hide in those trees, sounding a loud and pulsating chorus. In winter, the same neighborhoods are still and bare.

Mitchell is home to the world's only **Corn Palace**, or as old-timers term it, the world's biggest bird-feeder. The first Corn Palace was built in 1892 to celebrate the area's fertile farmland and to promote settlement. The success of the "Corn Belt Exposition," held each autumn in the whimsical corn-encrusted building, prompted the construction of new, larger structures in 1921, when it was officially christened "the Corn Palace," and again in 1937, when its Moorish-inspired minarets, turrets, and kiosks were added.

The present palace is decorated with 3,000 bushels of corn, grain, and native grasses and, odd as it is, that's what pulls camera-toting motorists off I-90 and into downtown Mitchell each summer. The building hosted virtually every touring Big Band in the 1930s, 1940s, and 1950s, and top-name performers such as Bob Hope and Andy Williams. One can only imagine the harsh words some stars must have had for their booking agents upon discovering themselves at this venue.

(following pages) Mitchell's famous Corn Palace is covered with grain, native grasses, and thousands of ears of corn, fashioned to create colorful illustrations.

When the American bandmaster and composer John Philip Sousa was invited to "Play the Palace" for the thirteenth annual festival in 1904, he quickly telegraphed his South Dakota admirers with the four-word retort, "What is Corn Palace?" Apparently that question was answered satisfactorily, because Sousa and his band arrived at the city's train depot that fall. Even then, the world-touring bandmaster remained skeptical and unbudging in the seat of his Pullman car until concert organizers brought him $7,000 in cash. Sousa and his band then played a series of twelve concerts.

Each year, before crowds gather for country western concerts and the carnival atmosphere surrounding the **Corn Palace Festival** (605-995-8427) at the end of August, crews strip the decorative murals from the building's exterior and begin to create new ones using thousands of bushels of local corn. This is precise work that carries a price tag of about $110,000. Throughout the summer, workers build up the murals by applying corn of varying types and colors to wooden panels on the exterior, following instructions printed on roofing paper attached to the panels. When completed, the murals, designed by a local artist, depict life on the prairie through mosaics of such things as windmills, grazing cattle, and horse-drawn plows.

The Palace's exterior panels are changed and adapted to a new theme each year, but the permanent interior panels, also in colored corn, remain the most exceptional work. Six of them, including a mural depicting the area's bountiful pheasant hunting, were designed between 1948 and 1971 by Oscar Howe, a Yanktonai Sioux painter whose geometrically abstract designs earned him critical acclaim and worldwide recognition. *604 North Main Street; 605-995-8427.*

The **Middle Border Museum–Oscar Howe Art Center**, a mile south of the Corn Palace, provides an in-depth look at the artist's work in other media. Howe served as Artist Laureate of South Dakota and taught at the University of South Dakota until his death in 1983. His visionary, vividly colored paintings are inspired by Indian life and spirituality, but also reflect modern influences. Displayed in a gallery dedicated to him, his works testify to his lifelong ambition to inspire fellowship between Native Americans and whites. Also at the museum is a large collection of art by other hands, Native American exhibits, horse-drawn

Redecorating the Corn Palace is a cob-by-cob job that begins in the early spring and ends in late summer in time for the Corn Palace Festival. (Greg Latza)

Winter counts, like this one by Lone Dog, served as historical records. Each winter,
a pictograph representing the year's events was added to a buffalo skin.
(South Dakota State Historical Society, Pierre)

vehicles, and early farm implements. The Leland Case Gallery contains sculptures, prints, and paintings by artists such as Gutzon Borglum, Harvey Dunn, and James Earle Fraser, while the Charles Hargens Gallery has oils and sketches by the artist whose work graced the covers of numerous books and who was considered the Norman Rockwell of South Dakota. *1300 East University Avenue; 605-996-4111.*

Once travelers have visited the Corn Palace, many check out the 4,000 dolls displayed directly across the street in an English-style castle called the **Enchanted World Doll Museum**. And as doll museums go, this one, with antique and modern dolls displayed in fairy tale settings, is worth a stop, for the collector or for girls between four and eleven. Tomboys, however, have been known to fidget. *615 North Main Street; 605-996-9896.*

Mitchell is also the home of **Dakota Wesleyan University** (1200 West University Avenue; 800-333-8506), a small liberal arts school on the city's south side, and an 85,000-square-foot branch of **Cabela's** (Exit 332 off I-90; 605-996-0337), the hunting and fishing outfitter, that is already drawing 1.5 million people off the interstate a year—as big a draw as the Corn Palace.

Those who venture north of town to the shores of Lake Mitchell will discover the state's lone National Archaeological Landmark. The **Mitchell Prehistoric Indian Village**, a town site dating back to about 900 B.C., provides a rare glimpse into the lives of prehistoric peoples who vanished from the northern Great Plains in the thirteenth century, possibly as the result of an extended drought. Continuing research at the site, which also is designated a National Historic Landmark, has revealed a place where as many as 1,000 seminomadic hunters and gardeners stalked buffalo, built lodges, raised vegetables, and protected one another from hostile bands of warriors. You can also take a relaxing walk over a swinging bridge or stop by a hunter's lodge, a museum, and the visitors center. *Guided tours are available. On the shores of Lake Mitchell, just north of Mitchell—signs and yellow banners mark the way; 605-996-5473.*

THE NORTHEAST

The rolling hills and prairie potholes of South Dakota's northeastern sector are interspersed with lakes, several state parks and recreation areas, and two national wildlife refuges. Drained by the valleys of the Big Sioux and James Rivers, then sliced across the top by the curves of the Bois de Sioux River, Big Stone Lake, and the Minnesota River, the northeast has many terrains. In the region's eastern reaches, near the Minnesota border, tree-lined lakes lie between gentle hills that drop into shallow ravines with thickets and wildflowers. Closer to the Missouri in the western part of this quarter, the land is drier, and cattle ranches are more common than farms.

The more than 120 lakes in this region were formed when glaciers from the last ice age scoured and gouged the earth as they slowly receded across northeastern South Dakota 11,000 years ago. Glaciers also left deposits of debris, sand, soil, gravel, and rock—up to 400 feet deep over the bedrock in spots—forming the rough, arrowhead-shaped range of hills that blankets the state's eastern ridge. These **Coteau des Prairies** (Hill of the Prairies) were home to several succeeding Indian cultures. Burial mounds, shards of pottery, and hand tools are evidence of the Woodland People who lived in the region around A.D. 1200.

Sioux Indians made their way here by traveling west from the woodlands of present-day Minnesota. They found the Paha Tanka (Great Hills) of northeastern South Dakota teeming with elk, buffalo, deer, and antelope. Rugged, timber-covered hills and ravines provided easily defended campsites and an abundance of fish-filled lakes, wild fruits and vegetables, and fuel. The Sioux inhabited this region for about a century before the first white men—French fur traders exploring the western frontier—discovered its bounty.

■ JOSEPH NICOLLET

In 1838, the U.S. Secretary of War engaged a French-born mathematician and astronomer, Joseph Nicollet, to survey the area. In producing his "mother map," Nicollet also became fascinated with the gentle grandeur of eastern South Dakota, its broad prairiescapes, lush river valleys, grasslands, and wildflowers:

THE NORTHEAST

May I not be permitted in this place to introduce a few reflections on the magical influence of the prairies? . . . Their sight never wearies . . . to ascend one of its undulations, moving from wave to wave over alternate swells and depression; and finally to reach the vast interminable low prairie, that extends itself in front, be it for hours, days, or weeks, one never tires. . . . It is then they should be visited; and I pity the man whose soul could remain unmoved under such a scene of excitement.

Nicollet realized that by mapping this region he was setting in motion a chain of events that would destroy the lives and livelihoods of the American Indian, and he had profoundly mixed feelings about what he was doing: "Then it was I bade a last adieu to the unconstrained liberty of the [Indians], who, it requires no great foresight to anticipate, will soon have to yield to the restraints of civilization."

Nicollet's map was published four years after his journey ended and in the same year as his death. Although all his maps have been proven highly accurate by modern aerial surveying, Nicollet received little attention until his journals were translated from French to English and published in 1976. Today, the Frenchman's efforts are memorialized by the 75-foot-tall Nicollet Tower, a gift from a handful of Sisseton senior citizens. The observation tower and interpretive center are near Sisseton at I-29 and State Highway 10.

■ SETTLEMENT

As Indian tribes were forced westward by treaties and U.S. cavalry troops, European immigrants followed, encouraged by railroad promoters and land agents, who hoped to attract new settlers, establish new towns, and increase commerce. Promising a paradise of blue sky and soft soil to any bundle-laden immigrant just off the boat, land agents would cajole, ingratiate, bribe, and otherwise use any means at their disposal to talk pioneers into heading for the townsite that they represented. And with increasing rail access, larger waves of settlers came.

Merchants followed and constructed stores and liveries. Newspaper editors brought presses and printed land notices, newsy bits, deeds, and drivel. Bankers built vaults. Connecting all these tiny towns—delivering supplies and departing with cattle, crops, and cash—was the railroad. So important was rail service in the last half of the nineteenth century that established communities dismantled whole

SETTLING A NEW CLAIM ON THE SOD

It was a marvellous adventure. By noon we were up amid the rounded grassy hills of the Sisseton Reservation where only the coyote ranged and the Sioux made residence.

Here we caught our first glimpse of the James River valley, which seemed to us at the moment as illimitable as the ocean and as level as a floor, and then pitching and tossing over the rough track, with our cars leaping and twisting like a herd of frightened buffaloes, we charged down the western slope, down into a level land of ripened grass, where blackbirds chattered in the willows and prairie chickens called from the tall rushes which grew beside the sluggish streams.

Aberdeen was the end of the line, and when we came into it that night it seemed a near neighbor to Sitting Bull and the bison. And so, indeed, it was, for a buffalo bull had been hunted across this site less than a year before.

It was twelve miles from here to where my father had set his stakes for his new home, hence I must have stayed all night in some small hotel, but that experience has also faded from my mind. I remember only my walk across the dead-level plain next day. For the first time I set foot upon a landscape without a tree to break its sere expanse—and I was at once intensely interested in a long flock of gulls, apparently rolling along the sod, busily gathering their morning meal of frosted locusts. The ones left behind kept flying over the ones in front so that a ceaseless change of leadership took place.

There was beauty in this plain, delicate beauty and a weird charm, despite its lack of undulation. Its lonely unplowed sweep gave me the satisfying sensation of being at last among the men who held the outposts,—sentinels for the marching millions who were approaching from the east. For two hours I walked, seeing Aberdeen fade to a series of wavering, grotesque notches on the southern horizon line, while to the north an equally irregular and insubstantial line of shadows gradually took on weight and color until it became the village in which my father was at this very moment busy in founding his new home.

My experienced eyes saw the deep, rich soil, and my youthful imagination looking into the future, supplied the trees and vines and flowers which were to make this land a garden.

I was converted. I had no doubts. It seemed at the moment that my father had acted wisely in leaving his Iowa farm in order to claim his share of Uncle Sam's rapidly-lessening unclaimed land.

—Hamlin Garland, *A Son of the Middle Border*, 1917

towns and reassembled them next to the new railroad lines. Those communities stubborn enough not to move are all ghost towns today.

■ MADISON   *map page 97, C-5*

Founded in 1875, the town of Madison stands northwest of Sioux Falls at the intersection of U.S. 81 and State Highway 34. The small town is home to Dakota State College, founded in 1881 as the state's first normal school. On campus is the **Smith-Zimmerman Heritage Museum** (221 Northeast Eighth Street; 605-256-5308), with its displays of farm implements and household items dating from settlement of the area following the Homestead Act of 1862.

Just a few miles west of Madison on State Highway 34, the little **Prairie Village** re-creates the early settler's way of life. Open from Memorial Day to Labor Day, this is the place to sample a way of life that endures only as a distant memory except in a few places such as this. A sod house squats on one corner of this living museum and the opera house where Lawrence Welk got his start sits just past the livery stable. Authentically restored all the way down to the 1893 steam

Rural life along State Highway 34.

carousel and its hand-carved wooden horses, Prairie Village is a bit of a movie set, but kind of a kick. The people of Madison, by the way, are modern and friendly and less inclined to leave you feeling pinched for your dollars than their counterparts manning the host of attractions along the interstates. On the last full weekend in August, the looms and farm tractors are in full gear for the **Prairie Village Steam Threshing Jamboree**, a festival with demonstrations of horse-powered feed grinding, antique tractor plowing, grain threshing, rug weaving, quilting, and spinning.

Other towns in the northeast host festivals commemorating their sodbusting founding fathers and mothers. **Webster** hosts the **Sodbuster Fest**. In **Miller**, residents go to the **Old Settlers Picnic**, and in **Lonetree, Sodbusting Days** is a grand event. Many sodbusting communities were formed by immigrant German, Norwegian, Swedish, and Czech groups who built their own churches and supported their own ecclesiastical schools and hospitals. Some northeastern South Dakotans remember these ethnic roots, as in **Eureka** (on State Highway 10 in the extreme northwestern part of the region), where each September residents hold a **German Schmeckfest**. Costumes and dances are authentic, beer flows freely, and wursts are the best pick of the day.

Old-time fiddlers do their thing at the South Dakota State Fair.

■ FLANDREAU AND VICINITY *map page 97, D-5*

In recent decades, South Dakota has participated in a different sort of gold rush: gambling. For years the state had permitted pari-mutuel betting on dogs and ponies, but in the late 1980s video lottery machines were legalized, and voters approved limited-stakes gambling in Deadwood in order to raise the necessary funds to preserve the town's Wild West character. But it took Congressional action to bring games of chance to the Indian reservations, a move to which South Dakota responded enthusiastically.

The **Royal River Casino** (607 South Veterans Street; 800-833-8666) lies 26 miles north of Sioux Falls in the town of **Flandreau,** east on State Highway 32 from I-29's Exit 114. The casino building lacks both the Wild West flavor and Victorian architecture of its counterparts in Deadwood and the pizzazz of the mega-casinos of Las Vegas and Atlantic City, but because of its proximity to Sioux Falls the Royal River attracts thousands of visitors to its games of chance: bingo, blackjack, and poker games, along with 250 incessantly ringing slot machines. If you drop by on your birthday with your I.D., you can try to grab some swirling cash in the Birthday Booth.

As with other Indian casinos in the state, and indeed the nation, this Santee Sioux tribe-owned hotspot has brought new economic prosperity to a reservation once plagued by joblessness and despair. Visitors to Flandreau today will find a revived community of 2,300 residents that was first settled in 1869 by 25 Christian Santee Sioux families. The reservation is also the site of a school widely attended by Indian children. Visitors may question the marriage of reservations and gaming as if something had been lost, some soul or mystique. But in South Dakota, whose reservations have traditionally been among the poorest areas in America, there is a new outlook, a new mood, and it shows on the faces of those who live there.

The **Moody County Museum Complex** (706 East Pipestone Avenue; 605-997-3191) displays antiques and collectibles from the area's pioneer past, and the county courthouse and community center contain numerous murals of Indians and homesteaders who participated in the community's 120-year history. Flandreau has several historic houses of worship, including the **First Presbyterian Church,** the oldest continuously operating church in South Dakota.

Flandreau's location on the Big Sioux River is scenic and uncrowded and each year, on the third weekend in July, residents celebrate their heritage in authentic costumes and traditional ceremonies at the **Santee Sioux Powwow.** *605-997-3891.*

■ BROOKINGS *map page 97, D-5*

Twenty-three miles north of Flandreau and 49 miles north of Sioux Falls on I-29 stands another community named for a settler and known for its tree-lined boulevards and university campus. In the 1940s, Brookings was a sleepy town of 6,000 residents whose future was tied to South Dakota State University, which in turn depended on the largesse of the ag-dominated state legislature. But when a few thousand education-hungry servicemen returned home following World War II, the town took off. Even though its population is just over 18,000, Brookings is home to more quality artwork and museums than its past, population, or location would appear to warrant.

Born in Woolwich, Maine, **Wilmot W. Brookings** earned his degree from Bowdoin College, then became one of South Dakota's pioneers in August 1857. In February 1858, acting as manager of a land company, Brookings set out on horseback from present-day Sioux Falls to establish a town at Yankton. Fifty miles later, a severe blizzard struck and the temperature plummeted to -30°F (-34°C). Already in danger of frostbite and death, Brookings compounded his problems by falling from his horse and landing in the Split Rock River. Wet and unprotected, he realized that his only hope for survival rested in a return trip to Sioux Falls in darkness. His feet were frozen when he finally reached the settlement. Under the most primitive of conditions and with only a butcher knife, a small saw, and no anesthetics, Dr. J. L. Phillip performed the first amputation in the history of what is now South Dakota.

Even with both legs gone below the knee, Brookings cast his lot with the Dakota pioneers and, because of his education, soon became a leading force in the territory. In a half-century of service to the state, Brookings was among the first members of the Squatter Legislature, was named governor of the Dakota Territory, served as associate justice, published the *Sioux Falls Leader,* organized a railroad, served as a member of the state constitutional convention, and worked variously as promoter, owner, and director of six major banks and companies in the state.

■ SOUTH DAKOTA STATE UNIVERSITY *map page 97, D-5*

Today, the city that bears Brookings's name is quaint and would be resoundingly quiet if it weren't for the close to 10,000 students who attend South Dakota State University, the state's largest educational institution. Founded in 1881, the university, with its botanical gardens, museums, and cultural and social organizations, is the focal point of the town. With programs in 200 majors, minors, and options, the university offers more than 6,000 courses annually, as well as bachelor's, master's, and doctoral degrees. Because of its beautiful setting and strong academic program, the university is popular and attracts a high percentage of out-of-state students. About three-quarters of the students enrolled at SDSU are South Dakota residents, with the balance coming from 46 other states and 41 foreign countries.

South Dakota State's chief rival is the University of South Dakota at Vermillion. Brookings students like to say that the highest point in South Dakota is Harney Peak (7,242 feet), and that the lowest point is at Vermillion, especially where the USD football team plays. So much for collegiate wit.

The **South Dakota Art Museum,** on the SDSU campus, houses works by two of South Dakota's finest artists. One is Harvey Dunn, the son of sodbusters and a painter who produced a vivid, though sometimes overly romantic, account of the good moments in the life of a prairie homesteader. In those paintings, viewers find little of the sod houses and tarpaper shacks, the fierce winters and dry summers, and the ceaseless, tedious labor that filled life on the South Dakota frontier. Classic, romantic, and beautiful, the paintings illustrate the all-is-right-with-the-world version of life that Laura Ingalls Wilder described in her series of pioneer adventure books.

An art teacher at South Dakota Agricultural College (now SDSU), which Dunn began attending in 1901, saw promise in his work and recommended that he enroll in the Chicago Art Institute. After taking classes in Chicago he studied with Howard Pyle, a leading illustrator of the day, and went on to have a significant career himself, his work appearing in *Scribner's,* the *Saturday Evening Post,* and other popular magazines. He left more than three dozen paintings to SDSU.

The second important artist represented in the museum is Oscar Howe, a Sioux Indian whose work derives from traditional Indian painting techniques but also reveals influences of twentieth-century European movements. Born on the Crow

Creek Reservation in 1915, Howe recorded the life, history, and legends of his people, the Yanktonai Sioux. His vision was powerful, mystical, modern, colorful, and commanding, and his life and work have served as an important model for other aspiring Indian artists.

In addition to the collections of paintings by Dunn and Howe, the museum exhibits the works of contemporary South Dakota artists and the handiwork of all the Sioux tribes, with examples of porcupine-quill embroidery, beadwork, eagle-feather headdresses, and intricately carved ceremonial pipes from the Crow, Dakota (eastern Sioux), Kiowa, Ojibwa (Chippewa), and Yakima tribes.

Delicate and refined work of a different tradition can be found in the museum's collection of Marghab embroidery, produced on the Portuguese islands of Madeira. Given to the museum in the late 1970s by Emile and Vera Way Marghab, the collection is displayed in a custom-built room, with specially designed lighting and climate controls. Vera Way was raised in South Dakota before she became a concert pianist and met and married Emile Marghab, a native of Cyprus. In Madeira, the two founded a linen company, the Casa Marghab, where Vera designed each of the company's offerings.

Harvey Dunn's The Prairie is My Garden *(1950) reveals the artist's romantic vision of prairie frontier life. The painting would make a perfect illustration for one of Laura Ingalls Wilder's idealized tales of settlers and sodbusting. (South Dakota Art Museum, Brookings)*

When political unrest hit Portugal in 1978, Casa Marghab was closed and Vera selected the South Dakota State Museum to receive her complete collection of embroidered linens—1,918 pieces, including 282 designs. Vera herself later returned to Watertown, South Dakota. Collectors from around the world regard Marghab linens as the measure of excellence among such embroidered pieces. *Medary Avenue at Harvey Dunn Street; 605-688-5423.*

Boosters of SDSU's **McCrory Gardens** (Sixth Street and 22nd Avenue) bill it "as the prettiest 70 acres in South Dakota," and at summer's peak it's hard to argue the point. With 14 formal theme gardens, including the newest Centennial Prairie Garden, the Children's Maze, and the Rock Garden, McCrory Gardens is a botanist's delight. In the adjacent **South Dakota Arboretum**, trees and shrubs are tested for tolerance to the state's uneven climate and varied soils.

Raising hardy plants is an appropriately calm activity in Brookings. Except perhaps on Friday nights when the frat houses and beer halls gear up for another party, it's rather subdued here—the Sunday morning church bells may be one of the noisiest events of the week.

■ OAKWOOD LAKES STATE PARK *map page 97, C-4*

North of Brookings, prairie potholes dot the landscape, marking one end of the northeast's chain of hundreds of clear blue lakes. Twice each year, these waters along the Central Flyway are visited by millions of ducks. Oakwood Lakes State Park, 20 miles northwest of Brookings on State Highway 30, is surrounded by native hardwoods and made up of eight lakes with 3,000 acres of water. Remnants of early habitation by the Woodland People—the Paleo-Indians who raised corn and beans in the Great Plains as long ago as 1000 B.C.—are found in 10 burial mounds within the park. Later, Sioux Indians called this area *Tetankaha*—"Home of the Great Summer Lodge." Also here is the cabin of the first white man to settle in the area, restored as a reminder of the rugged life of that era.

Fortifications built by soldiers following the Minnesota Uprising and later used as an Indian scout outpost for Fort Sisseton—a fort 93 miles north (see "Fort Sisseton")—are still visible in the park. Legend has it that an Indian princess was drowned in one of Oakwood's lakes by the warriors of her tribe because she had warned her soldier lover of an impending Indian attack.

■ DE SMET *map page 97, B-4/5*

Thirty miles west of Oakwood Lakes State Park on U.S. 14, near the shores of Mud Lake and Lakes Henry and Preston, is the hamlet of De Smet. De Smet traces its history to the coming of the railroad, and its name to a Jesuit missionary who spent his life among the Sioux Indians. This town of 1,200 has, in addition to a wonderfully renovated railroad depot, several paintings in a series by De Smet native Harvey Dunn. In his lifetime, Dunn painted more than 30 oils depicting pioneer life in South Dakota.

In viewing several of those works now displayed at the **Hazel L. Meyer Memorial Library,** it's difficult not to notice Dunn's tendency to glamorize prairie life. His technique is refined and unfaltering, but his subjects are too content, too happy to portray accurately the ceaseless toil it took to conquer the land and the forces of nature. Dunn's paintings primarily capture the good things about homestead life—the occasional day of sunshine when the plow didn't break, the wind didn't blow, and the wildflowers were in full bloom.

Each year during the last three weekends in July, De Smet gives thanks to author Laura Ingalls Wilder. A resident of De Smet from the age of 12 until she was 27, Wilder immortalized prairie living in her series of pioneer adventure books and described De Smet in one of them—*Little Town on the Prairie.* On these weekends, the town celebrates the pioneer way of life: actors re-create scenes from Wilder's books in an outdoor pageant and children can take free rides on a horse-drawn wagon.

Visitors can ramble through the **Surveyors' Shanty** (101 Olivet), the Ingalls' first home in De Smet, or the frame **Ingalls Homestead** (210 West Third Street) that Pa Ingalls built in 1887, where many of his hand-crafted items are on display. Or they might stroll under the cottonwood trees planted by Mr. Ingalls that today tower over the little town. *605-692-2108.*

Despite the bustle of tourists who retrace the life of Wilder and her family, the town remains relatively tranquil. Building facades and costumed attendants may reveal concessions to the tourist trade, but the residents remain hospitable and genuinely friendly.

(following pages) The sky rather than the land creates the striking scenery in eastern South Dakota.

■ HURON *map page 97, A-4/5*

Had it not been for the persistence of its residents a century ago, Huron, west of Brookings on U.S. 14, might have remained just another town along the rail. Surveyors for the Chicago & Northwestern Railroad first set up camp here in 1879. By the mid-1880s, the citizenry was promoting the town as a candidate for territorial capital (they succeeded) and, later, state capital (they failed). But though they were unable to garner the commerce that hosting the state government would have brought, they more than made up for it by building a strong agricultural economy. Huron remains an important regional hub, with many manufacturing concerns, shopping centers, and health facilities.

Huron's **Campbell Park Historic District** (Fifth to Ninth Streets Southwest) preserves nearly a hundred structures from the end of the nineteenth century, many of them modest but well-kept residences in Queen Anne and Colonial styles. A wonderful, flowing sculpture celebrates the contributions made by women to the state. Called *Spirit of Dakota,* it stands outside the **Crossroads Convention Center** downtown.

In 1904, Pierre won the prize of being selected as the permanent state capital, but that same year Huron was chosen as the site for the annual state fair. Each August this town of 12,000 experiences a population explosion with the opening of the **South Dakota State Fair** (800-529-0900), which takes place on the edge of town. What's billed as the world's largest pheasant, tipping the scales at 22 tons (it's fiberglass), greets visitors along the highway as they arrive for grandstand entertainment, exhibits, carnivals, and the opportunity to see neighbors and discuss local politics.

Four-H'ers show their best bulls, dairy cows, and calves for a week, then, following judging, watch their beloved animals sold at auction. Cowboys and cowgirls ride in rodeo performances, hoping to earn cash prizes offered in saddle bronc, bull riding, and barrel racing. In the exhibition halls, blue ribbons hang from the best-looking tomato, the most impressive squash, the loveliest flower arrangement, and the finest painting. Vendors hawk hot dogs and lemonade to fairgoers wandering among the midway carnival rides. The songs of country western stars fill the night and mingle with the musty smells emanating from the sale barns and beer tents.

A DIFFERENT KIND OF PRAIRIE

Beyond the Big Sioux there were no more fields, no houses, no people in sight. There really was no road. . . .

Laura said to Mary, "This prairie is like an enormous meadow, stretching far away in every direction, to the very edge of the world."

The endless waves of flowery grasses under the cloudless sky gave her a queer feeling. She could not say how she felt. All of them in the wagon, and the wagon and team, and even Pa, seemed small.

All morning Pa drove steadily along the dim wagon track, and nothing changed. The farther they went into the west, the smaller they seemed, and the less they seemed to be going anywhere. . . .

. . . Now they were in Dakota Territory going farther west. But this was different from all the other times, not only because there was no cover on the wagon and no beds in it, but some other reason. Laura couldn't say how, but this prairie was different.

. . . There was really almost no difference in the flowers and grasses. But there was something else here that was not anywhere else. It was an enormous stillness that made you feel still. And when you were still, you could feel great stillness coming closer.

All the little sounds of the blowing grasses and of the horses munching and whooshing in their feedbox at the back of the wagon, and even the sounds of eating and talking could not touch the enormous silence of this prairie.

—Laura Ingalls Wilder, *By the Shores of Silver Lake,* 1939

Laura stands in the middle of the back row in this Wilder family portrait. (South Dakota State Historical Society, Pierre)

■ HAYTI'S FARKLEBERRY FESTIVAL *map page 97, C-4*

Most of the early settlers of South Dakota learned to make do with what they had. There weren't many cries for public assistance, maybe because there was none to be had. Many of today's South Dakotans maintain the same make-do ethos. In fact, in one community on the shores of Lake Marsh, residents became so concerned with what they didn't have that they decided to invent something that no one else had. The 371 good-humored townspeople of Hayti (pronounced "HAY-tie"), 50 miles northwest of Brookings on U.S. 81, needed a gimmick to increase the community's commerce: Lake Marsh itself wasn't attracting any throngs of visitors, and even interest in the annual community celebration, called "Town & Country Days," was waning.

Enter Gordon Hanson, a Hayti native and teller of numerous "Ole and Lena" jokes. In 1986, the long-time South Dakota journalist discovered the mythical farkleberry, which any serious botanist would know claimed roots in its relative —the whortleberry. Thus was born Hayti's Fall Farkleberry Festival, which oddly enough was conducted in July. For nearly a decade, the rest of South Dakota tried to separate farkle-fact from farkle-fiction. The event is no longer held in Hayti, but you can still get a smile by ordering farkleberry pie with your coffee. On the way out of town, don't miss the world's only farkleberry test plot. It'll be on your right.

■ WATERTOWN AREA *map page 97, C-3*

Almost 30 miles north of Brookings on I-29 and just east on State Highway 22 is **Lake Cochrane**, one of the few spring-fed lakes in South Dakota and a wonderful body of water that still retains the kind of clarity it had when glaciers created it some 11,000 years ago. The 400-acre lake features campsites, boating, and swimming in a picturesque setting of woods and water. More sailing and windsurfing is available farther north, on lakes closer to Watertown.

About 20 miles northwest of the Lake Cochrane Recreation Area lies Watertown, a center of regional commerce, near the shores of Lakes Kampeska and Pelican. The founding of Watertown occurred in 1871, after the old Winona and St. Peter Railroad Company had completed a line from Minnesota to the east shores of Lake Kampeska, which proved an ideal site for a township.

The town was originally called Kampeska, but two brothers from Watertown, New York, are credited with providing the current name. Watertown was the home of Arthur Calvin Mellette, the Dakota Territory's last governor and the state of South Dakota's first governor. An attorney and editor from the East Coast who moved to the Dakota Territory in 1879, Mellette was appointed territorial governor by President Benjamin Harrison, and in 1883 he built a red-brick Italianate home in Watertown. He was elected South Dakota's first governor by a wide margin in 1889, and during his two terms in office, he tried to increase commodity prices paid to farmers and mitigate the effects of drought.

Following Mellette's term as governor, one of his best friends, the popular state treasurer W. W. Taylor, absconded with $367,000 of the state's money and left for an extended South American holiday. As one of Taylor's bondsmen, Mellette was liable for a portion of the loss. The former governor attempted to avoid scandal and restore confidence in state government by voluntarily surrendering to the state all of his family assets, including real estate and his home in Watertown. A short time later, a disillusioned Mellette moved his family to Kansas. He died there a year after leaving his beloved South Dakota.

The 1885 **Mellette House,** left in a state of decay for many years, has since been restored, thanks in large measure to the actions of concerned Watertown residents and the donation of the Mellette family's original furnishings, family portraits, and heirlooms. Visitors will find the house reconstructed and appointed as it was when it served as the cultural and political center of the region in the 1880s and 1890s. *421 Fifth Avenue Northwest; 605-886-4730.*

A good place to start a Watertown tour is at the **Redlin Art Center,** near the intersection of I-29 and U.S. 212. The center, which opened in 1997, exhibits 130 original works by artist Terry Redlin, a widely collected painter of wildlife and Americana. The $10 million facility also houses a planetarium, private offices, and the visitor information center of the Glacial Lakes Association. *1200 33rd Street Southeast; 605-882-3877.*

Another Watertown attraction is the **Bramble Park Zoo** (State Highway 20; 605-882-6269), home to 400 mammals, reptiles, and birds. Six miles north of town, gambling action—blackjack ($100 limit), poker games, slot machines—takes place 24 hours a day at the **Dakota Sioux Casino** (16415 Sioux Conifer Road; 800-658-4717), operated by the Sisseton-Wahpeton Sioux Tribe.

■ LITTLE FELLOW OF CLARK   *map page 97, B-3*

Perhaps because crime is low and news is scarce, South Dakotans tend to nurture legends. One such apocryphal story, the "Little Fellow," involved a young lad from Clark (west of Watertown on U.S. 212) and William F. "Big Bill" Chambers, a brakeman on the Chicago & North Western Railway, in the 1880s and 1890s. The boy was the son of either transient railroad cooks or poor homesteaders who lived in a shack along the tracks between Clark and Elrod, South Dakota.

Each morning, as the train passed near Clark, the 13- or 14-year-old boy would stand alongside the tracks, waving to all the railroad men on board. And the railroad men always waved back. But in 1888 the boy contracted smallpox and died that August.

After several weeks of not seeing the boy, the men noticed a small, bald mound on the prairie sod near the place where he had always stood. Upon inquiring, the crew learned that the boy had died and been buried in a plain wooden box near the railroad tracks—the spot the Little Fellow had requested—and the parents had disappeared. Beginning in 1889, Big Bill Chambers tended the grave every Decoration Day (Memorial Day) for 40 years. Today, the friendship of the "Little Fellow" and the rail crews is still honored at the annual Memorial Day celebration in Clark by a gathering of area residents, railroad buffs, and a local minister at the boy's gravesite 5 miles east of Clark on U.S. 212.

■ WAUBAY NATIONAL WILDLIFE REFUGE   *map page 97, C-2*

Tucked in a quiet area of the world midway between Watertown and Sisseton, surrounded by the waters of the Blue Dog, Hurricane, and Enemy Swims Lakes, lies Waubay National Wildlife Refuge. Waubay, appropriately named by the Sioux as "a nesting place for birds," contains 4,650 acres of prairie potholes separated by rolling hills and 700 acres of oak forest. On State Highway 12, 13 miles west of I-29, Waubay attracts a variety of migratory waterfowl, including Canada geese, mallards, and blue-winged teal. Rare white pelicans and pairs of western grebes gather on its lakes and ponds as well, and other wildlife species have been attracted to the refuge since it was established in 1935. White-tailed deer are common in the upland areas, while Chinese ring-necked pheasants, gray partridges, and sharp-tailed grouse are abundant, but less commonly seen. In the coulees and timbered areas, beavers, muskrats, minks, raccoons, foxes, skunks, and badgers make their dams and dens. *605-947-4521.*

■ HARTFORD BEACH *map page 97, D-2*

Century-old hardwood trees shade the confines of Hartford Beach State Park, 12 miles north and 2 miles west of Milbank on State Highway 15. On the shores of the 38-mile-long **Big Stone Lake,** Hartford Beach is a 300-acre park with fishing, sailing, waterskiing, and skin diving. Hiking trails lead to the sites of early-day fur-trading posts, Indian villages, burial mounds, and overlooks with striking vistas. The park also manages a 100-acre wilderness island in Big Stone Lake. Those who are able to get there by boat and like old-fashioned camping (there's no running water) will find the island a quiet retreat from the RVs and busy campgrounds of Hartford Beach. *605-432-6374.*

■ FORT SISSETON *map page 97, B-1*

In the quarter-century preceding the Civil War, immigrants flocked to Minnesota, Iowa, and the Dakota Territory to build their settlements. Not surprisingly, this infuriated the people who already lived there. To make amends, the U.S. government signed treaties with the Indians, agreeing to set aside certain lands for their use and pay them annuities in currency and supplies. Soon the self-sustaining Indian way of life vanished and the Indians were reduced to accepting handouts.

In 1862, Sioux chief Little Crow led a rebellion against settlers in eastern South Dakota and southern Minnesota. Subsequently, the U.S. government cracked down on "hostile" Indians and built a network of forts for the defense of soldiers and settlers. (Georgia State University Foundation, Pullen Library)

During the Civil War, the government ignored its treaty obligations. When months had passed with no disbursement of goods and cash to the Indians, numerous bands of Sioux began to starve. Their complaints were met with little sympathy and no response, however. One storekeeper remarked, "If they're hungry, let them eat grass."

On August 18, 1862, Little Crow, leader of the lower Sioux, declared war. Before his rebellion (which came to be known as the Minnesota Uprising, or Massacre) was quelled, 800 white men, women, and children were massacred in southern Minnesota, the Dakota Territory, and northern Iowa. The deaths sent chills down the backs of settlers in the West, and Washington felt compelled not to meet its original treaty obligations, but to provide a show of force that would cost it far more than fulfilling earlier promises would have.

The policy shift resulted in the creation of the Military Department of the Northwest. Its mission was to combat roving bands of "hostile" Indians (those refusing to stay on specified lands) and to provide security to the region's beleaguered settlers. A network of forts was built to provide a safe haven for soldiers and settlers and a supply chain for the growing army stationed in the West. In 1864, three companies of the Thirteenth Wisconsin Volunteers were dispatched to locate a site for a fort in northeastern South Dakota, which had seen conflict with Indians. Army officers agreed that the Coteau des Prairies region, with its rich supply of water, timbered valleys, fuel, and clay, was an ideal area, and they set about building **Fort Wadsworth** (now known as **Fort Sisseton**).

Following construction of its officers quarters, barracks, a hospital, stables, magazine, an oil house, and sawmill, Fort Sisseton became a center of activity in northern South Dakota and the army's newest stronghold on the frontier. Its officers authorized whites to trade with Indian tribes and provided agricultural supplies and seeds to friendly Indians.

On special occasions, particularly official visits from generals and dignitaries from the East, white tablecloths, champagne, and solid-silver services were brought out, and military orchestras performed. At one such event in the summer of 1865, Gen. John N. Corse and his staff made their official inspection tour, arriving from Fort Snelling at St. Paul, Minnesota. According to Fort Sisseton researcher Karen Karie:

> A buffalo hunt was arranged for them by all the officers of the post. The party numbered nearly a hundred and was led by Gabriel Renville, the Indian scout, who conducted them to the vicinity of Buzzard's Roost,

where they encountered an immense herd of buffalo—25,000 to 30,000 strong. . . . One of the general's aides, a young lieutenant, borrowed the finest and fastest horse and bragged that he would show the Indians how to hunt buffalo with his Colt revolvers. . . . The young officer began the chase and in doing so, became so excited that he dropped one of his revolvers and shot his horse in the back of the head with the other, thus putting himself out of the hunt.

Fort Wadsworth was renamed Fort Sisseton for a local Indian tribe in August 1876, after officials learned that there was already a Fort Wadsworth in New York state. Although the fort was the site of no major battles and bears no distinctive place of honor in the annals of military history, it served its purpose by discouraging hostilities between white settlers and the Sisseton and Wahpeton bands of the Sioux.

Thanks in large measure to reconstruction funded in the 1930s by the Works Progress Administration and its subsequent designation as a state park, Fort Sisseton remains one of the best preserved military posts in America. On its grounds, 10 miles southwest of Lake City, stand more than a dozen original and rebuilt structures, including barracks, officers and doctors quarters, and a guardhouse. The visitors center is open in summer (the park is open all year), and on the first weekend in June, the **Fort Sisseton Historical Festival** (605-692-2108), a re-creation of pioneer life in the 1860s, takes place. Reminders of warring days—shooting matches, tomahawk throws, and cannon and cavalry demonstrations—are presented, as are an arts and crafts fair, costume balls, and cook-outs.

Besides Fort Sisseton, the **Stavig House Museum** (112 First Avenue West; 605-698-4561), built by Norwegian immigrants in 1916, and the **Joseph N. Nicollet Tower and Interpretive Center** (State Highway 10 and Golf Course Road; 605-698-7672), which displays the "mother map" created by the French mapmaker and has wonderful views from the tower, are worth a visit.

■ SISSETON AREA   *map page 97, C-1*

Sica Hollow State Park, 15 miles northeast of Sisseton off State Highway 10, has preserved the favored campsites of the Dakota bands that once roamed the Great Plains. Although the species most important and sacred to the Dakota hunting parties—bison, wolf, and bear—have been pushed out by almost 150 years of

settlement, the park still provides a habitat for white-tail deer, wild turkeys, marmots, beavers, minks, raccoons, and songbirds. *605-448-5701.*

The park reawakens each spring with warm (and often wet) days and chilly evenings. By midsummer, the high humidity of eastern South Dakota accounts for hot, sweaty days and mild nights. September and October, when the park's 220-odd species of plant life display brilliant colors, are the best months to visit. Drive the 3-mile-long road that winds through ravines and along wooded hillsides, or, if you prefer hiking, walk the **Trail of Spirits,** a National Recreational Trail. Here, in spring and summer, sylvan wildflowers blanket the forest floor and woodland wildlife abounds.

Roy Lake State Park, along State Highway 10 between Sisseton and Britton, is remote and idyllic. On site are a state-owned resort (605-448-5498) on a 1,500-acre lake, campgrounds, picnic areas, cabins, concessions, and a footbridge to interpretive trails on Roy Island. Evidence of a prehistoric Indian village has been discovered on the shores of the lake, and archaeologists have linked artifacts found there to those of the Great Oasis Culture, which occupied the region about A.D. 900–1300.

(above) Today, three local beauties take part in an 1890s fashion contest and parade in the town of Bryant.

(opposite) An 1893 brochure promises the good life for those willing to relocate to "the next big city" of Sisseton.

■ BROWNS VALLEY MAN

On October 9, 1933, William Jensen was having gravel hauled from the municipal gravel pit to the driveway of his grain elevator in Browns Valley, a small farming community on the South Dakota–Minnesota border about 8 miles southeast of Sisseton. As the dumptruck spread its load, Jensen discovered several small bone fragments that appeared human. Further examination of the gravel uncovered a small brown flint spearhead.

Jensen got in his car and hurried to the gravel pit, where he found a worker loading a second wagon with gravel. Jensen sifted through the sediment, and his fingers uncovered a grayish stone knife. Nearby, in a 7-foot-high bank, he found the front of a human skull, jawbones, teeth, and finally, the remaining undisturbed skeletal fragments of what would become known as the Browns Valley Man.

Jensen lent the skeleton to the University of Minnesota for examination, and several scientific articles were published about the find. He later insisted that the skeleton be returned to him, and in 1950 the amateur archaeologist, fearing the theft of his greatest find, hid the remains in his fruit cellar. There the Browns Valley Man remained for the better part of four decades, sitting in a cardboard box, locked in a dark, damp cellar.

In 1987, following Jensen's death, the remains were rediscovered and sent to the state archaeologist at Hamline University in Minnesota. Carbon dating conducted in 1990 placed the age of the remains at 9,160 years old. As one of the "Paleo-Indians" who first inhabited North America, scientists contend, the Browns Valley Man stood 5 feet, 5 inches tall, and was between 25 and 35 years old at the time of his death.

Nine thousand years after he was buried with his skinning knives and finely crafted spear points, and nearly 60 years after his chance rediscovery, scientists confirmed that the Browns Valley Man was one of only a half-dozen sets of human remains dating from the early habitation of the continent, and arguably the oldest and most complete remains of a human ever found in the Western Hemisphere.

■ ABERDEEN   *map page 97, A-2*

The landscape of farmland and hills 100 miles west of Sisseton is dotted with myriad town sites and ghost towns, the majority of which were "sold" to eager settlers by even more eager railroad promoters during the Great Dakota Boom of 1878–1887. This was the period when pioneers who had spent months or years building their prairie towns sometimes moved their whole communities—buildings, homes, and all—onto the new railroad routes.

Aberdeen, located by the Milwaukee Railroad in a fertile valley of the James River in 1880, fared better than most. The town's setting was not vastly different from the Scottish Highlands community from which Aberdeen took its name. The town quickly became known as the "Hub City," given the network of rail lines that extended from it like spokes on a wheel.

Because of its excellent rail facilities, Aberdeen became a wholesale and shipping center, with large warehouses close to the tracks. The city expanded as the agricultural industry grew, and diversified into a manufacturing and service center. With increased trade and affluence, the community became a cultural center, offering "the best hotel accommodations between Minneapolis and the West Coast," and theaters that hosted entertainers and touring musicians, as well as political speakers, including Theodore Roosevelt, William Jennings Bryan, William McKinley, and later Franklin D. Roosevelt.

Aberdeen's 40 churches, representing 25 denominations, maintain the faith of the Scandinavian, German, Russian, and British immigrants who first settled the region. On the seamy side, a half-dozen strip bars, more than in any other town in the state, testify to the community's raunchier side. Although residents of this city of 25,000 voted a resounding "no" in 1993 to a state initiative to expand gambling in Deadwood and on South Dakota's Indian reservations, it's still probably harder to find a crisp dollar bill in Aberdeen than in any casino in the state.

Aberdeen also offers family-oriented entertainment. **Storybook Land** (2216 24th Avenue Northwest; 605-626-7015), a children's fantasy park, has more than 50 larger-than-life exhibits such as Captain Hook's ship, as well as impressive gardens. The Yellow Brick Road and greeters dressed as Dorothy, the Scarecrow, the Tin Man, and the Cowardly Lion are an homage to former Aberdeen resident L. Frank Baum, the author of *The Wonderful Wizard of Oz*. Just outside park gates is **Wylie Park,** with more than 200 acres of grassland, a variety of wildlife, and picnic and swimming areas. Animal compounds board bison, sika deer, elk, Barbados sheep, whitetail and white fallow deer, longhorn steers, goats, and ducks.

More than 3,000 students attend **Northern State University** in Aberdeen. Founded in 1901, the Neoclassical buildings of the campus stand on 52 tree-shaded acres in the center of town.

Sand Lake National Wildlife Refuge is home to prairie chickens—as well as hundreds of other species of wildlife and waterfowl.

Aberdeen's history is preserved and recounted in the **Dacotah Prairie Museum** (21 South Main Street; 605-626-7117), which contains the **J. L. Zietlow Telephone Pioneer Museum,** and at **Centennial Village,** just north of town on Old U.S. 281. In addition, the 17 impressive residences of the **Aberdeen Highlands Historic District** can be found between 12th and 15th Avenues on Main Street.

■ SAND LAKE NATIONAL WILDLIFE REFUGE *map page 97, A-1*

Twenty-seven miles northeast of Aberdeen (take U.S. 12 east to County Road 16, then 20 miles north through the town of Columbia), Sand Lake has a 100-foot tower similar to the one at Waubay. Forty miles of roads wind through Sand Lake's 21,451 acres, but the real story is off the road where hundreds of species of wildlife and waterfowl live amid grassland, forest, lake, and marsh. Except for howling prairie winds that whip through the tall grass and cattails like a comb through a child's hair, the refuge is exceptionally quiet. Even in the midst of summer, when the number of visitors to South Dakota may approach the number of full-time residents, you can hear only the honking of a few thousand ducks.

■ SAMUEL H. ORDWAY MEMORIAL PRAIRIE

Since settlement of the prairies, fences have hemmed in wildlife and overgrazing has damaged or eliminated many of the native grasses. Fast-moving grass fires that once rejuvenated the prairie by restoring nutrients and eliminating thickets and saplings have been all but eliminated.

In 1978, perceiving how man's interference was endangering the native grassland, the Nature Conservancy carved out the Samuel H. Ordway Memorial Prairie, a 7,800-acre tract of native grasses 50 miles northwest of Aberdeen—nonetheless a relatively small haven for the prairie grasses that once characterized all of eastern South Dakota. Elevations here are measured in inches rather than feet, and even on a calm day it's so windy that even a seasoned cowboy strolling through will trade his Stetson for a baseball cap.

L. Frank Baum, author of The Wonderful Wizard of Oz, *may have been inspired by South Dakotan tornadoes rather than Kansan ones. This twister—the first ever photographed—swept past Howard, not too far from Baum's Aberdeen home, on August 28, 1884. (South Dakota State Historical Society, Pierre)*

CASHING IN HIS CHIPS

Al Neuharth founded USA Today *and was at one time chairman of Gannett. Now a multimillionaire media mogul, he started out a poor country kid from South Dakota.*

I got my first job promotion when I was nine years old. Not a raise, but a big promotion.

I was promoted from harvesting cow chips by hand—that's manure to city folks—to herding cattle on horseback on the parched prairies of my grandfather's farm in South Dakota.

That was like going from garbage collector to grand marshal.

The pay was the same. No money. Just board and room for the summer.

It was 1933. Depth of the Depression and the Dust Bowl days.

My grandmother, Katharina, leaked the good news about my promotion. She came to pick me up in Grandpa's Model A Ford on my last day of school in the fourth grade.

Al Neuharth's humble South Dakota origins.
(South Dakota State Historical Society, Pierre)

"Allen, Grandpa's gonna give you the new job you want. You'll have your own horse to herd cattle. It's because you did such a good job picking up cow chips last summer," Grandma gushed. "But don't let on I told you. . . . "

[Grandpa] was a gritty German who figured everyone should be treated alike and made to earn their way. I had been lobbying him all winter to give me a bigger job the next summer. But I lobbied Grandma to lobby for me, too. And that's what got me my promotion.

When we got to the farm and Grandpa made my new job official, he just said, "You did a good job with the cow chips last summer. Now, let's go pick out a horse so you can get to herding the cows."

My promotion as a kid taught me:

- If you have a lousy job, you're more likely to get promoted out of it if you buckle down and do your best, rather than be a wimp and do your worst.

- It works to cultivate friends in high places who will help get you promoted— even your grandmother.

—Al Neuharth, *Confessions of an S.O.B.*, 1989

C E N T R A L
S O U T H   D A K O T A

The swath of land that sandwiches the Missouri River from Chamberlain in the south to Mobridge in the north comprises central South Dakota. Its largest city, Pierre, is the state capital, chosen for no other good reason than its perfectly central location. On the eastern side of the Missouri is rolling Midwest farmland, with small towns established by Civil War veterans and northern Europeans in the nineteenth century. On the western side lie the vast, dry grasslands typical of the Great American West, where spread two large Indian reservations, the Cheyenne River and the Standing Rock. Down the middle runs the Missouri, the great dividing line of the state. Mellowed by four earthen dams and pooled into giant reservoirs that have submerged more than 900 square miles of land, the river stretches 435 miles through the heart of South Dakota. In central South Dakota are two of the so-called Great Lakes of South Dakota, Lakes Oahe and Sharpe, man-made monuments culled from the river that are, incidentally, visible from space, according to native son and Space Shuttle astronaut Sam Gemar. The waters of the river and its lakes wash more than 3,000 miles of shoreline and lap at the sites of frontier forts and the ruins of fur traders' outposts.

■ HISTORY ON THE MISSOURI

Although often commenting in their journals on the Missouri's beauty, explorers Lewis and Clark cursed its sandbars as surely as the men under them who bare-knuckled boats and supplies upstream during their 1804 expedition. On good days, the expedition made from 15 to 20 miles. The corps often stopped to investigate what lay behind the bluffs, to hunt, to collect berries, and to make measurements of wind, water, and temperature. Some of the trip must have been fun: when the explorers spotted their first prairie dog village, they attempted to dig to the bottom of one of the holes. When they gave up on that hole, they proceeded to pour five barrels of water into another hole without filling it. According to their journals, they found the surrounding prairies beautiful, teeming with game and inviting further exploration. But because of strong headwinds, nagging sandbars,

CENTRAL SOUTH DAKOTA

A   **B**   **C**   **D**

NORTH DAKOTA

0   20   40 Miles
0   20   40   60 Kilometers

Elevation
in feet

| 7,242 |
| 6,000 |
| 5,000 |
| 4,000 |
| 3,000 |
| 2,000 |
| 962 |

Kenel
Pollock
Herreid
McLaughlin
12
10

Standing Rock Indian Reservation
63
Sitting Bull's Grave
1806
1804
Lake Oahe
Mound City
Selby
83
271
Eureka
10
47
Hosmer
247
253
Ipswich
45
Aberdeen
281
12

Mobridge
Klein Museum
Sacagawea Monument
20
Bowdle
Roscoe
12

Timber Lake
Lake Moreau Recreation Area
Akaska
Swan Creek Rec Area
Hoven
47
Onaka
20
Onida
20
20

Cheyenne River Indian Reservation
West Whitlock Rec Area
Seneca
Faulkton
212

2
La Plant
212
Parade
Eagle Butte
63
Lake Oahe
East Whitlock Rec Area
Gettysburg
Dakota Sunset Museum
1804
Redfield
212

Cheyenne River
Little Bend
Bush's Landing
Agar
Onida
83
47
Lake Louise Recreation Area
45
Bonilla
28

Triple U Buffalo Ranch
1806
Cow Creek Rec Area
Spring Creek Rec Area
Blunt
Harrold
Highmore
14
Miller
26
26

Hayes
14
Fort Pierre
PIERRE
Oahe Dam
La Framboise Island
Farm Island Recreation Area
South Dakota Cultural Heritage Center, Discovery Center and Aquarium & State Capitol Building
Washington
Wolsey

Midland
14
Fort Pierre National Grassland
83
Stephan
34
Crow Creek Indian Reservation
Golden Buffalo Casino
1806
Fort Thompson
34
Wessington Springs
281

Murdo
90
63
Pioneer Auto Museum and Antique Town
Vivian
Presho
Lower Brule Indian Reservation
47
Kennebec
Reliance
Oacoma
90
50
Lake Sharpe
Chamberlain
Gannvalley
45
Crow Lake
Kimball
11
Plankinton
90

White River
53
83
St Joseph's Indian School
45
Stickney
281

44
Hamill
47
Iona
42
Corsica

Mosher
44
Witten
49
Dixon
Platte
44

Carter
Winner
18
Colome
53
183
Gregory
Burke
18
50
Yankton Indian Reservation
Lake Andes
18

Mission
18
Rosebud Indian Reservation
83
Keya Paha
Lake Francis Case
Bonesteel
47
Pickstown
18

NEBRASKA

PASSING THE MOUTH OF THE WHITE RIVER

15th of September, 1804

At the confluence of White River with the Missouri is an excellent position for a town; the land rising by three gradual ascents, and the neighbourhood furnishing more timber than is usual in this country.

After passing high dark bluffs on both sides, we reached the lower point of an island towards the south, at the distance of six miles. The island bears an abundance of grapes, and is covered with red cedar: it also contains a number of rabbits. At the end of this island, which is small, a narrow channel separates it from a large sand island, which we passed, and encamped, eight miles on the north, under a high point of land opposite a large creek to the south, on which we observe an unusual quantity of timber. The wind was from the northwest this afternoon, and high, the weather cold, and its dreariness increased by the howlings of a number of wolves around us.

—The Journals of the Expedition of Lewis and Clark, 1804

and strong currents, the crew was often forced to use tow ropes and manhandle their boats and supplies in their upriver voyage through South Dakota.

The river was also a challenge to early settlers. South Dakotans like to claim that when early settlers first saw the Ol' Muddy they didn't know whether to drink it or plow it. And each spring, flooding forced nearby farmers to create dams with countless sandbags. In these early years of the Dakota Territory, the river also served to separate whites and Indians. Until, of course, white settlers crossed the river, intruding on Indian lands. Then, for the protection of traders and sodbusters, forts and frontier outposts were built at regular intervals along the muddy shore.

No bridges crossed the river until after the railroads arrived in the nineteenth century. Between 1924 and 1926, the federal and state governments erected five highway bridges, opening western South Dakota to rapid expansion, increased tourism, and new interaction between the major population centers at the extreme edges of the state. When massive dams were built on the Missouri between 1946 and 1963, backing up and widening the river, much of the land that Lewis and Clark viewed during their first two months in South Dakota was submerged.

■ EAST OF THE MISSOURI

Government officials, railroad promoters, newspaper editors, and land agents who came to the state in the mid-nineteenth century cast central South Dakota as prime farming land—"the sole remaining paradise in the western world." Germans, Norwegians, Irish, and a handful of Hutterites took the bait, claimed the land, and quickly found out how unsubstantiated the promoters' grandiose claims really were. Today, mile after mile, the wind blows down creek-cut coulees trodden only occasionally by cattle searching for forage and pheasants looking for a sheltered place to raise their young. Along the river, trees provide homes for eagles, osprey, and hawks that feed on field mice, rabbits, and other varmints that sneak through the ravines for a fresh drink of water each day. The only human inhabitants of this place, descendants of the homesteaders, reside in ranch houses sometimes set miles apart and most often hidden from the road by shelterbelts planted generations earlier. Rest assured, though, that they're home. Making a living on this land requires perseverance and a close relationship with the local banker.

In September 1804, explorers Lewis and Clark traveled this stretch of the Missouri River, near today's Chamberlain.

A journey through this region is as bland as travel gets—a 70-mile sleepwalk through farmland and cow pastures interrupted by a scant half-dozen interchanges signaling other farming communities. Because of the straight-lined roadway and unchanging scenery, it's not unusual to see a South Dakotan with a paperback or a newspaper draped across the steering wheel as he races across the state. Almost as common are unplanned lane changes by motorhomes and semis whose drivers are drowsing at the wheel. Some say this monotony must be the reason books on tape were invented.

Close to the Missouri, rangeland—rolling hillsides and sparsely wooded ravines, dotted with beef cattle—gradually appears. The small towns differ little from their counterparts in eastern South Dakota. Main Street businesses provide the essentials (real shopping is reserved for excursions to Mitchell and Sioux Falls), and town residents mingle with their rural neighbors in coffee klatches at the corner café. Wander in for a farmhand breakfast, and—whether or not you want to—you'll probably hear why the sheriff stopped at the Taylor's place Tuesday, who fell off the bar stool Saturday at the Dew Drop Inn, and whose "outfit" (pickup) was parked behind the Seed-E Motel Friday night while his wife was visiting her mother in Yankton.

■ CHAMBERLAIN   *map page 127, C-5*

As you crest the bluffs of the Missouri River above the town of Chamberlain on I-90, an unexpected panorama unfolds. It's best viewed from the state rest stop on the south side of the interstate, where walking trails lead out to the edge of the bluffs. In summer, you can stand on a knoll 300 feet above the water and get your first whiff of wind cooled by the river, then filtered through dry prairie grasses. In spring, a subtle green tint clings to rolling hillsides gently sloping to the water's edge. By late summer and early fall, green is replaced by autumn golds and reds; the brittle grasses crackle underfoot. In winter, the same vantage point reveals an arctic tundra, scoured and reshaped daily by almost incessant frozen winds that whip the snow and send any semblance of powder scurrying for Nebraska.

On September 15, 1804, the Lewis and Clark Expedition passed the mouth of the **White River,** just south of Chamberlain, and paused the following day to let the crew rest and the baggage dry out after three days of heavy rains. Along the bluffs of the

GRILLED MEDALLIONS OF BUFFALO
WITH PEACH CHUTNEY

(Serves 6)

18 medallions of buffalo, 2 oz. each
$^1/_2$ cup of olive oil
2 cloves of garlic, minced
1 T. of basil

$1^1/_2$ tsp. of crushed bay leaf
juice of one small lemon
$^1/_4$ tsp. freshly ground black pepper
salt to taste

Combine all ingredients except the buffalo in a food processor until mixed thoroughly. Pour mixture into a bowl and add medallions. Marinate for 4 hours.

PEACH CHUTNEY
(makes 4 cups; freezes well)

1 16 oz. can sliced peaches in heavy syrup
1 cup white sugar
1 cup firmly packed brown sugar
1 28 oz. can diced tomatoes, drained
1 cup white vinegar
$^1/_2$ cup raisins
2 cloves garlic, finely chopped
$1^1/_2$ large onions, thinly sliced

2 T. crystallized ginger, thinly sliced
1 fresh lemon, thinly sliced with seeds
    removed, but peel remaining
1 Scotch bonnet pepper, seeds
    removed, chopped very fine
$^1/_2$ tsp. ground cloves
$^1/_2$ tsp. ground cinnamon
1 T. mustard seed
dash of salt

Using an enameled pot, add syrup from peaches (set peaches aside), and add all other ingredients. Cook over high heat and bring mixture to a boil, stirring constantly. Continue to boil for about one-half hour, or until mixture thickens. Add peaches and return to boil. Allow to thicken, but do not allow peaches to break apart. Set aside to cool.

Remove medallions of buffalo from marinade. Grill medallions until rare or medium. Remove from grill, and top with chutney. Serve.

—Ruth Johnston, *The Buffalo Cookbook*, 1994

Missouri, the explorers' hunters killed buffalo, elk, deer, and pelicans. On September 17, after being confined to the boat for several weeks, Lewis set out on foot to explore the countryside along the river. The short, rich prairie grasses reminded him of a "beautiful bowling green" on which he spotted wolves and polecats and, circling above on the air currents, a number of hawks. The famed explorer, who would commit suicide only five years later, was altogether pleased by the scenery and was impressed by a nearby buffalo herd that he estimated numbered 3,000.

The town of Chamberlain stretches out along the east bank of the Missouri. Named for Selah Chamberlain, director of the Milwaukee Railroad in 1880, at the time the town was founded, it's a ramshackle and random place with little to distinguish it from the hundred other South Dakota communities that were founded as steamboat stops and railroad sidings. Its southern city limits have been extended to the interstate, where small town entrepreneurs hope the visibility of a few fast-food restaurants will pull motorists from the road.

The town's economic strength, though, continues to rest in the fertile soils of surrounding farmlands and in visiting hunters and fishermen. Each fall, as the buds of winter wheat paint a deep green cast on the fields, sportsmen stalk pheasants, grouse, prairie chickens, turkeys, geese, and ducks, while big-game hunters bag antelope, mule deer, and whitetail deer. When combined with thousands of fishermen who frequent the 107-mile-long Lake Francis Case, hunters, motorists, and area residents keep Chamberlain prosperous and its 2,300 residents busy filling coolers, pumping gas, and selling groceries.

Nonhunters—and you'll find few of them in South Dakota—enjoy *viewing* the state's wildlife. On nearly any drive off the main highways or any trek along a river bluff or through a wooded ravine, visitors can spot ring-necked pheasants, hawks, eagles, and a variety of waterfowl. Deer, antelopes, and coyotes are active in the early morning hours and at dusk in any season.

Chamberlain's **St. Joseph's Indian School** opened in 1927 as a school for Sioux Indian children. It provides general education courses, as well as studies in the Lakota language and culture, for approximately 200 students enrolled in grades one through eight. Originally founded with the intention of re-educating Indian children in Christian American culture and values, St. Joseph's and similar reservation schools were the products of progressive, liberal reformers who believed Indian children should be encouraged to integrate with the rest of white America. Too

Central South Dakota offers numerous fishing opportunities. Here Steve Nelson snags a walleye from Lake Oahe.

often these schools succeeded only in creating a confusing, painful atmosphere for children unaccustomed to living away from their families. They were required to speak English, adhere to rigid time constraints, spend long periods indoors, and study Christian doctrine, often under the eye of overly severe nuns and priests.

Today, the school's **Akta Lakota Museum** (605-734-3452) provides a vivid look at a way of life that has vanished from the Great Plains. Across the river from Chamberlain—in its sister city, Oacoma—most travelers stop at **Al's Oasis**. This immense restaurant offers unexceptional food, including cuts of buffalo that it once tackily touted as having been taken from the same herd that appeared in *Dances With Wolves*.

■ LOWER BRULE AND CROW CREEK

Turn off I-90 onto State Highway 50 to switch from four-lane-interstate speed to a pace suitably slow to explore the interior of South Dakota. Twenty miles north of Chamberlain on State Highway 50 are two of the state's seven Indian reservations. The Lower Brule and Crow Creek Reservations are separated only by the Missouri, the former tribe's land falling on the west, the latter's on the east of the natural divide. In the heart of these reservations, the river makes a curious 24-mile loop to form what is known as the Big Bend of present-day Lake Francis Case. When steamboats began to ply the river after 1831, passengers welcomed the bend as a chance to relieve some of the boredom of river travel. At one end of the loop, they would disembark, walk the mile and a half of prairie to the other end of the loop, then wait for the steamer to make its way around the river.

The two reservations are alike in appearance. Both hug the rolling river bluffs and extend outward onto the prairie about 125,000 acres. For a century there was little to do here but watch the sun rise and set. Today, as on so many of the nation's reservations, the sound of slot machine payoffs interrupts the monotony of prairie winds and slow-moving rivers. On the Lower Brule Reservation, legalized gambling provides numerous jobs for tribal members and revenues for tribal government. The **Golden Buffalo Casino** (321 Sitting Bull Lane; 605-473-0556) attracts a large number of buses filled with the farm crowd from Iowa, Nebraska, Minnesota, and North Dakota, as well as in-state residents who would never consider a trip to Vegas or Atlantic City. But with the gaming hall close by and a friend or two to go with, a quick trip to the reservation becomes a perfectly acceptable form of entertainment. It's somehow fitting that these tribes can turn a profit from their white neighbors. The Indians say that life is a circle, and cash payments made from gambling revenues to each eligible member of the tribe lends some validity to the claim.

The Sioux celebrate their own heritage with powwows on both reservations each August. The **Lower Brule Fair and Powwow** (605-473-5561) is held at Lower Brule; the **Crow Creek Powwow** (605-245-2221) is held at Fort Thompson.

■ PIERRE *map page 127, B-4*

In 1743, two sons of the French explorer Pierre Gaultier de Varennes, Sieur de La Verendrye, became the first whites known to have ventured into present-day South Dakota. After stumbling across the hostile, wind-blown prairie, the adventurers came upon the Missouri River and stopped to survey the view from one of the bluffs. There, above what is now Fort Pierre, the brothers left an inscribed lead plate that claimed the land for their king, Louis XV.

The plate stayed on that grassy bluff for 170 years, an undiscovered record of the first visit by whites to South Dakota, until a group of children playing on the hillside in 1913 accidentally unearthed it and placed it in the proper hands. Today the **Verendrye Plate,** which remains in remarkably good condition despite its age, can be viewed at the South Dakota Cultural Heritage Center in Pierre. State Highway 34 follows the Missouri to the northwest and roughly retraces the path of the La Verendrye brothers, early fur traders, and explorers Lewis and Clark. In nearly the exact geographic center of the state, that highway passes through Pierre.

Citizens of South Dakota will know you're an outsider almost as soon as you open your mouth—at least if you pronounce the capital's name as it's spelled. If you do, you'll draw a slightly condescending smile and a polite correction. The capital city of South Dakota is not pronounced like the name of the French explorer, but like the word "pier."

Pierre became the state capital by default more than anything else. Shortly after South Dakota acquired statehood in 1889, the choice of the capital city was put to a vote. Those backing Pierre as the best choice claimed that the community's location in South Dakota's geographic center would result in equal representation in the capital to all areas of the growing state. The argument may have made sense to some, but not to most. After several ballots, numerous bribes, and a lot of cajoling, South

Dakotans designated Pierre as the capital, but only because competition among Mitchell, Huron, Chamberlain, Sioux Falls, and Watertown was so fierce that no one could form a coalition to locate the capital anywhere else. Even then, South Dakotans didn't get a capitol building constructed until 1910.

Today, Pierre is off the beaten track, although a new four-lane highway now connects it to I-90. It may well be America's most isolated state capital. For eleven months of the year, it's even without legislators, a sleepy town of 13,800 residents who are content to perform their state and federal government jobs, stop at the store, and go home. During the remaining month, which also happens to be the year's coldest, legislators gather for their annual session and transform the city into a hotbed of lobbying efforts, hospitality rooms, and partisan politics. A couple of hundred insurance agents, farmers, ranchers, businesspeople, homemakers, lobbyists, and lawyers debate the merits of naming a state fossil or changing South Dakota's appellation from "The Sunshine State" to "The Mount Rushmore State," as well as more momentous issues.

Debate in Pierre often occurs between two very large "interest groups": South Dakotans living on the west side of the Missouri, and those living on the east side. Residents of the state refer to each other as either "East River" or "West River" folk—an important distinction to South Dakotans. Depending on your disposition and which side of the river you're on, your neighbors can be either too rough and regular or, conversely, too urban, and liberal enough to belong in a suburb of Minneapolis. The denser population of the eastern half of the state means it dictates what happens in mundane daily matters such as school-funding formulas and mining regulation, and that sometimes sticks in the craw of West River residents who have their own opinions about education and employment.

Partisan and geographic politics aside, South Dakotans managed to construct one of the most impressive **State Capitol** buildings in the country, even if they did model it after Montana's. For a state with a penchant for the practical, its grandeur, elegance, and expense were quite a statement. After 70-odd years of use, it had grown a bit shabby, but a restoration completed in time for the state's centennial celebration in 1989 rendered it beautiful once again. The building has mosaic floors, marble staircases, stained-glass skylights, scagliola columns, and artwork from the early nineteenth century. The exterior is made of Marquette sandstone and Indiana bedford limestone, and the foundation is South Dakota boulder granite. The dome is solid copper.

The interior features Greek and Roman designs and stenciling, as well as several massive murals depicting the state's beginnings. In the rotunda are four fine bronze sculptures by Black Hills artist Dale Lamphere. On the grounds are a man-made lake, several sculptures, an eternal flame, and the governor's official residence. The latest addition to the grounds is a powerful memorial to the late Gov. George S. Mickelson and seven staff members and state leaders who all died in the fiery crash of a small plane in April 1993. The memorial, a massive reproduction of Korczak Ziolkowski's sculpture *Fighting Stallions,* was a gift from the people of South Dakota.

Every year on the day after Thanksgiving, a few dedicated South Dakotans arrive at the capitol armed with hundreds of handmade ornaments, ready to carry on a Christmas tradition. Together, they decorate nearly three dozen spruce, pine, and cedar trees that line the halls and adorn the rotunda. Each tree is decorated according to a different holiday theme. The results are dazzling: by the time state employees arrive on Monday morning, the halls are bathed in a warm glow of holiday lights and color.

Looking up into the ornate dome of the capitol building in Pierre.

■ A R O U N D   T O W N

Nothing outside of the capitol grounds in Pierre appears to have been laid down with much thought or planning. As with so many South Dakota towns, inexpensive land is plentiful, and most people like to put some space between themselves and their neighbors. Residential and commercial districts sprawl. The layout of the downtown district seems random and spans a mere four or five square blocks, with a commercial strip extending past it for a mile in either direction. In summertime, petunias planted on virtually every boulevard in town add color to drab facades, but still fall short of providing any continuity to the place.

Nonetheless, there are some bright spots in Pierre. The South Dakota State Historical Society's museum at the **Cultural Heritage Center** (900 Governor's Drive; 605-773-3458), a modern building bermed and covered with native grasses to blend in with the surrounding prairie, houses fine displays exploring the state's history. The exhibits are less stuffy than one might expect, and they effectively describe the settlement of South Dakota in the context of the rest of the nation's development. An advertisement that sought Catholic missionaries for Indian reservations in the state reminds visitors of what early settlement probably entailed:

> WE OFFER YOU: No salary; No recompense; No holiday; No pensions.
> But: Much hard work; A poor dwelling; Few consolations; Many
> disappointments; Frequent sickness; A violent or lonely death;
> An unknown grave.

Also worth a visit is the **Discovery Center and Aquarium** (805 West Sioux Avenue; 605-224-8295). This science playground has more than 50 self-guided, hands-on exhibits and activities, as well as a fresh water aquarium featuring species native to Missouri River waters.

■ LAKE OAHE AND ITS DAM   *map page 127, A/B-2/3*

In 1962, President John F. Kennedy traveled to Pierre to dedicate the **Oahe Dam.** Two decades later, the massive earth-rolled dam (ranked second largest in the world, for those who keep track) remains an outstanding example of what can be done with an unlimited budget, a couple of hundred dump trucks, and an over-abundance of dirt. About 7 miles north of the city, the Lake Oahe Project was built and is maintained by the Army Corps of Engineers, which hasn't always been

CASEY TIBBS, BRONCO BUSTER

1929–1990

America's greatest bronco buster was born in a log cabin on a remote family homestead 50 miles northwest of Fort Pierre, near the banks of the Cheyenne River. He grew up breaking horses, and at the age of 14 started riding in South Dakota rodeos. A year later, Casey Tibbs was trailing bucking stock on the national circuit; by 19, he had become the youngest man ever to win the world saddle bronc riding championship. In the 1950s, he won a total of six saddle bronc riding crowns—a record still unmatched—plus two all-around cowboy championships and one bareback riding championship.

Success in the rodeo arena brought him new opportunities, such as his syndicated newspaper column, "Let 'er Buck." He wrote, produced, and starred in several movies, and he worked regularly as a stuntman in television and film. Casey was feted on the television show *This Is Your Life* in 1958, the same year that he took a rodeo troop to perform at the World's Fair in Belgium. In 1973, he and his troop introduced rodeo to Japan.

On August 10, 1989, "C.T." was honored at the Pro-Rodeo Cowboy Hall of Fame in Colorado Springs by the dedication of a larger-than-life bronze statue of himself atop a bucking horse named "Necktie." During his speech, the ailing star glanced at the imposing sculpture, called *The Champ*, and said, "Thanks for making me look so good . . . Hell, I *was* good."

The life of Casey Tibbs is commemorated in displays at the National Buffalo Association headquarters in Fort Pierre and the South Dakota Cultural Heritage Center in Pierre. The Silver Spur Bar on Main Street, Fort Pierre, still turns on the light over his portrait each night, and, for the abstemious, another statue of C.T. stands two blocks away on U.S. 83.

Casey Tibbs.
(South Dakota State Historical Society, Pierre)

known for its ability to blend dams with the surrounding environment. This one is no exception, being visible from several miles away. Its power plant (tours are conducted daily in the summer months) houses seven of the globe's largest generators, and its water intakes occasionally create whirlpools on Lake Oahe. During the huge floods in the Midwest in the summer of 1993, South Dakota residents escaped relatively unscathed because of the dam at Lake Oahe.

As incongruous as this great lake seems with the surrounding prairie, it is now a fixture of South Dakota and backs up water well into North Dakota. Lake activities include sport fishing, pleasure boating for high-powered craft and leisurely houseboats, and (due to persistent prairie winds) some of the best freshwater windsurfing east of Oregon's Columbia River Gorge. Sailboat regattas color summer days on Lake Oahe, sleek sheets passing the anchored boats of walleye fishermen.

In the fall and winter, the lake's location on the Central Flyway, covering a vast north-south slice of the central United States, attracts millions of Canada geese and ducks, some of which end up on the holiday tables of hunters. Younger, lighter geese often use the Missouri as a rest stop in late October and early November before colder weather forces them farther south. But, as many as 300,000 other Canada geese, most of which are older, larger, and less inclined to fly a cou-

Lake Oahe. (Greg Latza)

An aerial view of Oahe Dam. (Greg Latza)

ple of thousand extra miles, make the Pierre area their home all winter, relying on open water and leftovers from the irrigated cornfields near the river to sustain them through the coldest months. Other birds, including mallard ducks, whooping cranes, and sandhill cranes, use the Missouri River as a stopping place during their annual spring and fall migrations, and eagles often can be found wintering in the giant cottonwoods below the Oahe Dam.

■ FISHING LAKE OAHE

In every season, and in almost every type of weather, fisherman can be found on the waters of Lake Oahe, staring into its depths, watching their rod tips, and occasionally glancing at the horizon, aware that sudden squalls can make this body of water treacherous. In general, they come for the walleye, which often grow to as much as 10 pounds, as well as the chinook salmon (introduced in 1982), the trophy northern pike, and the solitude. Surrounding the Oahe are bluffs that are so round, so barren, and normally so brown that they appear as tan derby hats on the horizon. The isolation of this lake has often been equated to "fishing on the moon."

Access areas are provided along the entire river, but most are found on its east side. West-bank access is limited by a lack of roads near Oahe. Facilities are scarce and first-class resorts are nonexistent. Among the most popular marinas on Oahe are the Spring Creek/Cow Creek Area near Pierre, Bush's Landing near Little Bend off State Highway 1804, and Whitlock's Area, near U.S. 212 south of Mobridge. Nearly everyone, including all of the successful fishermen on this stretch of river, uses boats, and the fishing vessels tend to be deep hulled to counteract the high waves. Bank fishing is seldom fruitful. Inexperienced fishermen will find that hiring a guide, who most often comes with a boat, will increase their chances of success and enjoyment.

Guides, who can be found for hire at marinas and through fishing publications, local brochures, bait shops, and even the bulletin board at area supermarkets, are inexpensive, and they know the parts of the river that don't show up on the map. Because of the sheer size of Lake Oahe, their boats are often equipped with Citizen's Band radios in addition to Global Positioning Systems and the standard depth finders, beer coolers, and live bait wells. The radios are used to stay in touch with other guides and marinas to monitor the best fishing locations at any given time.

Fishermen tend to be courteous and helpful, as long as they're not annoyed by greenhorns. Most have trailered their boats to the Missouri, and at night you won't find them frying fish over an open campfire with a tent pitched in the background. If they're not staying at one of the area's low-priced motels, it's likely these fishermen are luxuriating in a well-stocked motor home or fifth-wheel trailer, complete with a microwave, fridge, and queen-size bed. Still others will stay on their boats, which generally range from 16-foot speedboats to 40-foot cabin cruisers.

Unfortunately, several years of drought have caused water levels on Lake Oahe to drop, and because a smaller surface means less habitat, fish populations have been affected. Rainbow smelt are less plentiful, and the small walleye that prey on them are growing more slowly than before, not fast enough to replace the larger walleye taken by fishermen. Access to the lake has suffered too, and boat ramps have had to be extended to reach water level. *For more information on fishing, regulations, and the status of Lake Oahe, call 800-445-3474.*

For the nonfisherman, **La Framboise Island** and **Farm Island Recreation Area**, both near Pierre, offer excellent hiking trails with views of the river, waterfowl, and wildlife. Parking is provided and both islands are accessible to the handicapped.

■ WEST ACROSS THE RIVER

The town across the bridge from Pierre, **Fort Pierre,** claims 1,900 residents and a history that dates back to the origins of the state. The settlement was founded in 1832 by the American Fur Company. In 1839, the company sent Pierre Chouteau up the Missouri River to establish trade with the Indians. Chouteau piloted his steamboat, the *Yellowstone,* to the mouth of the Bad River and began trading with Indians from nine Sioux tribes. An average of 17,000 buffalo hides valued at three to four dollars each were traded each year, then shipped to eastern U.S. and European markets where they were made into hats and coats. The focus changed in 1855, when the government bought the fort for use in quelling Indian attacks on white settlers. Even though nothing of the fort remains today, and cows graze in the area of the original cottonwood stockade, the National Park Service designated the site as a National Historic Landmark in 1991.

A century ago, when Fort Pierre was the cattle-shipping capital of South Dakota, dusty Texas cattlemen drove their longhorns to Fort Pierre's stockyards for shipment by rail to eastern markets. The town still clings to its rough-hewn image: crowds at bars and restaurants sport a variety of apparel from cowboy hats and faded jeans to golf shirts and pinstripe suits, and rowdy groups of weekend sportsmen mingle with the "suits" from the state capital. Before the capital city issued several "on-sale" (drinking on site) liquor licenses in the early 1960s, Fort Pierre's **Silver Spur Bar** was the major social center in central South Dakota, reputably having the highest volume of on-sale liquor business in the state. The establishment's owner, the wry Irish O'Leary, bequeathed a large share of the Silver Spur to the local Catholic church in his will. When O'Leary died, church leaders, uncomfortable with their windfall, quickly and quietly sold the bar.

Fort Pierre still attracts big crowds to the Silver Spur and the Hop Scotch Club, the only bar in central South Dakota featuring nude dancers. Because Pierre is located in the Central Time Zone and Fort Pierre is in the Mountain Time Zone, at closing time serious tipplers often race across the Missouri River bridge for an extra hour of imbibing, particularly when the state legislature is in session.

Beyond those two establishments, the nucleus of Fort Pierre's business district is a bank, a taxidermist, and the **Chateau** (110 North Deadwood Street; 605-223-2402), a down-home restaurant whose barbecued steaks and onion rings make a trip across the river memorable.

■ WINNER   *map page 127, B/C-6*

Fifty-five miles west of the Missouri River on State Highway 44 is Winner, the home of more than 3,100 souls who have an uncommon habit of being nice. Like the residents of Mobridge and Watertown, Winnerites are a hearty lot of ranchers and small businessmen who tend to leave out-of-towners thinking they must have just dropped a $20 bill on the floor and failed to pick it up. There's nothing distinctive about the town other than the people, unless it's the large number of pheasants that live on its outskirts and make Winner a hunting headquarters during the fall season. Too small for a megamall or fast-food chain restaurants, Winner is one of those out-of-the-way places that still has family-owned businesses: restaurants, bars, a drugstore, a barbershop, and a service station. The local Elks Lodge is still the best place to meet the town's movers and shakers, and they're likely to buy the first round just because you showed up.

Fort Pierre from an early sketch. (National Archives)

Part of the set for Dances with Wolves, *near the Triple U Buffalo Ranch. (Paul Jones)*

■ NORTHWARD THROUGH THE PRAIRIE *map page 127, A-3*

When the movie star Kevin Costner began searching America for buffalo herds and a landscape unchanged since the 1860s as the setting for an epic movie he planned to make about the West, he discovered South Dakota and the **Triple U Buffalo Ranch.** With a herd of buffalo 3,500 strong and 60,000 acres of open plain and unscarred horizon, the ranch provided the ideal setting for that film, *Dances with Wolves,* the story of a young Civil War officer assigned to the frontier and his first encounters with its Sioux Indian inhabitants.

To visit the ranch, travel 31 miles northwest of Pierre on State Highway 1806. You won't be able to saddle up and ride through the largest privately owned herd of bison in the world, but much of the ranch's perimeter is accessible by car. A little imagination can transport a visitor back to the nineteenth century, when great herds of these snorting beasts roamed all of the Great Plains. You can also visit the ranch's gift shop and purchase buffalo souvenirs and meat.

The landscape north of Pierre is typical of central South Dakota. A windswept range unfolds for miles, populated with grasshoppers and the occasional herd of deer or buffalo. The few ranchers who inhabit this region eke out a living on land that supports very little but sagebrush, cockleburs, and fence posts.

Northeast of Pierre on U.S. 14 and 83 are the small communities of **Blunt, Onida,** and **Agar,** which have a combined population of 1,200. Each one has seen better days. Residents are courteous and friendly, but the towns themselves are a little dreary.

■ GETTYSBURG   *map page 127, B-2*

Five miles east of U.S. 83 on U.S. 212 is Gettysburg, a town founded by Civil War veterans who joined immigrants in scrambling for some of the last land open for homesteading. Many of the area's early settlers jumped off the train at Pierre and headed north for open ground. Once there, they built their sod shanties and began breaking the ground and planting crops. Most of that marginal farmland has been

Railroad under construction near Gettysburg. (South Dakota State Historical Society, Pierre)

returned to pasture, but much of it cannot support more than a few head of cattle. Gettysburg's 1,300 residents, huddled in an old town surrounded by rolling prairie hills, enjoy its tranquility and are undismayed by its remote location.

At the town's **Dakota Sunset Museum** (205 West Commercial Avenue; 605-765-9480), artifacts from the numerous Mandan and Arikara campsites that once dotted the nearby prairies and river bluffs are displayed. The surface of Medicine Rock, a large flat limestone boulder displayed in the museum, is carved with handprints, footprints, and bird and animal tracks, as if to signify all that has passed its way. Early Indians believed the rock to be sacred and left gifts of colored cloth, tobacco, beads, and herbs as offerings to the Great Spirit.

■ MOBRIDGE *map page 127, B-1*

About 50 miles north-northwest of Gettysburg at U.S. 12 and State Highway 20 is Mobridge, standing on a sharply curved bank of the Missouri River and across from both the Standing Rock and Cheyenne River Indian Reservations. In the summer of 1906, as Milwaukee Railroad crews labored to build a bridge across a horseshoe bend in the Missouri River, an unknown telegrapher sent word of their location as succinctly as possible. His abbreviated dots and dashes, intended to convey "Missouri Bridge," gave Mobridge its name.

Construction of the bridge allowed trains to start hauling hopeful homesteaders to the last of the open range. It's a wonder that early settlers didn't head for greener pastures, because the weather here is brutal, but a knot of tough-as-nails settlers

The first bridge traversing the Missouri River in South Dakota was built at Mobridge in 1906. The name of the town was derived from a telegraph operator's abbreviation of "Missouri Bridge." (South Dakota State Historical Society, Pierre)

stuck it out, and in that is the essence of Mobridge: you'd have to travel to extreme northwestern South Dakota to reach another community as isolated as this one. Just the same, it is aboundingly clear that you'd be hard pressed to arrive in another South Dakota town as eager to greet you. Nowhere will you find such back-slapping, friendly folk. Or maybe they're just surprised that you came at all.

The town itself is not unlike a hundred others. Its storefronts have aged and there is little sign of improvements, save a $2 million upgrade to the 50-bed hospital, which happens to be the town's major employer. But familiarity breeds comfort, a large part of Mobridge's charm. Walk into **Rick's Cafe** (117 Main Street; 605-845-5300) and local color surrounds you. It is owned by Rick Christman, who once won the New York City Chili Cook-Off, and its decor smacks of Rick's Cafe Américain in the classic film, *Casablanca*. Try the hamburgers and count the misspelled words on the handwritten signs tacked to the walls. The **Wheel Restaurant** (820 West Grand Crossing; 605-845-7474) has a more refined atmosphere, great food, and a view of Lake Oahe. At the same address, in the Wrangler Motor Inn, is the **Windjammer Lounge** (605-845-3641), with its superb view.

Bud Livermore (above) reflects on a stormy sunset sky over the central South Dakota plains (opposite).

The **Klein Museum** has a fine collection of early Native American beadwork, headdresses, clothing, tools, and early photographs. The museum houses doctor and dentist offices, a parlor, a law office, a kitchen, a bedroom, and other rooms with period furnishings of the early 1900s. Outdoors are an original schoolhouse and a post office, plus a log cabin with a collection of old and new toy tractors inside. Open from April through October. *1820 West Grand Crossing; 605-845-7243.*

The **Scherr-Howe Arena** is jammed for high school basketball games every Friday night in the winter. Named for Jim and Bill Scherr, brothers who became hometown heroes when they competed as Olympic wrestlers in the 1980s, and for celebrated South Dakota artist Oscar Howe, the arena is still in use a half-century after it was constructed. The custodian gladly lets visitors gaze at 10 of the most unusual murals in the state. Painted by Howe under a Works Progress Administration grant in 1942, the murals represent the artist's early realistic work—not the abstract, colorful movement that defines his later painting—and portray the history of the Plains Indians who inhabited the Mobridge area, from traditional ceremonies and depictions of everyday Sioux life to the arrival of the missionaries. Of these 30-foot-tall murals, one, called *Sundance*, merits mention: Lakota Indians sing and pound their drums in the background, while a Sioux warrior with the skin of his breasts pierced performs a sacred dance ritual in which a participant dances in the sun until overcome by a trance vision. It is a powerful painting filled with pain and pride, themes that resurfaced frequently in Howe's subsequent work. *212 Main Street; 605-845-3700.*

■ SITTING BULL COUNTRY

Long before engineers and bridge builders came to the prairie north of Pierre and near the town of Mobridge, the land was home to the Arikara and later to Sioux Indian tribes, as well as to Sitting Bull, North America's most famous medicine man and Indian leader.

Sitting Bull was born in this rolling terrain in 1831, on the Grand River a few miles west of Mobridge—and he is buried at the same place. During his life, Sitting Bull was alternately praised as a hero and condemned as a coward by his own people. Sitting Bull was not a hereditary chief, but gained the power he possessed through his undying resentment of white encroachment on tribal lands and his ability to convey that message in a powerful and sometimes eloquent way. Credited with masterminding Indian strategy at the Battle of the Little Bighorn, Sitting Bull had to live in exile in Canada for several years following Custer's defeat. Later, he starred in Buffalo Bill's Wild West Show as it toured the United States and Europe, signing thousands of autographs for the then-princely price of 50 cents each. Even in death, he remains controversial, mysterious, and a continuing reminder of Native Americans' proud struggle for independence.

In 1881, Sitting Bull returned from exile with his starving band of sympathizers and surrendered to the U.S. Army. He was placed under house arrest on the Standing Rock Indian Reservation in extreme southern North Dakota, where he grudgingly submitted to reservation life and the humiliation that he feared most—dependence on the U.S. government for all he wore and all he ate. Even after a long period of quiet drudgery and brief stints tending a small garden plot with his compatriots, Sitting Bull was still regarded as a "hostile" by Indian officials who feared his power and his potential to arouse the anger of reservation Indians.

When the Ghost Dance religion came to South Dakota (see the "HISTORY" chapter), offering Indians hope that they might rid themselves of the whites and welcome home the buffalo and their departed brothers, Sitting Bull did nothing to quell the dancing among his people. This angered government officials who, in turn, concluded that the Ghost Dance would lead to hostile action against whites and that the aging Sitting Bull was responsible and should be arrested.

Fearing that the use of Union soldiers in the arrest of Sitting Bull would result in unnecessary bloodshed, military officers assigned the task to 42 Indian policemen. As dawn approached the Dakota plains on December 15, 1890, the "metal breasts," so called because of the badges on their chests, swept into Sitting Bull's encampment. They found him asleep on the floor of his cabin with his two wives, and rousing him, told him he was under arrest. Sitting Bull, 59 years old, reconciled himself to imprisonment and slowly shuffled from his cabin at gunpoint. As he came into view, he found the entire camp surrounding his home. Braves harassed the Indian policemen. Women screamed and called upon the men to drive the police from the camp. And finally, Sitting Bull's son Crowfoot taunted his father for submitting to the will of the police.

That was enough, and in his last act of defiance, Sitting Bull loudly proclaimed that he was not going anywhere. In the ensuing struggle between reservation police and Sitting Bull's warriors, the chief was shot twice in the back and killed.

As the firefight continued, its smoke obscuring the fallen bodies of those mortally wounded, the horse that had accompanied Sitting Bull in the Wild West Show sat down, lifted one leg, and performed circus tricks. When the smoke cleared in the gray dawn light, seven members of Sitting Bull's faithful bodyguard lay dead, scattered among four bodies of Indian police. Army troops arrived a short time later, restored order, and loaded the bodies of the policemen and the chief like cordwood on a supply wagon, Sitting Bull on the bottom, and transported them to nearby Fort Yates. There, with no ceremony and little respect, the army buried Sitting Bull in a corner of a post cemetery, interred in a rough wooden box. When Fort Yates was abandoned as a military post years later, the bodies of soldiers buried in the cemetery were removed and Sitting Bull became the lone occupant of an all but abandoned graveyard in a place he never knew.

In 1953, descendants of Sitting Bull sought permission from North Dakota authorities to remove the Sioux leader's remains from the neglected gravesite at Fort Yates to a new memorial near Mobridge. When their request was denied, the group alerted the Indian agent at Fort Yates, and, in his presence, took the bones. The descendants buried them on a high bluff 5 miles from Mobridge on U.S. 12, close to Sitting Bull's home grounds. Following the removal, North Dakota officials were incensed. But a U.S. circuit judge ruled that only the family and the federal government could determine where the great Sioux leader would finally rest.

At the site today, a seven-ton granite bust of Sitting Bull by the late Korczak Ziolkowski, the sculptor of the Crazy Horse Memorial, looks out over a horseshoe bend in the scenic Missouri River valley where the chief once

Sitting Bull's grave site near Mobridge.

roamed. Although isolated by the changed route of the highway and mowed only occasionally, this desolate memorial nonetheless conveys the resiliency, intelligence, and quiet pride of a great Sioux leader.

■ STANDING ROCK AND CHEYENNE RIVER INDIAN RESERVATIONS *map page 127, A/B-1/3*

Approximately 70,000 Sioux live in South Dakota—as much as three times the population 200 years ago—and of the state's nine Sioux tribal governments, six have reservation boundaries. Reservations within the state cover about 5 million acres, or about 10 percent of its total acreage. Just west of Mobridge on U.S. 12 is the Standing Rock Indian Reservation, 843,000 acres of vastness and desolation that extend north into North Dakota. Past the reservation's southern border lies the Cheyenne River Indian Reservation, the second largest of South Dakota's Indian reservations, with 1,396,000 acres.

Together these two enormous reservations cover a tract larger than Delaware, with none of that state's diversity. Although residents use the medical and retail services of Mobridge to the east and Pierre to the southeast, there is little interaction between the white and Indian worlds. For the most part, the two remain indifferent to one another.

These two reservations are among the most sparsely populated areas in South Dakota and cover three counties of remote grasslands and mind-numbing tundra-like expanses. Motorists traveling the two main arteries, U.S. 212 and U.S. 12, through the two reservations should check the condition of their vehicles before attempting a cross-country trek. Except for the asphalt and gravel roadways and an occasional community, this land has changed little since the Civil War era. Residents live far apart in small towns, most with fewer than 500 people, with names that echo the area's Native American past: Thunder Hawk, Eagle Butte, Whitehorse, Green Grass, and Iron Lighting. Each of the burgs is marked only by reduced speed zones, cigarette stops, and gas pumps.

Look-alike government housing dots the prairie—the paint, though fading, in stark contrast to the brownness of the surrounding land.

VISITING GRANDMOTHER ENGLAND

In the late 1870s, Black Elk toured with Buffalo Bill's Wild West Show, performing across the United States and abroad. In his life story as told to John G. Neihardt, he describes crossing the "big water" and spending "six moons" in a very big town called London, where Queen Victoria attended a command performance.

They put us all on a very big fire-boat, so big that when I first saw, I could hardly believe it; and when it sent forth a voice, I was frightened. There were other big fire-boats sending voices, and little ones too.

Afterwhile I could see nothing but water, water, water, and we did not seem to be going anywhere, just up and down; but we were told that we were going fast. If we were, I thought that we must drop off where the water ended; or maybe we might have to stop where the sky came down to the water. There was nothing but mist where the big town used to be and nothing but water all around. We were all in despair now and many were feeling so sick that they began to sing their deathsongs. . . .

❖ ❖ ❖

One day we were told that Majesty was coming. I did not know what that was at first,

but I learned afterward. It was Grandmother England. . . . She was little but fat and we liked her, because she was good to us. After we had danced, she spoke to us. She said something like this: "I am sixty-seven years old. All over the world I have seen all kinds of people; but to-day I have seen the best-looking people I know. If you belonged to me, I would not let them take you around in a show like this."

—John G. Neihardt,
Black Elk Speaks, 1932

Black Elk. (South Dakota State Historical Society, Pierre)

SOUTH-CENTRAL
AND BADLANDS

Vast swaths of South Dakota are without civilization. Across miles of open plain, scarred over ages by creek-cut coulees and incessant winds, few signs of human habitation exist. So it is with south-central South Dakota—an area bounded on the north by I-90, on the east by the Missouri River, on the west by the Black Hills, and on the south by South Dakota's border with Nebraska. Except for the relatively populated Black Hills region, the West River area has only about two people per square mile.

Much of the south-central plains lacks any one measure of distinction. Formed by the same lift that created the Rocky Mountains, the land slants east and drains into the Missouri River. Unlike the flat basins and gently rolling hills of lowland eastern South Dakota, the topography of the plains is high buttes, deep canyons, and badlands. Surprising changes occur in this landscape, which encompasses everything from cool wooded ravines and lazy rivers to grasslands and some of the most god-forsaken country man has ever seen.

The South Dakota journalist Bob Mercer claims that western and eastern South Dakota essentially grew up as twins separated at birth by the Missouri River and the vast Indian reservations that have historically run down the middle of the state. In the 1870s and 1880s, when Yankton, Bismarck, and other communities fought to be named the Dakota Territory capital, nonconformists in western South Dakota sought to break away and form their own separate territory to be called Lincoln. As the region grew, its residents developed two distinct personalities. By and large, residents of western South Dakota are a bit less mainstream and a lot more down to earth than their eastern counterparts who, they sense, probably look down their noses at the West River residents' less refined ways. Even in 1993 an eastern South Dakota public relations worker—who might consider a new vocation—said, "I believe the East River and West River people are different in the ways of their women. The women on the West River chew tobacco and the women on the East River don't." Truth is, only a few western South Dakota women chew tobacco, but they're hell on whiskey and cigars.

■ HISTORY

The first inhabitants of this land were hunters of the giant bison herds that roamed the Great Plains. Not surprisingly, white settlement of this infertile region came late. While the fertile farmlands of eastern South Dakota attracted sodbusters after the 1861 establishment of the Dakota Territory, the plains west of the Missouri were designated for Indians under treaties with the U.S. government. But when the bison herds were gone, living off this land became extremely difficult for the Sioux, and only when they turned to the Black Hills could the Indians find game to supplement the government's rations.

In the 30 years following the initial gold rush to the Black Hills, enormous areas of western South Dakota still remained remote and untouched by white settlement. In the 1880s, the main routes to the Black Hills from the east were two wagon trails leading to Deadwood: one from Bismarck, North Dakota, and one from Fort Pierre in central South Dakota. The first rail line into western South Dakota came not from Sioux Falls, but from Chadron, Nebraska, through Buffalo Gap in 1885–86. No railroads directly connected eastern and western

When George Catlin painted this scene, tens of millions of buffalo roamed the Great Plains. (Buffalo Bill Historical Center, Cody, Wyoming. Gift of Paul Mellon)

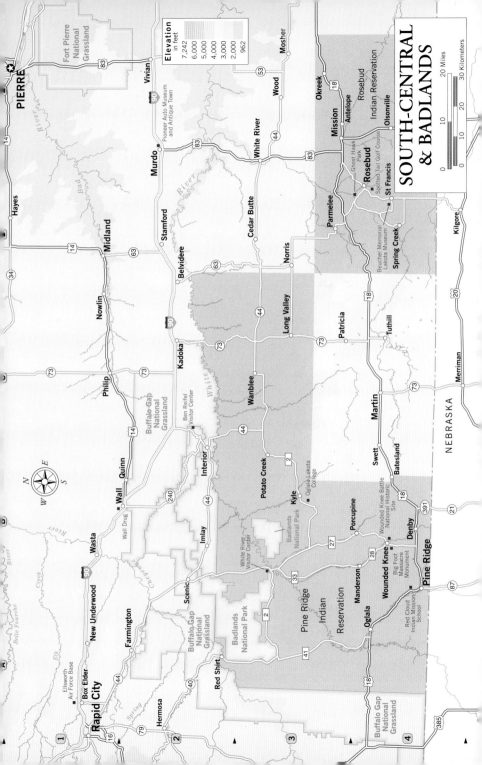

SOUTH-CENTRAL & BADLANDS

Elevation in feet

| 7,242 |
| 6,000 |
| 5,000 |
| 4,000 |
| 3,000 |
| 2,000 |
| 962 |

0   10   20 Miles
0   10   20   30 Kilometers

PIERRE

Fort Pierre National Grassland

Hayes

Midland

Nowlin

Philip

Kadoka

Wall   Quinn

Wasta

New Underwood

Box Elder

Ellsworth Air Force Base

Rapid City

Farmington

Hermosa

Scenic

Imlay

Interior

Ben Reifel Visitor Center

Buffalo Gap National Grassland

Wall Drug

Red Shirt

Buffalo Gap National Grassland

Badlands National Park

White River Visitor Center

Badlands National Park

Pine Ridge Indian Reservation

Oglala

Pine Ridge

Red Cloud Indian Mission School

Buffalo Gap National Grassland

Vivian

Murdo

Pioneer Auto Museum and Antique Town

Stamford

Belvidere

Long Valley

Wanblee

Potato Creek

Kyle

Oglala Lakota College

Manderson

Wounded Knee

Big Foot Massacre Monument

Denby

Porcupine

Wounded Knee Battle National Historic Site

Mosher

Wood

Okreek

Mission

Antelope

Olsonville

Rosebud Indian Reservation

Rosebud

St Francis

Spotted Tail Golf Course

Ghost Hawk Park

Parmelee

Spring Creek

Beuchel Memorial Lakota Museum

White River

Cedar Butte

Norris

Patricia

Tuthill

Martin

Swett

Batesland

Kilgore

Merriman

Kigore

NEBRASKA

White River

Bad River

Cheyenne River

Belle Fourche River

Spring Creek

Elk Creek

N   E   S   W

South Dakota until 1906–07, when the bridge at Mobridge went up. Public high-way bridges didn't span the Missouri until 1924, with one at Mobridge first and later others at Forest City, Pierre, Chamberlain, and Rosebud.

In 1904, the Rosebud Indian Reservation was opened to homesteaders—the last government land lottery in the United States and yet another affront to the Sioux tribe. Widespread white settlement came to western South Dakota outside the Black Hills, and homesteading occurred on other reservations throughout the ensuing decade. In 1907, Edith Eudora Kohl (née Ammons) and her sister, Ida Mary, joined more than 100,000 others who contracted "homestead fever" and sought a stake near "the land of the Burnt Thigh," otherwise known as the Lower Brule Indian Reservation, then located around present-day Gregory County on the west side of the Missouri. The exploits of the two young women, both in their twenties and as "timid as mice," are told in *Land of the Burnt Thigh*, published in 1938 by Minnesota Historical Society Press. A classic account of the quiet, heroic settlers of this vast region, the book offers rare insights into the legions of women who sought their own simple investment in the future by "proving up" their own land claims. The sisters ran a newspaper, taught school, operated a post office and general store, helped others who had come to settle, and found time to battle prairie fires, rattlesnakes, and raging blizzards—all in an effort to keep 160 acres. Edith Kohl's narrative pales in comparison with those of other noted prairie writers, such as the Pulitzer Prize–winner Hamlin Garland, but her descriptions of the carnival atmosphere surrounding the opening of the Rosebud Indian Reservation portray both the naiveté and the desperation of many pioneers who sought to settle land in South Dakota.

In the first decade of the twentieth century, thousands of single women "marched" as homesteaders into western South Dakota. Some sought a prudent investment, some sought a husband, and still others sought a way to support themselves and several children after the loss of a spouse through death, divorce, or desertion. Claim records indicate that nearly 12 percent of all homesteaders were women—and committed women at that. Those same records reveal that 42.4 percent of the women proved up their final claims, while only 37 percent of their male counterparts did the same.

LAND LOTTERY AT ROSEBUD

At the stroke of midnight a cry went up from the registrars. At 12:01 under the dim flicker of coal-oil lanterns and torches hung on posts or set on barrels and boxes, that most famous of lotteries began. The uproar and confusion of the hours before midnight were like a desert calm compared with the clamor which broke out. Registrars lined both sides of the street. 'Right this way, folks! . . . Register right here!' And there, on rough tables, on dry-goods boxes, anything upon which a piece of paper could be filled out and a notary seal stamped thereon, the crowd put in their applications as entries in the gamble, raised their right hands and swore: 'I do solemnly swear that I honestly desire to enter public lands for my own personal use as a home and for settlement and cultivation, and not for speculation or in the interest of some other person. . . .'

In the excitement and chill of the October night, fingers shook so that they could scarcely hold a pen. . . . Into the slits in the huge cans which held the applications dropped a surprising number of items. People became confused. . . . And some, shaking uncontrollably with excitement, were barely able to drop their applications in at all.

And somewhere, off in the dark spaces beyond the flickering lights, lay the million acres of land for which the horde was clamoring, its quiet sleep unbroken.

—Edith Eudora Kohl, *Land of the Burnt Thigh*, 1938

■ ROSEBUD INDIAN RESERVATION *map page 157, D/E-3/4*

Of the estimated 70,000 Lakota (Sioux) living within South Dakota, about three-fourths claim reservation residence. Two Indian reservations in this region, Rosebud and Pine Ridge, cover well over two million acres amid the sticky gumbo soil and the buffalo and western wheat grasses. Most urban Indians in the state either live on reservations part-time or make frequent visits to them to maintain cultural and family ties, while they take advantage of employment and educational opportunities offered in towns and cities. In western South Dakota, where few employment opportunities exist close to the reservations, the Lakota tend to be among the most disadvantaged people in the United States.

Eighteen miles west of Winner on U.S. 18 is the 882,000-acre Rosebud Indian Reservation, once home to an early Native American leader who strove for peace between Indians and whites. Following a series of conflicts in the 1850s between Indians and the U.S. Army, Spotted Tail (Sinte Gleska) of the Brules became a proponent of peace. As a chief of the Brules, a sub-tribe of the Teton Sioux, Spotted Tail was certain that his tribe would not emerge victorious against the superior numbers and weapons of the white soldiers. After he persuaded most of the members of his tribe to sign the Fort Laramie Treaty in 1868, which created the Great Sioux Reservation though further diminishment of what was once an eight-million-acre Sioux stronghold, the Brules were moved from Nebraska to land near the Missouri River in South Dakota, where they were encouraged to take up farming. When tribesmen refused, Spotted Tail traveled to Washington and attempted to persuade the Secretary of the Interior to relocate the agency farther west and to preserve Sioux hunting lands in the Black Hills. Spotted Tail was allowed to move his agency, but the Sioux goal of saving the Black Hills was derailed by the discovery of gold in them and the subsequent rush of white settlers. This further angered the Brule Sioux, and many left the reservation to join hostile bands, including that of Spotted Tail's nephew, Crazy Horse. These bands, under the leadership of Crazy Horse and Sitting Bull, ultimately toppled Custer at Little Bighorn, after which Crazy Horse returned to an agency, Sitting Bull fled to Canada, and Spotted Tail selected the site of a new agency near Mission. This new agency was first named for the peace-seeking Sioux leader, but later was changed to Rosebud Agency.

The landscape of the Rosebud Indian Reservation hasn't altered much since the days when Spotted Tail rode bareback over its grassy buttes and into its quiet creek beds. Only two main highways now bisect what was once marked only by buffalo herds and a few Indian ponies. If you stand on a rise in the surrounding prairie, buffeted by the ceaseless winds, the low drone of a few passing vehicles is the only indication you'll have that modern man has ever visited this place. Were you to fly over it on a moonless night, only a few yard lights would stare back from the darkness.

Electricity and plumbing have come to the main buildings in the communities of the Rosebud Reservation. But in the outback, where gravel roads and a few dirt tire tracks lead the way to the horizon, there are few amenities. Dirt-floored shanties, mobile homes, and brightly painted government houses are found at the

A lone schoolhouse graces the high plains in the western part of the state.

end of those lonely, litter-lined roads, and little else. In the few towns—really just wide spots in the road—such as Okreek, Mission, Olsonville, St. Francis, Rosebud, and Parmelee—children go to school each morning and grown-ups to coffee, just as in every other rural town in South Dakota. The town of Rosebud, southwest of Mission, is the location of the reservation's only medical center and of Sinte Gleska College, the state's only college on an Indian reservation, which offers courses in Native American studies and liberal arts degrees. Just west of Rosebud in Crazy Horse Canyon is **Ghost Hawk Park,** about 50,000 acres of stark beauty. Southwest of town, the nine-hole, grass-green **Spotted Tail Golf Course** gives residents one of the few opportunities to tee off in south-central South Dakota.

■ ST. FRANCIS

During his presidency (1869–77), Ulysses S. Grant attempted to establish the first peace policy toward Native Americans. Meanwhile, various Christian missionaries had established their churches on most reservations. To simplify his supervision of the reservations, Grant's policy assigned each reservation one and only one Christian denomination. The Rosebud Reservation was first designated

Father Buechel, a Jesuit priest who wrote a number of books in the Lakota language and introduced their culture to many non-Indians. (Marquette University Archives, Milwaukee)

Sioux dolls from the collection of the Cultural Heritage Center in Pierre. (South Dakota State Historical Society, Pierre)

Episcopalian, but Spotted Tail argued that many of the Brules had already been converted to Catholicism by Father De Smet. In addition to acquiring Catholic status for his tribe, the Brule chief was able to persuade U.S. authorities to allow the construction of a Catholic mission, which was finished in 1885 by Franciscans and Jesuits who had been expelled from Germany by Prince Otto von Bismarck. These missionaries also plowed adjoining fields and planted trees. By 1900, with 500 students enrolled in elementary and vocational education, the St. Francis Mission in the present-day town of St. Francis had become the largest Indian mission school in America, and it eventually expanded to include a full high school curriculum.

Although many priests have stood at St. Francis's altars and blackboards, one of the most remarkable was Father Eugene Buechel, a Jesuit who took an intense interest in the Sioux and introduced their culture to thousands of non-Indians. Buechel collected artifacts and photographs, deciphered the Lakota language, compiled a Lakota-English dictionary and a grammar, and wrote a number of other books in Lakota. His collection is the cornerstone of the **Buechel Memorial Lakota Museum** (350 South Oak Street; 605-747-2745) on the campus of the St. Francis Mission and School. Preserved there are a variety of Teton Sioux materials, including photographs of Spotted Tail, as well as a 300-plant herbarium.

LAKOTA BOARDING SCHOOL

It is almost impossible to explain to a sympathetic white person what a typical old Indian boarding school was like; how it affected the Indian child suddenly dumped into it like a small creature from another world, helpless, defenseless, bewildered. . . .

Oddly enough, we owed our unspeakable boarding schools to the do-gooders, the white Indian-lovers. The schools were intended as an alternative to the outright extermination seriously advocated by generals Sherman and Sheridan, as well as by most settlers and prospectors over-running our land. "You don't have to kill those poor benighted heathen," the do-gooders said, "in order to solve the Indian Problem. Just give us a chance to turn them into useful farmhands, laborers, and chambermaids who will break their backs for you at low wages." In that way the boarding schools were born. The kids were taken away from their villages and pueblos, in their blankets and moccasins, kept completely isolated from their families—sometimes for as long as ten years—suddenly coming back, their short hair slick with pomade, their necks raw from stiff, high collars, their thick jackets always short in the sleeves and pinching under the arms, their tight patent leather shoes giving them corns, the girls in starched white blouses and clumsy, high-buttoned boots—caricatures of white people. When they found out—and they found out quickly—that they were neither wanted by whites nor by Indians, they got good and drunk, many of them staying drunk for the rest of their lives.

—Mary Crow Dog with Richard Erdoes, *Lakota Woman,* 1990

Lakota students pose with a nun on the reservation.
(Marquette University Archives, Milwaukee)

■ MURDO   *map page 157, E-2*

Forty-five miles north of Mission at the intersection of U.S. 83 and I-90 is Murdo, home to 612 residents and a collection of rare, classic vehicles, from a 1902 Oldsmobile to one of Elvis Presley's motorcycles. These are housed in the 10-acre, 39-building **Pioneer Auto Museum and Antique Town** (503 East Fifth Street; 605-669-2691), which is worth a stop for anyone interested in the finest cars America has produced, as well as other collections ranging from fine china to hand organs. Among the 250 antique cars are the 1948 Tucker used in the movie *Tucker* and one of the General Lees used in *The Dukes of Hazard.*

■ BEEF AND BUFFALO
Traveling in south-central South Dakota can be a serenely pleasurable experience. A full moon can light the prairie on a summer night. In winter, that same moon can cast a glow across a windswept tundra, silhouetting coyotes, deer, and antelope as they forage for food. And on some nights the unexpected happens, the occasion no one planned. Such was the case in the mid-1950s when Beef met buffalo.

Stanton Uhlir had grown up in the area of **Kadoka,** a small town of ranchers about 50 miles west of Murdo. As long as anyone around those parts can recall, Stanton had always been big. By the time he reached high school, his friends were kidding him that he would have to use the truck scale at the grain elevator just to be weighed. Stanton's bulk earned him the nickname "Beef," and his 6-foot-6-inch height earned him center spot on the Kadoka High basketball team. Even though the team never won the State B championship, Stanton's heroics on the court are legendary in the community. More than family and friends still remember the night Kadoka traveled to the Corn Palace in Mitchell to compete for the State B Consolation Championship. It was Stanton's last game in high school, his tennis shoes would be put in the closet for the winter, and the graduating senior undoubtedly hoped to end his career with a bang. When the final buzzer sounded that night in 1950, Beef had scored an incredible 50 points—a record that still stands in South Dakota B basketball.

Following graduation, Stanton headed off to South Dakota State University to earn a degree in agriculture. A bum knee sidelined him from sports, but following graduation he came home to Kadoka with a new degree and a real desire to teach veteran farmers how to manage their land. As the newest agent for the Agriculture,

Stabilization and Conservation Service, Stanton traveled the back roads, conducting classes in all the small communities of south-central South Dakota.

One winter night, after teaching a small group of White River farmers and ranchers the latest in tillage techniques, Beef headed for home in his big old Buick. It was nearly midnight when he spotted the lights of Murdo over the northern horizon. Friends say Big Beef was probably thinking about stopping "for a hook or two" before making the last leg into Kadoka, but perhaps he was just mulling over the next day's schedule, or dreaming about a soft pillow and a warm bed.

As his speeding Buick crested a rise in State Highway 83, Beef probably had a microsecond to analyze what lie before him—a herd of bison that had broken a fence and found a firm footing on the asphalt roadway. Buffalo have been known to outrun horses, but these didn't budge. What happened next has been described as the "crimson splash." The Buick bashed into the buffalo and neither prevailed. The car was totaled. Two buffalo were killed instantly and more than half a dozen were wounded. Miraculously, Beef wasn't hurt—a testament to his 300-pound frame. After assessing the situation, Stanton decided that Murdo was close enough to call for help and he elected to hoof it to town.

As he slid from the mangled car into the surrounding darkness, he detected a strange sound over the escaping steam of his broken radiator. Two bulls, each about seven times heavier than the Big Beef, were less than pleased by the introduction of a car into their world. The death of others in their group and the pungent smell of fresh bison blood splashed on frozen ground had excited them, and they were mad. Beef slowly backed to the car as the bulls pawed the pavement and snorted their intentions. Beef knew when he was licked.

About an hour later, another motorist was driving up State Highway 83 when he came upon a sight even stranger than Beef had literally run into. There, in his headlights, was a man sitting on top of a wrecked car with dead, bloodied, and angry buffalo all about. "His buddies gave him a hard time about those buffalo until the day he died," Beef's uncle, Vernon Uhlir, says with a chuckle. "But there aren't too many people who can run into a herd of buffalo and live to tell about it. The pure size of Big Beef, he was just solid. To visit with him, you'd think he was as mean as anyone in the world. But inside he had a heart of gold and he was just like a big kitten." Stanton died in September 1990, but around Kadoka, the story of Beef and the buffalo lives on.

West of Kadoka, I-90 passes through one arm of 590,000 acres of rolling prairie known as **Buffalo Gap National Grassland.** Early morning and dusk are the best times to roam the grasslands in search of the deer, antelope, grouse, wild turkey, and prairie dogs that live there. On the northern edge of this section of the grassland is the town of **Wall**, home to massive Wall Drug. (See "How Many Miles to Wall Drug?" on page 174) Known around the world, at least by name, the store dominates the local economy in this tiny town.

■ BADLANDS NATIONAL PARK   *map page 157, A/B-2/3*

Just south of Wall, the landscape changes quickly. Rolling grasslands abruptly give way to chiseled spires, ragged ridges, and deep canyons—the setting for the Badlands, the strangest area in the state. So stark is Badlands National Park that it has been described as "hell with the fires burned out." In this land so ruthlessly ravaged over the ages by the wind and rain, the ridges, gullies, spires, and knobs are a powerful reminder of the forces of nature. Their fossil-laden soils, which erode with each new season, offer mementos of giant beasts that once lurked in the region.

The plains suddenly give way to the ragged buttes of the Badlands south of Wall.

According to Jay Shuler, a National Park Service naturalist who studied and wrote about the park in the 1980s, the Badlands are the result of

...A natural history that began about the time the dinosaurs died out, sixty-five million years ago. The shallow Pierre Sea, which divided the continent into eastern and western land masses, drained away, making North America whole again. A jungle developed on the exposed seabed, transforming the dark mud and shale to a bright yellow soil. From about thirty-seven million years ago to twenty-three million years ago, the climate gradually became cool and dry. Intermittent sediment-loaded floods swept over the area, depositing layer upon layer of volcanic ash and mud. Between floods, plant-eating mammals fed on the lush vegetation, and some fell prey to a variety of flesh-eaters. Their bones were buried by the sediments and fossilized. These fossils comprise the best and most complete record of the Oligocene Epoch, the Golden Age of Mammals, which had reached the species diversity and body size to occupy the living space left vacant by the dinosaurs.

About half a million years ago erosion began to slice through the prairie and the fossil-rich layers of mudstone beneath it, creating a landscape so chaotic and spectacular—so difficult to travel across—it came to be called the "Badlands." The word badlands then became the generic geologic term for all barren, severely eroded landscapes, whether in Montana or Mongolia, on the Moon or Mars.

The French fur traders who explored the western United States in the early 1800s referred to the area as *les mauvaises terres à traverser,* or "bad lands to travel across." The Lakota labeled it *mako sica,* or "land bad." Despite the harshness and apparent inhospitable topography of the Badlands for these more recent arrivals, this area has been supporting humans for more than 12,000 years. Ancient mammoth hunters were the first to visit the Badlands. Much later, the Arikara came to the area around the White River—which today runs through Pine Ridge Reservation—because of the huge herds of buffalo that darkened the grasslands. Later still, the Lakota drove out those rival bands, and they dominated the region for about 100 years. By the mid-nineteenth century, trappers, followed by other Europeans, soldiers, miners, homesteaders, and cattlemen, had supplanted the Lakota.

BADLANDS "ARCHITECTURE"

In 1935 Frank Lloyd Wright traveled through South Dakota and was greatly moved by the unique landscape of the Badlands. In this letter to Robert Lusk, a Huron newspaper publisher, Wright reveals his reverence for natural forms and his appreciation for their apparent architectural qualities.

Dear Bob:

Speaking of our trip to the Big Bad Lands, Black Hills, and Spearfish Canyon: I've been about the world a lot and pretty much over our own country; but I was totally unprepared for that revolution called the Dakota Bad Lands. From Mitchell, Paul Bellamy was driving a fair seventy over the brown Dakota prairie to reach the Bad Lands before sunset. About four, afternoon, something came into view that made me sit up straight and look at Bellamy to see if he saw what I saw. "Oh," said he, "you've seen nothing yet." But I had. What I saw gave me an indescribable sense of mysterious otherwhere—a distant architecture, ethereal, touched, only touched with a sense of Egyptian, Mayan drift and silhouette. As we came closer a templed realm definitely stood ambient in air before my astonished "scene," loving but scene-jaded gaze. The streamline working on a vast pleateau of solid cream white clay, something like "calichi," had sculptured this familiar world into one unfamiliar but entrancing.

Endless trabeations surmounted by or rising into pyramid (obelisk) and temple, ethereal in color and exquisitely chiseled in endless detail, they began to reach to infinity spreading into the sky on every side; an endless supernatural world more spiritual than earth but created out of it. As we rode, or seemed to be floating upon a splendid winding road that seemed to understand it all and just where to go, we rose and fell between its delicate parallels of rose and cream and sublime shapes, chalk white, fretted against a blue sky with high floating clouds; the sky itself seemed only there to cleanse and light the vast harmonious building scheme.

—letter from Frank Lloyd Wright, 1935

(following pages) Badlands National Park. (Robert Holmes)

Despite efforts to tame this vast wasteland, the Badlands soon became regarded as a geologic wonder worthy of preservation. Authorized by Congress in 1929, Badlands National Monument was proclaimed by President Franklin D. Roosevelt in 1939 "to preserve the scenery, to protect the fossils and wildlife, and to conserve the mixed-grass prairie."

In 1976, the size of the monument more than doubled with the addition of 133,300 acres of the **Pine Ridge Indian Reservation,** which is administered by the National Park Service by agreement with the Oglala Sioux Tribe. Then, in 1978, Congress recognized the enduring value and uniqueness of the Badlands by elevating it to National Park status.

Altogether, these banded pinnacles, sawtooth spires, and steep canyons cover 244,000 acres in the state's southwestern region. The Badlands formations can be eerie to some, picturesque to others. The **Ben Reifel Visitor Center** at **Cedar Pass** (9 miles south of I-90 on State Highway 240; 605-433-5361) and the **White River Visitor Center** in the southerly Stronghold Unit (off BIA [Bureau of Indian Affairs] Highway 27; 605-433-2878) help visitors become acquainted with the area. Few paved roadways exist within the park; many areas are accessible only by four-wheel-drive vehicle or on foot or horseback.

In 1976, Congress set aside 64,250 acres of the park as the **Sage Creek Wilderness Area.** Although this roadless area is protected from development, it is open to hiking, backpacking, and other activities. The only trails within the wilderness are the ones created by the tread of bison, so hikers, who have been known to get lost in the maze of canyons and layered cliffs, are encouraged to purchase a topographical map before adventuring into the backcountry. There are several other caveats for those who leave the comforting confines of air-conditioned autos during a visit to the Badlands. Climbing the Badlands formations can be dangerous, as slopes are often steep and crumbly. Weather can change suddenly, and lightning, hail, high winds, and sun require caution during the summer—take water along, even on short hikes. Bison can be extremely dangerous. A large bull often weighs as much as a small car and can travel nearly as fast. Venomous prairie rattlers are common within the park.

As dangerous as an excursion into the Badlands may sound, these few simple precautions can guarantee a wondrous experience. The Badlands are among the last vestiges of one of the world's great grasslands, and even today they support thousands of species of wildlife and plants. Prairie grasses once covered nearly a quarter of the United States, from southern Alberta, Canada, almost to Mexico and from the Rockies to Indiana. Much of that grassland has vanished beneath the plow, but in the Badlands those strains of grass still billow in a timeless wind, and wildflowers still bloom in the crags and crevices of this harsh landscape.

From afar, this terrain can appear dead and dry. Up close, it is teeming with life. In every draw that drains the surrounding prairie, plant life is either blooming or awaiting a warm sun to spread its color. In the spring, the bloom of the star, sego, and gumbo lilies mirrors the receding snowdrifts, just an instant before the earliest of the wildflowers, the pasqueflower, bursts into bloom. From June through August, prairie coneflowers lift their bright yellow petals above the short grasses, while plains pricklypear and Missouri pincushions provide colorful, close-to-the-ground displays. All told, nearly 50 different grasses and almost 200 types of wildflowers grow in the Badlands.

Although summer temperatures may top 100 degrees F (38°C), and in winter the wind chill regularly drops below zero, an abundance of animals call the Badlands home. Hundreds of prairie dogs busily build their "towns," while badgers, bobcats, foxes, and coyotes may linger nearby, eager to make a meal of one of them. Antelope and Rocky Mountain bighorns, the latter introduced into the park after the extinction of the native Audubon bighorn, are often found on the rocky cliffs or grazing on the grassy tables, while mule deer favor the wooded draws. Cottontails and jackrabbits race through the tall grass, careful to avoid the prairie rattlers, yellow-bellied racers, and bullsnakes scavenging for food. White-throated swifts and cliff swallows nest on the faces of cliffs, and rock wrens build their homes in the crevices. Golden eagles have been known to rear their young on high, inaccessible buttes within the park, while the burrowing owl prefers ground level and often builds its nest in prairie dog holes. On the grasslands, long-billed curlews search for insects to the song of the western meadowlark. In late spring and early summer, small cinnamon-colored calves join the park's 500 head of bison.

Sunrise and sunset induce a panorama of color in this seemingly barren land. Light plays with the layers of sedimentation in the rock, casting varying hues of purples, reds, grays, and golds in contrast to the deep greens of the prairie grasses. At night these lands far away from the glow of city lights provide the ideal spot to view the stars. The sky is commonly so clear that satellites can be seen in orbit around the Earth. A full moon can illuminate the way for starlight hikers as the ragged ridges draw a wicked line against the horizon.

HOW MANY MILES TO WALL DRUG?

You could walk clear across South Dakota and still know nearly every step of the way how many miles you were from the tiny high-plains community of Wall. Catchy, and sometimes corny, phrases are attached to virtually every billboard along the route: "Have You Dug Wall Drug?" and "Who Has the Gall to Bypass Wall?" are two standards. Then there are signs that inform motorists they've missed the place.

The signs were the brainchild of Ted and Dorothy Hustead, who, back in 1936, were owners of little Hustead Drug Store on Main Street in Wall. One sizzling Sunday afternoon, Dorothy observed the cars zooming out of the Badlands and heading for Rapid City on unpaved U.S. 16. Those tourists, thought Dorothy, were probably hot and thirsty, and here she sat with a mountain of ice and no customers. Why not put up roadside signs strung along the fencerows reading "Free Ice Water/Wall Drug/Wall, S.D."?

In short order, her husband had boards painted, postholes dug, and signs planted along the neighboring highway. Before he returned to the store, customers already had arrived for their free ice water. The rest, as they say, is history. At last count, there were more than 3,000 Wall Drug signs in all 50 states. In fact, Wall Drug signs have been posted around the world, including Italy, Holland, England, Wales, Germany, India, and Africa and even in the Arctic Circle. In World War II, a Wall Drug sign was suspended from the harbor bridge in Sydney, Australia, and a helicopter-mounted sign noting that it was 10,659 miles to Wall Drug survived the Tet Offensive in Vietnam in 1968.

Today, Wall Drug in Wall takes up a full city block and sells far more than pharmaceuticals. South Dakotans and many regular, cross-state travelers have grown up enjoying the drugstore's two "cowboy bands"—actually animated mannequins—who perform every 15 minutes or so. Wall also serves some of the best pancakes and donuts in the state and sells Black Hills gold jewelry, Native American arts and crafts, books, and fine Western apparel and tack. In summer, it's hard to find a parking spot among the out-of-state cars, motorhomes, and motorcoaches that clog the narrow streets of this small town. In winter, uniformed personnel from nearby Ellsworth Air Force Base and warmly clothed ranchers sit side by side enjoying coffee and donuts.

*The famous "jackalope," part rabbit and part antelope,
is one of the many tourist attractions at Wall Drug.*

■ PINE RIDGE INDIAN RESERVATION

The southern half of Badlands National Park lies within the Pine Ridge Indian Reservation, the home of the Oglala Sioux. With 1,772,212 acres, the reservation is second in size only to Arizona's Navajo Reservation. And it is nearly as desolate, as evidenced by any South Dakota map. Amid a smattering of towns with names such as Red Shirt, Potato Creek, Porcupine, and Wanblee, visitors find an abundance of buttes with monikers like Buzzard, Eagle Nest, Snake, and Slim.

Shannon County, which covers more than two-thirds of the Pine Ridge Reservation, consistently ranks among the poorest counties in the nation. In 1999, 52.3 percent of its inhabitants were below the poverty line. Unemployment, officially 17.3 percent according to the 2000 census, is generally estimated to be much, much higher, and alcoholism and infant mortality rates are also high.

The towns and their residences reveal the poverty of the region. Adults sit on porches and steps with little to do, as their children play in grassless yards. The trading posts, stores, gas stations, and laundromats are the center of activity, except during the powwows, when the whole town turns out to celebrate.

Eight miles from the White River Visitor Center, the **Cuny Table Cafe** (605-455-2957) serves what are inarguably the best Indian tacos in South Dakota. Served on fry bread (instead of a hard tortilla) and filled with seasoned ground beef, lettuce, and cheese, they're best eaten with a fork. Three miles west of **Kyle,** on BIA Highway 2, **Oglala Lakota College** (605-455-6000), the area's only four-year accredited college, has a bookstore with a respectable collection of Native American literature. The major community celebration—the **Wazi Paya Oyate Festival and Kyle Fair**—is held in mid-August.

On the reservation's extreme southern edge, near the border of Nebraska, is the town of **Pine Ridge,** home to the **Oglala Nation Fair and Rodeo,** held on the first weekend in August. The three-day rodeo and four-day powwow include drum and dance contests, and golf, horseshoe pitching, and softball tournaments. The **Sioux Nation Shopping Center** offers a lean selection of groceries, hardware, clothing, books, and arts and crafts.

The **Red Cloud Indian Mission School** (605-867-5491), a few miles north of Pine Ridge on U.S. 18, presents the Indian Art Show, a collection of 200 works of art representing 30 different tribes. Forty paintings from the school's permanent collection are on display. The Indian star quilts are exquisite, and the gift shop sells genuine bead and quill work at reasonable prices.

Brandon One Feather at a powwow at Pine Ridge Reservation.

A rare photo of a dejected-looking Chief Sitting Bull, with his wife and two babies (white woman unidentified), shortly before his murder at Standing Rock Reservation on December 15, 1890. (Center for Western Studies)

■ BATTLE AT WOUNDED KNEE

In the south-central area of Pine Ridge, in a place few but avid historians and Native Americans ever visit, is the town and National Historic Site of Wounded Knee. East of town on BIA Highway 27, near the silent hardwoods of Wounded Knee Creek, is a simple stone marker honoring those slain here on a cold winter day in 1890. But to those who live on the reservation, and to those who drive past this solitary pinnacle on a regular basis, the soul of the nation may well be buried here.

In the years immediately following the loss of the Black Hills to the U.S. government, some Sioux leaders resisted the removal of their people to reservations and agencies that the treaties demanded. Big Foot, known to some as Spotted Elk, was a hereditary chief of the Minniconjou Sioux of the Cheyenne River Reservation. Regarded as an outstanding chief and a strong believer in the way of life the Indians had known prior to the arrival of the whites, Big Foot eagerly accepted the Ghost Dance religion, taught by the Paiute religious leader Wovoka. Big Foot encouraged his people to faithfully perform the ceremony and by so doing rid themselves of the whites, welcome back their departed warriors, and return to a way of life robbed from them over time.

On December 15, 1890, the Sioux spiritual leader Sitting Bull was killed on the Standing Rock Indian Reservation in north-central South Dakota. As tension

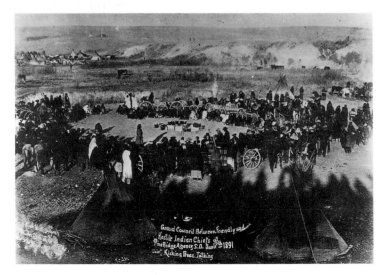

A Grand Council between Indian chiefs at Pine Ridge on January 17, 1891, just two and a half weeks after the Massacre at Wounded Knee. (Center for Western Studies)

mounted among Indians throughout South Dakota, Chief Big Foot decided to leave his encampment on the shores of the Cheyenne River and journey with his band to Pine Ridge, where he hoped to join Red Cloud, another Lakota chieftain. En route, Big Foot was joined briefly by more than 40 of Sitting Bull's warriors who had fled Standing Rock following the shooting of their leader. As he neared Wounded Knee in the dead of winter, the exhaustion, cold, and the 150-mile trek had clearly taken a toll on his band of followers—350 men, women, and children.

On December 28, Maj. Samuel Whitside and about 200 members of the Seventh Cavalry (the regiment wiped out at the Battle at Little Bighorn in 1876) caught up with Big Foot's band and escorted them into camp along Wounded Knee Creek, where they were joined by 300 additional troops. Whitside and his officers made plans to disarm the Indians the next morning, take many of the warriors prisoner, and transport them to Omaha, Nebraska, for detainment. Suffering from pneumonia and exhaustion, Big Foot willingly acceded to the demands.

The next morning, December 29, 1890, the army of 500 surrounded the Indian camp. At its center, a white flag was hoisted as a sign of peace, while Big Foot lay in

(above) Participants prepare at dawn for the next leg of the annual Wounded Knee Memorial Ride, which retraces the route taken by Big Foot and his band before the massacre. (opposite) The memorial to those killed at Wounded Knee on December 29, 1890.

DEC. 29, 1890
CANKPE OPI EL WONA
WICASA TE TEWICAKTE CA EPE KTA

23 SPOTTED THUNDER
24 SHOOTS THE BEAR
25 PICKED HORSES
26 BEAR CUTS BODY
27 CHASE IN WINTER
28 TOOTH ITS HOLE
29 RED HORN
30 HE EAGLE
31 NO EARS
32 WOLF SKIN NECKLACE
33 LODGE SKIN KNOT KIN
34 CHARGE AT THEM
35 WEASEL BEAR
36 BIRD SHAKES
37 BIG SKIRT
     TWIN TURTLE
38 BLUE AIR
39 PASS WATER IN HORN
40 SEABBARD KNIFE
41 SMALL SIDE BEAR
42 KILLS SENECA
43 KILLS SENECA

a heated army tent. Though the Indians were ordered to give up their weapons, only a few guns were surrendered, so officers began searching tepees. This alarmed the Indians, and in the commotion, a shot was fired. Soldiers responded with a barrage of bullets, killing nearly half of the warriors in the first round of gunfire. Then the rapid-fire Hotchkiss guns opened up, firing on the Indian camp. In only a few minutes, about 200 Indians were dead. The bodies of unarmed women and children were found as far as 3 miles from the initial confrontation, shot down as they ran for their lives across the plains. Twenty-five of the military men were killed. Big Foot was shot down in the first volley, his body photographed for posterity. (He was buried in a mass grave with the other victims of the Massacre at Wounded Knee.) That night, a sudden blizzard passed through, covering the bodies in a thick blanket of snow.

In the following days, newspapers and government officials referred to the confrontation as a "battle," but it was none other than wholesale slaughter. Within a year, the army had awarded 23 Medals of Honor to members of the Seventh Cavalry for "valor" shown in the carnage. But there was no cover-up of this affair. Even whites were incensed, and from this point on, the systematic extermination of the Indian people ended. With the earlier deaths of Sitting Bull and Crazy Horse, and the final tragedy at Wounded Knee, settlement of the last true frontier in the West was assured. The blood in the snow at Wounded Knee melted in the spring of 1891, and as it thawed and ran across the prairie in a thousand rivulets, it carried with it a way of life for the American Indian.

"The Wounded Knee Massacre marks a major turning point in world history," former Harvard University instructor turned Oglala Lakota College official Patrick Cudmore wrote in the *Rapid City Journal* on the hundredth anniversary of the tragedy. "It symbolizes more than just the massacre of Chief Big Foot's ragged band, more than just the ending of America's Indian Wars and more than just the closing of America's 'last frontier.' The deeper meaning of the Wounded Knee Massacre is that it symbolized the end of almost 400 years of unrelenting war against the indigenous people of the Americas. . . . "

■ TRAGEDY REVISITED AT WOUNDED KNEE

In April 1973, violence returned to Wounded Knee when members of the **American Indian Movement** (AIM) took 10 hostages and barricaded themselves in the Sacred Heart Church at Wounded Knee. The occupation at Wounded Knee, whose

This photograph of plaintiffs suing for the return of the Black Hills to the Sioux was taken in 1923. The recovery of some of those lands continues to be debated in Congress today. (Marquette University Archives, Milwaukee)

perimeter included grounds where the approximately 200 Lakota had been massacred by U.S. troops 83 years earlier, followed a February 6 riot at the Custer County Courthouse. That protest was incited when a white man who had killed an Indian was charged with manslaughter rather than murder. Three weeks later, on the evening of February 27, a caravan of 40 cars headed to Wounded Knee where AIM members occupied several buildings and took the hostages in an effort to draw attention to the federal government's violation of the 1868 Fort Laramie Treaty and to alleged corruption in the tribal government and in the Bureau of Indian Affairs. Federal authorities soon circled the village and even called in armored personnel carriers. At the height of the confrontation, AIM members and supporters swelled to about 300 in number and exchanged hundreds of rounds of fire with federal marshals and BIA police. By the time the siege ended on May 8, after 71 days, only about 40 were left in the occupying forces, the rest having crept away exhausted and discouraged. The occupation resulted in the deaths of two members of the occupying force, Buddy Lamont and Frank Clearwater, as well as in injuries to nine others, including federal marshal Lloyd Grimm of Omaha, who was paralyzed from a chest wound.

Soon after the occupation of Wounded Knee ended, the Sacred Heart Church burned to the ground. From its ashes came change on the Pine Ridge Reservation. The siege raised international awareness of the plight of the Lakota people. Calls to return sacred lands in the Black Hills to the Lakota gained backers on the reservation and in Congress. The Oglala Sioux tribe formed its own police department, and the white governor of South Dakota declared a year of reconciliation between Indians and non-Indians.

Days after the first massacre at Wounded Knee, when the blizzard finally left southwestern South Dakota, U.S. soldiers dug a huge hole in the ground and buried many of the Indians killed at Wounded Knee in a common grave. Only a simple stone pillar marks the burial site. Descendants of the victims of the massacre have petitioned Congress to designate Wounded Knee as the nation's first tribal park. It seems only fitting that those who died in this place be remembered, perhaps finally putting the troubled spirit and the tragedy of Wounded Knee to rest.

(above) The Oglala Nation Powwow at Wounded Knee. (Paul Jones)

(opposite) Pale purple coneflowers grace the high plains.

B L A C K   H I L L S

After an expanse of seemingly endless prairies, South Dakota's Black Hills, the oldest mountains in America, unfold on the western horizon. At first appearing as a dark cloud on the edge of the rolling range, they gradually grow in size, casting a silhouette against the sky. Then the true height of the Black Hills becomes apparent. Eighteen of its peaks are higher than 7,000 feet, and they are capped by Harney Peak, at 7,242 feet.

Residents of neighboring Wyoming and Montana, proud of their own states' Rockies, often scoff at the size of the Black Hills. Wyoming's boosters once placed a billboard just over the Wyoming–South Dakota border that read, "You've Seen the Hills, Now Come See the Mountains." Meanwhile, South Dakota's northerly brother posted the self-effacing phrase, "North Dakota Proudly Announces the Completion of Its Mountain Removal Project." South Dakotans say it's all a matter of perspective. After all, Harney Peak is the highest point between the Rocky Mountains and the Alps.

Altogether, the Hills cover an area roughly 50 miles wide and 120 miles long. Two-thirds are in South Dakota, the remainder in eastern Wyoming. Within the Hills are four areas administered by the National Park Service: Mount Rushmore National Memorial, Wind Cave National Park, Jewel Cave National Monument, and Devils Tower National Monument, the latter located in extreme northeastern Wyoming.

About 60 million years ago—roughly the same time dinosaurs disappeared from the face of the Earth—an igneous intrusion below the flatlands formed the dome-shaped hills, as well as the labyrinth of large caves beneath. Lakota Sioux called them *Paha Sapa,* or "Hills of Black," and from afar, their pine-clad cliffs do appear as dark shadows. Within their borders, 1,000-foot limestone palisades flank streams bordered by quivering aspens and ponderosa pines. Lush forests are home to deer, elk, mountain lions, wild turkeys, Rocky Mountain goats, porcupines, raccoons, and bighorn sheep; and stream banks to beavers, muskrats, and minks.

To the Cheyenne Indians, who practiced their vision quests in the isolation of these wooded hills and valleys, and later to the Lakota Sioux, the Black Hills were sacred, far removed from the concerns of everyday life, a place of introspection, and connection with Wakantanka—the Great Spirit. One of the most

Crowds gather to watch a parade in Rapid City, circa 1900. (Center for Western Studies)

sacred places within the Hills was, and is, Bear Butte, a 1,200-foot conelike geo-logic rarity east of Sturgis. Both tribes also often avoided the Hills because of strange noises that emanated from within. Those noises can still be heard today, as wind whistles past the fingerlike granite spires of the Needles, and thunder crashes off hundreds of canyon walls during frequent spring and summer storms.

■ TRAVEL BY ROAD AND TRAIL   *map page 189*

Travel through the Black Hills is enhanced by fine touring roads. Hundreds of miles of scenic highways chase gurgling streams and weave their way through the pine-covered canyons of these mountains. Make no mistake, though. There are more curves on these roads than there are in a bronc rider's cowboy hat and enough hills to overheat your brakes. However, except in extreme weather condi-tions, most roads are well-maintained and passable in a family sedan.

Though highway travel is easy in the Black Hills, something about the windshield gets in the way of truly experiencing their beauty and ruggedness. They are best enjoyed close up, with dirt and pine needles underfoot. The 111-mile **Centennial Trail** spans the entire Black Hills from north to south. Dedicated during the state's centennial in 1989, the trail is intended to represent the diversity of South Dakota's landscape. Crossing prairie grasslands near **Bear Butte State Park** northeast of Sturgis, the trail gradually climbs into the Black Hills high country, skirting seven lakes and a myriad of streams, abandoned gold camps and ghost towns, through the **Black Elk Wilderness Area** and **Custer State Park,** before returning to the wildflowers and prairie pines at **Wind Cave National Park** near Hot Springs.

The attraction of this trail is not only its length and the variety of landscapes and geologic formations that users encounter, but the many access points and campgrounds along its route and the ways in which that trail may be traveled. The Centennial Trail's dozens of trailheads allow hikers, bikers, and horseback riders access to the pines, creeks, and coulees of **Black Hills National Forest.** Many portions of the trail follow the paths of long-gone flumes that carried water to town sites and gold-mining sluices in the late nineteenth century. As a result, hikers will discover a trail that is surprisingly level, with the exception of spots where small bridges and trestles have rotted and disappeared over time.

All of the trailheads have ample parking, but four of them are designated as "horse camps," allowing extra room for horse trailers for those who want to hoof it through the forest. Horseback riders are encouraged in all but Wind Cave National Park, and mountain bikers may use the majority of the trail, with the exception of Wind Cave and the Black Elk Wilderness Area. In winter, more than 600 miles of additional trails throughout the Hills are open to cross-country skiers and snowmobilers.

One of the most scenic and easily accessible portions of the trail begins at the **Flume Trailhead,** a half-mile south of Sheridan Lake on Forest Road 439. The trail follows the gentle shoreline of the lake before heading into the forest. Along the way, a spur trail takes hikers over the earthen dam and across a sturdy footbridge that spans Sheridan Lake's spillway. This segment of the trail, as well as the **Rapid Creek Trailhead** off U.S. 385 below the dam at Pactola Reservoir, are ideal for a quiet picnic or bobber fishing from shore. For a brochure on the Centennial Trail and information on other trailheads, contact the Black Hills National Forest Supervisor's Office (605-673-9200).

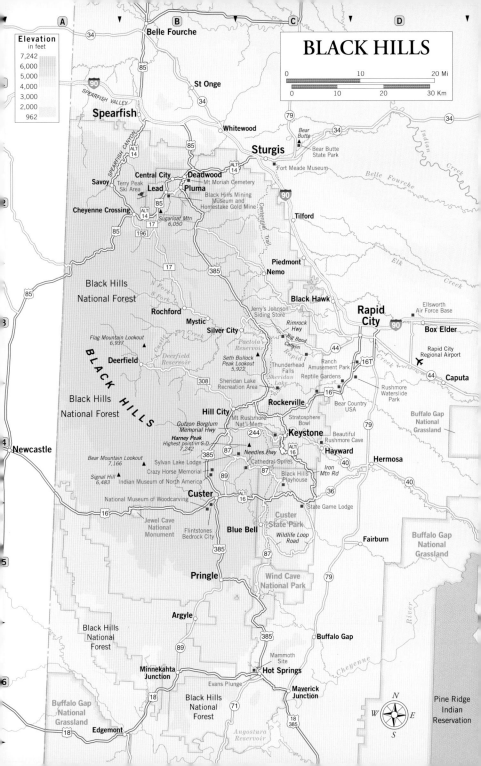

Trail rides and hikes are a favorite recreation for visitors to the Black Hills. (Paul Jones)

■ WEATHER

Extreme temperatures, at least by Midwest standards, are infrequent in this region, sometimes labeled the "Banana Belt" because of its warm temperatures. Yet winds known as "chinooks" often race through the Hills, melting snow, bringing a warm respite from winter—and causing some of the most abrupt changes in temperature to be found in the United States.

The most famous chinook was that of January 1943, when the greatest one-day variation in temperature ever recorded in the United States occurred in the northern Black Hills community of Spearfish. The mercury rose from 4 degrees F below zero (-20°C) to 45 degrees F above zero (7°C) in less than two minutes. So quick was the temperature change that large plate glass windows cracked throughout town, and cattle that had been standing on frozen ground had to work to stay on their feet in the slippery mud of feedlots. As the chinook's warm winds blanketed the town of Lead, thermometers soared to 52 degrees F (11°C). Meanwhile, less than three miles away, residents of the city of Deadwood still shivered in temperatures of 16 degrees F below zero (-27°C). In Rapid City, the thermometer at Montana-Dakota Utilities showed 9 degrees F (-13°C) at

10:30 A.M., and in the next half hour rose to 57 degrees F (14°C), then fell to 10 degrees F (-12°C). The following day, the *Rapid City Daily Journal* reported:

> The phenomenon was striking at the Alex Johnson Hotel corner at 11 A.M. On the east side of the hotel, winter was in all its glory, biting legs and faces, while around the corner on the south side, not 50 feet away, spring held sway.

■ RAPID CITY: GATEWAY TO THE BLACK HILLS

map page 189, D-3, and page 192

On the eastern edge of the Black Hills is Rapid City, a former cowtown that grew up to become the state's second-largest city and the eastern gateway to the Paha Sapa. At the intersection of I-90 and State Highways 44 and 79, the city is a regional shopping and medical center, and its 59,000 residents work in a variety of industries, from timber to tourism. Considering the state's low wage scale, they seem content to take part of their pay in blue skies, trout streams, and ponderosa pines. The dream of most blue-collar workers here is to be able to afford a house in the trees, where "you can hunt deer from your deck."

Rapid City was founded in 1876, when John Brennan persuaded a group of unsuccessful miners to establish a commercial center at the base of the Black Hills to provide supplies for the gold fields. Despite his best intentions, most stagecoaches and wagon trains continued into the heart of the Hills, where other settlements already were booming. Fortunately, in 1886 residents persuaded the Missouri, Fremont & Missouri Valley Railroad to lay tracks through town, and soon after, Rapid City began to prosper.

Topography determined much of its subsequent growth. Residential and commercial buildings wrapped themselves like a horseshoe around a large hill in the center of town, separating east and west. Today, residential development to the north and east is middle class and sprawling. Homes on the west and south sides tend to be newer and tucked in the pines or built on ridges that afford commanding views. **Skyline Drive** creeps down the hill's spine, providing an impressive vista of the entire community. Incongruously, replicas of seven life-size green dinosaurs guard the ridge at **Dinosaur Park,** a reminder of the Works Progress Administration crews that constructed these concrete kid-climbers in the 1930s.

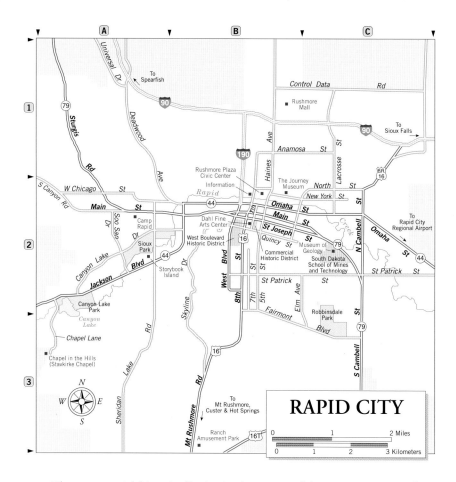

To Spearfish

Control Data Rd

Rushmore Mall

To Sioux Falls

Anamosa St

Rushmore Plaza Civic Center
Information

The Journey Museum

North St

New York St

Omaha St

Main St

St Joseph St

Quincy St

Museum of Geology

Commercial Historic District

South Dakota School of Mines and Technology

St Patrick St

St Patrick St

Fairmont

Robbinsdale Park

Blvd

Universal Dr

Deadwood Ave

Sturgis Rd

W Chicago St

Main St

Soo San Dr

Camp Rapid

Sioux Park

Canyon Lake Dr

Jackson Blvd

Storybook Island

Canyon Lake Park

Canyon Lake

Chapel Lane

Chapel in the Hills
(Stavkirke Chapel)

Skyline Dr

Lake Rd

Sheridan

Mt Rushmore Rd

West Blvd

8th St

7th St

5th St

Elm Ave

S Cambell St

N Cambell St

Omaha St

Haines

Lacrosse St

Creek

Rapid

Dahl Fine Arts Center

West Boulevard Historic District

To Mt Rushmore, Custer & Hot Springs

Ranch Amusement Park

To Rapid City Regional Airport

RAPID CITY

0   1   2 Miles

0   1   2   3 Kilometers

N
W   E
S

The **commercial historic district** in the center of downtown consists of 38 buildings constructed between 1881 and 1930. Typical of the period, they have flat roofs and were built of stucco, brick, limestone, and clapboard. Few have been restored to their original grandeur, which perhaps wasn't all that grand, but the **Buell Building** (Seventh and St. Joseph Streets), the **Firehouse Brewing Co.** (610 Main Street), and its next-door neighbor, the **Prairie Edge Building** (Sixth and Main Streets), have undergone substantial renovation.

The **Dahl Fine Arts Center** rotates exhibits of paintings and sculpture by area artists. One of its largest rooms is dedicated to a cyclorama of American history, a 180-foot-long, 10-foot-high mural. The push of a button brings on special lighting and narration and leads visitors around the room and through the evolution of the United States. *713 Seventh Street; 605-394-4101.*

Farther east on State Highway 79 South, the **Museum of Geology,** on the campus of the South Dakota School of Mines and Technology, provides a rare glimpse of prehistory. "Talking" dioramas narrate the history of the Badlands and the strange creatures that once inhabited the area. The museum's holdings also include what is possibly the finest collection of fossilized bones of giant dinosaurs, marine reptiles, and prehistoric mammals in the state, as well as extensive collections of rare and wonderful agates, fossilized cycads, rocks, gems, and minerals. (And in South Dakota, where several important institutions are engaged in the same activity, assembling the finest collection is no small task.) *501 East St. Joseph Street; 605-394-2467.*

The **West Boulevard Historic District** covers portions of 18 blocks southwest of the downtown business area. Its homes are set back from a wide, tree-lined boulevard, giving the area a stately and quiet atmosphere. Architectural styles include nineteenth-century Queen Anne and early twentieth-century Colonial.

(above) South Dakota's first brewpub opened in 1991 in Rapid City's old firehouse. (following pages) The brontosaurus in Dinosaur Park. (Both photos by Robert Holmes)

The **Journey Museum,** a $12.5 million state-of-the-art enterprise, opened in 1997. It's holdings—art, artifacts, and memorabilia come from five outstanding public and private collections. Inside a 48,000-square-foot building, the Journey takes visitors on a 2.5-billion-year trip through the history of the Black Hills. *222 New York Street; 605-394-6923.*

Live animals, nursery-rhyme displays, and play areas grace the grounds of **Storybook Island,** on Sheridan Lake Road between Canyon Lake Drive and Jackson Boulevard. The free children's park is Rapid City's most popular attraction, and its fountains, trains, castles, and children's theater make it a perfect side trip if you're traveling with kids. *1301 Sheridan Lake Road; 605-342-6357.*

Just a few minutes away on Chapel Lane Drive off State Highway 44 West stands the **Stavkirke Chapel**—a 1969 replica of the 850-year-old Borgund Church in Norway. The parklike setting and the church's unusual pegged construction and intricate wood carvings make this an interesting stop.

Rapid City hosts a variety of events, ranging from the **Black Hills Stock Show & Rodeo** in late January and early February and the **Central States Fair** in August to Broadway productions and International Basketball Association action. The arena of the massive **Rushmore Plaza Civic Center,** christened by Elvis Presley in "the King's" last performance, is the venue of choice for most community activities, concerts, and events.

Rapid City is not known for its nightlife, although a few sports bars and hideaways do keep city fathers from rolling up the streets at 7 P.M. **Woody's** (826 Main Street; 605-343-1931) is one of the town's liveliest nightclubs, with DJs and karaoke during the week and rock bands on weekends. Helping to maintain the festive atmosphere are billiards, darts, video lottery, arcade games, and nightly drink specials. The **Firehouse Brewing Company** (610 Main Street; 605-348-1915) is the city's only brewpub, and as suds at on-premise breweries go, the ones at the Firehouse rank with the best at similar establishments in Portland, Minneapolis, and Chicago. The lagers, ales, and stouts are best served with the brewery's traditional German fare—the smell of the bratwursts would make a Bavarian's tastebuds water. In good weather, local musicians regularly perform in the Firehouse's outdoor beer garden.

Just west of town on scenic State Highway 44 are two lovely places to eat and sleep: **Fireside Inn** (7 miles past Canyon Lake; 605-342-3900) and **Das Abend Haus Cottages and Audrie's Bed & Breakfast,** (23029 Thunderhead Falls Road; 605-342-7788).

■ **E L L S W O R T H   A I R   F O R C E   B A S E**   *map page 189, D-3*
Rapid City's economy receives a major boost from nearby Ellsworth Air Force
Base, 7 miles east of the city on I-90. Home to a third of the nation's B-1B
bombers, and one of the largest military installations in the United States,
Ellsworth also has some worthwhile activities for visitors. A low-cost tour of the
base takes participants near one of the strategic, low-level bombers, along the base
flightline, and stops to view restoration work being conducted on vintage aircraft
in one of the hangars. More entertaining, however, is the **South Dakota Air &
Space Museum,** just outside the Main Gate at Ellsworth. The museum's steadily
growing collection includes static aircraft, among them Gen. Dwight Eisenhower's
personal Mitchell B-25 bomber, a scaled-back version of the Stealth bomber, some
fighter planes, and cargo and utility aircraft. *605-385-5188.*

■ Sᴛᴜʀɢɪs   *map page 189, C-2*
The scene of the world's largest motorcycle rally, the tiny town of Sturgis is tucked
against the eastern foothills of the Black Hills about 30 miles north of Rapid City on
I-90. Sturgis is normally a quiet town of two-story storefronts and 6,500 people—
unless it's August. Then the town swells with the 400,000 bearded bikers who roar
in for the annual **Sturgis Rally & Races.** (See "Bikers' Bash," pages 198–199.)
    Sturgis has hosted one of the most interesting frontier attractions in the Hills
for more than a century: the **Fort Meade Museum** (State Highway 34; 605-347-
9822). Fort Meade opened as a peace-keeping fort in 1878, two years after the
Seventh Cavalry's disastrous defeat by the Sioux at Little Bighorn. Its initial mission was to keep whites out of the Black Hills in accordance with U.S. government
treaties with Indian tribes. When that proved impossible, its mandate was to protect white settlers and gold miners. Remnants of the defeated Seventh Cavalry,
minus Lt. Col. George Custer, eventually regrouped here, including Comanche,
the horse of Capt. Myles Keogh and the only living creature found by the U.S.
Army on the Custer battlefield following the massacre. The horse arrived at the
fort and was retired by its commander, Col. Samuel Sturgis.
    Colonel Sturgis had lost his son, Lt. Jack Sturgis, in the fateful 1876 fight
against the Sioux, and the story goes that the colonel had it in for Maj. Marcus
Reno, accused (and later acquitted) of negligence at Little Bighorn. Major Reno, a
confirmed drunk and carouser, developed a crush on the colonel's daughter, Ella.

BIKERS' BASH

It was "Bike Week" in the Black Hills in 1990—the fiftieth anniversary of the Sturgis Rally and Races—and I had just shared a few brews with a friend who was tending bar at the Pyramid Beer Gardens. The hot August sun scorched my retinas as I stepped onto Main Street, and, fumbling for my sunglasses, I saw that the curb was lined with Harley Davidsons of every era—an assortment of old-time Knuckleheads, Shovelheads, and Panheads mixed with the modern streamlined beauties called Wideglides, Softtails, and Dressers, complete with farings, luggage bins, stereos, and a lot of chrome.

The streets were packed for the fiftieth observance of the largest motorcycle rally in the world. Two-wheelers had traveled from around the globe to enjoy rock concerts, motorcycle racing, hill climbs, and scenic highways. The radio had warned local residents for weeks to brace for the expected 400,000 bikers for rally week. As I navigated the crowded street, suitably dressed in jeans and a black T-shirt, it appeared to me that the radio announcers had been right. Beards and bandannas were de rigueur, and from all the halter tops and short-shorts you'd think you were at Daytona Beach during spring break. The smell of stale beer and portable toilets mixed with motorcycle exhaust wafted over the sun-baked parchment, so it all stopped somewhat short of euphoria.

Vendors hawked a mountain of T-shirts to bikers from every state in the Union, 10 Canadian provinces, and more than three dozen foreign countries. As I walked down Main Street, watching biker women "headlight" tourists holding Sony camcorders, I wondered why they all came. Sometime between that thought and the speculation of how badly beaten a guy would get if he accidentally set one of these bikes on its side and triggered a domino-like catastrophe on Main Street, a strange thing happened. The crowd began to part for me. I was no longer bumping shoulders with hairy, badly groomed men who slept in sleeping bags and forgot to brush their teeth. They were literally stopping in front of me, stepping to the side, and smiling. Initially it was so odd and disconcerting that I thought perhaps my fly was down or I'd worn my Suzuki baseball cap. With a glance I dismissed each of those possibilities, but still they stared. Surely they didn't mistake me for the far grayer and infinitely more wealthy Malcolm Forbes, who used to like to bring his hot air balloons and Capitalist Tools to the rally each year.

After a block of continuous examination from passersby, I was frazzled. After all, nobody goes to a party with a half-million people—many of them Harley owners—

hoping to get noticed. Why were all these burly boys looking at me? My underarms began to get moist and I was grateful that, at the very least, my Right Guard was performing admirably. But still they looked, they smiled, they got out of the way. Finally, in a pure act of desperation just short of running screaming through the throng—I stopped and turned around.

There, behind me, following me step for step was one of the most beautiful women I had ever seen. I admit I don't recall her face, though I'm sure it was surrounded by blonde hair freshly rinsed with spring water and lemon. Come to think of it, the only thing I recall was her black, knee-high calfskin boots and the body paint, because that's all she wore. As she smiled, I think I saw perfect teeth, and I stepped aside and returned the grin like every other doorknob on the block, simultaneously feeling sorry for the next sorry sap who inadvertently walked in front of that woman.

—Tom Griffith

Imagine the rumble and the roar in downtown Sturgis when these gents (and ladies)
start their engines. (Greg Latza)

FROM CUSTER TO HIS SUNBEAM

My Darling Sunbeam—Your dear Bo can't send a very long letter, tho with volumes to say. After dinner, when we reach camp, I usually take an escort to search out a few miles of road for the following day, and when I return I am ready to hasten to my comfortable—but Oh so lonely—bed.

Reveille regularly at a quarter to three, so that it behooves one to go to bed early. Reynolds leaves in the morning for Ft. Laramie, so to-day is letter-day. I am going to explore in that direction some 25 or 30 miles. I take five companies with me. Two companies left this morning in another direction. Both absent three days.

Breakfast at four. In the saddle at five. First I have my official dispatch to attend to, then a letter to the "World."

The expedition has surpassed most sanguine expectations. We have discovered a rich and beautiful country. We have had no Indian fights. We have found gold and probably other valuable metals. All are well. I did not expect my wagon-train . . . and here it has followed me all the way.

—Lt. Col. George Custer, letter to his wife written from
Harney Peak, Dakota Territory, July 2, 1874

Colonel Sturgis refused to grant Reno permission to date his daughter, but that didn't stop Reno from ogling the young maiden through her bedroom window. When Colonel Sturgis discovered the "paneful" romance being conducted under his roof, he had Reno charged with window-peeping, which in military parlance translated into conduct unbecoming an officer and a gentleman. Reno was found guilty and was forced from the army. Eventually, he died penniless and was buried in a pauper's grave in Washington state. But the story didn't end there. In 1967, Reno's grandnephew petitioned the federal government for a review of the charges, and Maj. Marcus Reno received a full pardon, was restored to rank, and received an honorable discharge. His remains were then reburied with his comrades on the bluffs overlooking the Little Bighorn.

Fort Meade's history also encompassed events far more violent than a flirt and a court-martial. In June 1884, Alex Fiddler, "a white man of a desolate character," was jailed for beating and robbing a German immigrant. Shortly after his arrest and transport to the Sturgis jail, an angry mob forced his release and transported him to the nearest large tree, where they hanged him. The tree was referred to afterwards as "Fiddler's Tree." A year later, a trooper named Ross Hallon was arrested and accused of killing a local doctor. Another group of vigilantes visited the jail and told the guards it was time for dinner break. The next morning, Hallon's body was found hanging from Fiddler's Tree.

Historic documents are on display at the museum, among them original papers signed by Custer, Reno, and Sturgis. The most intriguing and poignant may well be letters written by common soldiers to their wives and children. In one such beautifully penned letter, dated June 8, 1876, Henry C. Dose, a trumpeter for the Seventh Cavalry, wrote his wife: "General Terry said that if we get Sitting Bull and his tribe soon, then we are going home, but if we don't we will stay three months and hunt for him. I wish for mine part we would meet him tomorrow." Little more than two weeks later, the meeting took place, and Dose lost his life.

In addition to letters, the museum displays old uniforms, guns, and photographs depicting the fort's history and the men—like the all-black 25th Cavalry unit, and the all-Sioux Indian Troop L of the Third Cavalry—who served here. In the mid-twentieth century, Fort Meade housed workers for the Civilian Conservation Corps and German prisoners of war before the Veterans Administration took it over in 1944.

Seven original buildings constructed in the 1880s still stand on the grounds, as well as other ones erected between 1904 and 1906. Three of the original stables survive, and some of the historic houses are now the residences of staff of the **Fort Meade V.A. Medical Center,** located on the grounds. Also here are the **South Dakota Military Academy's** officer training school and the **South Dakota National Guard,** which is working to restore two barracks.

■ SPEARFISH   *map page 189, B-1*

Nestled in a quiet valley on the northern tier of the Black Hills, about 15 miles northwest of Sturgis on I-90, is the idyllic community of Spearfish. Known for its beautiful location at the mouth of Spearfish Canyon, the town contains the Black Hills State University campus, an unobtrusive Main Street, and sleepy residential neighborhoods. Add low crime and unemployment rates, and a friendly, small-town atmosphere, and it's obvious why this was the fastest growing community in South Dakota in the late 1980s and early 1990s.

Spearfish first entered the history books in 1833, when a band of prospectors dodged Indian tribes and sneaked into the Hills in search of their fortune. Judging by the evidence today, it appears that this group truly "discovered" gold in the Hills 40 years before the Custer Expedition confirmed its presence. However, as the ragged party headed for home, they were spotted by Indians and attacked near Spearfish. In 1887, Spearfish stonemason Louis Thoen was on Lookout Mountain near town when he uncovered a rock on which had been scratched:

Came to these hills in 1833 seven of us DeLacompt, Ezra Kind, G.W. Wood, T. Brown, R. Kent, Wm. King, Indian Crow. All died but me Ezra Kind. Killed by Ind. beyond the high hill, got our gold in 1834. Got all gold we could carry, our ponys all got by Indians. I have lost my gun and nothing to eat and Indians hunting me.

Because dating the stone accurately has proved difficult, a few historians may doubt the authenticity of the **Thoen Stone**. Nonetheless, its presence has spurred queries into who really first searched for gold in the Black Hills. Today the Thoen Stone can be viewed, with its easily read etchings, at the **Adams Memorial Museum** (54 Sherman Street; 605-578-1714) in Deadwood.

The first pioneers came to Spearfish Valley in 1876, to take advantage of the steady streams of clear water, which flowed from nearby hills, and the rich black soils. Its first store opened in 1877, and the town's first school followed a year later. Spearfish Normal School, now Black Hills State University, graduated its first class in 1887. The **D.C. Booth Historic Fish Hatchery** (423 Hatchery Circle; 605-642-7730), one of the West's oldest such facilities, was established in 1896.

When the **Matthews Opera House** opened in 1906, it was immediately hailed as the focal point of an otherwise culturally bleak region. It hosted vaudeville in the 1930s, a shooting gallery in the 1940s, and summer stock in the 1950s. After its restoration in 1966, it became the summer theater of the local college. Refurbished and reopened in the late 1980s, the opera house continues its tradition with a mix of music, vaudeville, and comedy. Performances take place on most Mondays, Wednesdays, Fridays, and Saturdays from mid-June through mid-August. *614 Main Street; 605-642-7973.*

In 1932, one of Europe's oldest productions, the Luenen Passion Play, came to America from Germany. In 1939 it become a permanent Black Hills institution. More than 65 years later, the **Black Hills Passion Play** is still powerful. Staged three nights weekly from June through August in a 6,000-seat outdoor amphitheater, the

The Booth House at D.C. Booth Historic Fish Hatchery in Spearfish.

production uses 22 scenes and an ensemble of 250 actors and extras to reenact the last seven days in the life of Christ, taking the audience on a journey from Jerusalem to Gethsemane and the Ascension. *I-90, Exit 12, 100 St. Joe; 605-642-2646.*

As pretty as the town of Spearfish is, **Spearfish Canyon** is prettier. In any season, the limestone palisades that flank either side of U.S. 14A are breathtaking. A National Forest Scenic Byway, the road meanders along Spearfish Creek, past waterfalls, quaking aspens, sweet-smelling spruce, and ponderosa pines. For about three weeks each fall, the canyon fills with the colors of changing leaves that are as spectacular as any Vermont countryside. The upper reaches of the canyon provided the backdrop for the closing scenes in the movie *Dances With Wolves.*

■ DEADWOOD   *map page 189, B-2*

Gold was discovered near Deadwood in 1876, and within a year, 6,000 gold-hungry diggers had swarmed into the area to stake their claims. Soon came the camp followers—mule skinners, merchants, madams, card players, outlaws, and con artists. Among them was James Butler, alias Wild Bill Hickok—a sometime spy, scout, stagecoach driver, and sheriff—and his pal, Martha "Calamity Jane" Cannary Burke.

When Hickok heard of the 1876 gold rush, he left his new bride in Wyoming and galloped to Deadwood, where he hoped to relieve recently wealthy miners of some of their earnings at the gaming tables. Because Hickok was renowned as a gunman and marshall in the Kansas towns of Hays City and Abilene, Deadwood folks thought he might bring "a semblance of order to the lawless element of the camp," as the local newspaper stated at the time. But that wasn't to be. On August 2, as he sat in a poker game with his back to the door at Saloon No. 10, a hooligan named Jack McCall crept up behind Hickok and shot him in the back of the head. As McCall escaped, the dying Hickok fell forward, spilling pairs of black aces and eights on the table—a combination that forever after would be known as "the dead man's hand." Even though McCall was quickly captured and a vigilante jury was assembled, the defendant argued that Hickok had recently killed McCall's brother. To everyone's surprise, the jury acquitted McCall, who quickly left town. His freedom, however, was short-lived. After drunkenly bragging about his manipulation of the Deadwood jury, he was arrested by Nebraska authorities and turned over to a U.S. marshall in South Dakota. Just four months later, a

Standing left to right: Deadwood Dick, Edgar Howard, Charles R. Norden, Doc W. F. Carver, Buffalo Bill. Seated left to right: Capt. L. H. Norik, Pawnee Bill, and Diamond Dick Janner. (Center for Western Studies)

Yankton jury found McCall guilty of killing Hickok, and on March 1, 1877, he was hanged outside of town, his corpse buried in an unmarked grave.

Meanwhile, Hickok's body was laid to rest high above town at Deadwood's own Boot Hill—the **Mount Moriah Cemetery.** Even today, throngs of travelers visit the fenced gravesite. Nearby are the final resting places of other legends of Deadwood Gulch, including Calamity Jane, Preacher Smith, Potato Creek Johnny, and Madam Dora DuFran.

Two fires and a flash flood obliterated Deadwood three times in the next 10 years, and lawlessness continued. Finally, civilization came to town in the form of millionaire George Hearst (the father of William Randolph Hearst) and two fellow California investors. Together, they bought the Homestake Mine in the nearby town of Lead, and big industry entered the picture. Shafts thousands of feet deep were dug to reach ore deposits. Bankers built banks, publishers began printing

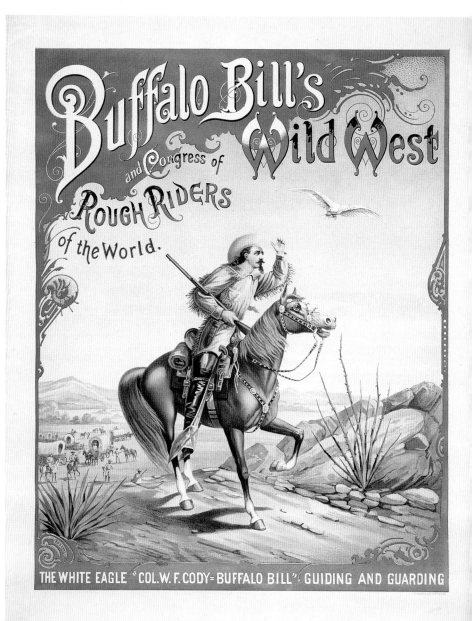

Poster advertising Buffalo Bill's Wild West Show, circa 1890.
(Buffalo Bill Historical Center, Cody, Wyoming)

newspapers, and wary merchants began constructing buildings using non-flammable bricks and stones. Many of those buildings still stand today.

When South Dakota gained statehood status in 1889, gambling was outlawed in Deadwood, but that didn't stop the betting parlors and brothels from conducting a steady trade right into the next century. Gambling flourished until a major crackdown in 1947, and discreet bawdyhouses continued operations until 1980. The city's reputation for exciting nightlife never did die, but by the late 1980s, Deadwood's historic Main Street had begun to take on the appearance of a dying town. Storefronts were boarded up. Once impressive Victorian facades were crumbling, and instead of a quaint Wild West business district, visitors encountered drab and virtually deserted streets in all but the busiest summer months.

That all changed in the fall of 1989 when legalized gambling returned. Between 1989 and 2003, more than $170 million in public and private funds were invested in renovating everything from the original period street lighting and cobblestone streets to area churches, museums, and downtown buildings, some of which required as much as $5 million in restoration work. What had been a town in steady decline is now a model of historic preservation, and the entire town is listed as a National Historic Landmark.

Rodeo fan in Deadwood during the Days of '76 Festival.

CALAMITY JANE

Martha Jane Cannary Burke, a.k.a. "Calamity Jane," has been the subject of so many stories and legends that it is difficult to distinguish fiction from fact. Notorious for drinking, smoking, sexual promiscuity, a foul mouth, and wearing pants, she was an ace shot, a part-time prostitute, and a one-time soldier (until a skinny-dipping episode ended her military career). Her claim to be a companion of Wild Bill Hickok, King of the Pistoleers, was enough to make her famous. But who *was* Calamity Jane?

Supposedly, she was born in 1852, in Iowa or Missouri, and moved west to Montana with her family. She eventually reached Deadwood, South Dakota, where she may or may not have known Bill Hickok, and acquired her significant reputation. According to her own story, she was at various times a Pony Express rider, an Indian fighter, a stagecoach guard, and a scout under Custer. In 1878, she is said to have ministered to victims of smallpox. She got married once, to a Mr. Clinton Burke in 1891, and had children both in and out of wedlock.

In her own day, Calamity Jane was somewhat of a legend. Dime-novel writers in the East, eager for a heroine and thrilled with the chance to hook someone up with

Calamity Jane looking somewhat tougher than Doris Day's Hollywood version. (Library of Congress)

Wild Bill Hickok, portrayed Calamity Jane as a femme fatale. Their Calamity possessed a graceful, womanly form, girlish beauty, and tresses of raven hair reaching down to a "peerless" waist. This Goddess of the Plains was always galloping out of the hills on her cayuse pony in time to notice deserving men on flagging horses pursued by thieves or Indians. With a couple of shots she'd knock out the villains, and the hero would turn around on his horse to see bad guys biting the dust, done in by a pretty little thing with a luscious figure and cherry red lips—a "wonderful little woman to have around in a calamity." The hero would then ask Calamity what her name was and whether she might want to get together. She'd answer, "If you want to find me, ask around. Everyone knows who I am," and she'd trot off into the hills. This is the Calamity Jane portrayed by Doris Day in the Hollywood version of the story.

The most frequently published photograph of Martha Jane Cannary reveals a plain and rather shabby woman in a slouch hat and a stained, fringed, buckskin jacket. The photograph published in this book shows a confident, physically powerful woman, nicely mounted and well dressed in mannish Western clothes.

Whoever she was in fact, Calamity Jane was one of the most infamous heroes of the West, a woman whose motto was, "Never go to bed sober, alone, or with a red cent left in your pocket." When she died in 1903, she was buried next to Bill Hickok.

—Jessica Fisher

Eighty gaming halls now line the streets of Deadwood. Tired, old, run-down stores on Main Street, worth less than $30,000 in 1988, suddenly sold for $1 million a year later. The negative aspects of the gambling boom include the displacement of nearly all the downtown retail outlets and the cacophony of slot machines stuffed in every nook, cranny, and convenience store.

The **Bullock Hotel** (633 Main Street; 605-578-1745) is one of the finest examples of historic restoration in South Dakota. Built in 1895 by Seth Bullock, the town's first sheriff and a close friend of President Theodore Roosevelt, it has the finest guest rooms in town, each appointed with nineteenth-century Victorian furnishings, as well as spacious gaming parlors with blackjack, poker, and one-armed bandits. The cut-stone building, with its fancy cupolas and cornices, is purportedly haunted by Bullock's ghost, which has shown up too frequently to be

Native American history interpreters at the Lakota encampment at Tatanka show how their ancestors used the buffalo for food, clothing, and shelter. (Tatanka)

easily discounted. Guests are more inclined to have a face-to-face encounter with actor/producer Kevin Costner, who often stays at the Bullock during his frequent visits to Deadwood, where he owns the **Midnight Star** (677 Main Street; 605-578-1555). This actually is three establishments in one—a casino on ground level, a richly wooded sports bar, **Diamond Lil's,** on the second floor, and **Jakes** (800-999-6482), arguably one of South Dakota's best restaurants, on the third tier. The costumes Costner wore in nearly all of his films—from *Field of Dreams* and *Dances with Wolves* to *Tin Cup* and *Open Range*—are on Diamond Lil's walls, but the real dream is the food at Jakes. The rib-eye with mushrooms sautéed in amaretto is a better bet than any poker game in town.

Costner's newest attraction, **Tatanka: Story of the Bison,** opened in 2003 a mile north of Deadwood. Dedicated to the American bison, it has a larger-than-life bronze sculpture of 14 bison being pursued by three Lakota horseback riders as its centerpiece. An interactive interpretive center explores the relationship between

211 BLACK HILLS 211

Miners have risked life and limb in their pursuit of gold in the Black Hills over the last century. (Adams Museum, Deadwood)

bison and man, and a replica of an 1840 Lakota encampment offers visitors a snapshot of what life might have been like for Native Americans on the Great Plains of yesteryear. The **Sweetgrass Grill at Tatanka** provides a chance to sample outstanding bison dishes, as well as bison hotdogs and stews. *100 Tatanka Drive, U.S. 85; 605-584-5678.*

A host of other Main Street casinos, including the **Silverado, Gold Dust, Four Aces,** and **Miss Kitty's** have invested hundreds of thousands of dollars to dazzle visitors as soon as they cross the threshold. Some casino owners have even bought their own limousines and buses to transport customers past the other establishments to their own front doors. But the real fun in Deadwood is often found in just roaming the streets, watching the tourists, and stepping in and out of doorways. **Durty Nelly's** Irish pub in the **Historic Franklin Hotel** (700 Main Street; 800-688-1876) hosts some of the best bar bands and jazz in the Black Hills. There's something half-cocked over at the **Old Style Saloon No. 10** (657 Main Street; 800-952-9398), which bills itself as the world's only museum with a bar, and after two shots of red-eye and a walk through sawdust, past walls and rafters jammed with thousands of artifacts, old photos, and even Wild Bill's wedding license, you may be hard-pressed to argue the point. Upstairs, at the **Deadwood Social Club** (605-578-3346), you'll discover a relaxed atmosphere, great steaks and pastas, and one of the best wine lists in the region. Across the street, even teetotalers stop in to admire the massive carved oak bar of the **Bodega** (662 Main Street).

In addition to the Bullock Hotel, a number of other casino hotels offer good rooms at fair prices. Each is served by the **Deadwood Trolley,** which rolls past nearly every important place in town about every 15 minutes. The **Mineral Palace Hotel** (601 Main Street; 605-578-2036) has fireside dining and one of the largest gaming complexes in Deadwood, while the **First Gold Hotel** (270 Main Street; 800-274-1876) attracts huge crowds each year because of its good food and friendly dealers. The **Deadwood Gulch Resort** (south of Main Street on U.S. 85; 800-695-1876) offers comfortable accommodations, pool, spa, and plate-sized T-bone steaks in a creekside location.

A 100-ounce gold bar from the
Homestake Gold Mine.

■ LEAD   *map page 189, B-2*

Most of the mile-high community of Lead (pronounced "Leed," as in an auriferous gravel deposit) sits perched on steep hillsides. For 125 years, it was dominated by the gray metallic Homestake Gold Mine, with its 8,000-foot-deep shafts and high hoist. Homestake commanded the region's economy for more than a century, and though mining companies continue to search for gold in the Black Hills, none has had the profound impact of Homestake, the longest continuously operating gold mine in the world.

Four fortune-hungry prospectors originally worked the Homestake claim, but quickly sold out to a group of capital-rich Californians who brought in the machinery necessary for large-scale ore mining in 1877. The company hired large numbers of immigrant miners from Italy, Great Britain, the Balkans, and Scandinavia, and quickly made South Dakota one of the leading gold-producing states.

As gold prices declined and production costs increased, the Homestake was closed for good in the fall of 2002 and crews began dismantling its age-old buildings. The next year, in May 2003, the National Science Foundation and a prestigious group of scientists identified the Homestake Mine as the ideal site for the nation's new National Underground Science Laboratory.

A company town, Lead has been marked throughout with the presence of gold mining on a colossal scale. Its massive "open cut" signifies the spot where an entire mountain was moved, scoop by scoop, in search of the precious metal. The **Homestake Gold Mine Visitor Center** (160 West Main Street; 888-701-0164) offers a view of the open cut, and from May through September mine surface tours expose visitors to the giant hoists, ore-crushing machinery, and final refining processes of this industry. The **Black Hills Mining Museum** (323 West Main Street; 605-584-1605) examines the history of the mining industry, from carbide lamps and timber stopes to compressed-air locomotives and gold-panning techniques.

As much as 15 feet of "white gold," also known as snow, falls at this altitude in the Black Hills each winter, bringing thousands of skiers to the Lead area for outdoor recreation. **Terry Peak Ski Area,** 3 miles southwest of Lead off U.S. 85, has a 1,100-foot vertical drop, more than 20 miles of ski trails, and beginner, intermediate, and expert runs. Nearby **Deer Mountain Ski Area** boasts a 700-foot vertical drop, 25 trails, and lighted night skiing.

■ SCENIC DRIVES FROM THE NORTHERN BLACK HILLS *map page 189*

Although virtually every paved highway, gravel road, and cow path constitutes a scenic byway, the roadway used to get from Point "A" to Point "B" can often mean the difference between a common road trip and an adventure. U.S. 385 from Lead winds through the heart of the Black Hills all the way to Nebraska, and it's a relatively quick and pretty drive past towering pines, rock outcroppings, **Pactola Reservoir** and **Sheridan Lake,** and the towns of **Custer** and **Hot Springs** farther south.

A road less traveled (which generally means a combination of cattle guards, gravel, and dust) will test your savvy and your vehicle's shocks. One of the best afternoon excursions in any season but winter takes motorists about 3.5 miles south of Lead on U.S. 85, then turns left onto County Road 17 to the all-but-abandoned town of **Rochford.** This is a winding route as the road traces the path of the North Fork of Rapid Creek for about 15 miles. (The suddenly faint or car-sick should take left turns on County Roads 216 or 255 for a 5-mile trip back to the blacktop of U.S. 385.) Rochford's answer to the "Megamall" in Minneapolis (and the town's lone retail outlet), along with the **Moonshine Gulch Saloon** and a number of deer hunters' shacks, make up the town. To continue, stay on County Road 17 for a couple of miles before it connects with County Road 187 to **Castle Creek.** At the bottom of the hill, the road leads past slate-lined slopes, ponderosa pines, and wildflowers to one of the loveliest creeks in the Black Hills, Castle Creek, meandering slowly from **Deerfield Reservoir** to its confluence with **Rapid Creek.**

Another road, **Rimrock Highway,** also known as State Highway 44 West, provides a splendid scenic drive through one of the prettiest canyons in the Black Hills, **Big Bend.** Leading west from Rapid City to its junction with U.S. 385, the highway follows Rapid Creek and some heavily stocked fisheries. A favorite with motorcyclists who love to visit the **Rimrock Tavern** and **Jerry's Johnson Siding Store,** the road has many curves but is well-maintained. A half-mile past the well-marked **Thunderhead Falls** turn-off, the highway leads through the wicked and wonderful canyon. (Some say Big Bend was the site of a thunderous locomotive collision in 1907, but no one seems able to find the disaster's exact location.) On the steep canyon wall, remnants of a flume that carried water to Rapid City are still visible, and at various times, bighorn sheep, goats, and deer have been spotted, as have rattlesnakes, minks, muskrats, beavers, and a variety of waterfowl.

A view of Harney Peak's summit, at 7,242 feet the highest point between the Rockies and the Alps.

Chilly Rapid Creek, with its alternating slow and fast currents, is a popular place for inner-tubers, as well as for fishermen who wet their lines and waders in search of elusive brown trout. In South Dakota, public access to creeks and rivers can be gained at most bridges, or by asking landowners permission to cross their private property. Those same waterways are regarded as a public thoroughfare up to the high water mark, even if they flow through private property. Consequently, once in the water, fishermen and tubers can proceed unimpeded.

Creekside residences are plentiful in the canyon, and many original home builders took advantage of an abandoned railroad right-of-way on which to construct their houses. The **Crouch Line** was often called "the crookedest railroad in the world." Along its 30-mile path between Rapid City and **Mystic**, the railroad crossed Rapid Creek 110 times, and the train made the equivalent of 14 complete circles in one trip. Nearly every rail was bent to fit the curves of the canyon, and locals joked that the bends were so sharp that the brakeman in the caboose could pass a chew of tobacco to the engineer manning the locomotive. The railroad, a dream of Charles D. Crouch, was founded in the early 1890s and was closed in 1947. Few signs of it exist today.

■ RAPID CITY TO RUSHMORE   *map page 189*

Along U.S. 16 south of Rapid City—the road to Mount Rushmore—travelers encounter myriad private tourist attractions ranging from drive-through wildlife parks and go-cart tracks to RV resorts and waterslides. One of the oldest is **Reptile Gardens** (5 miles south of Rapid City; 800-335-0275). Founder Earl Brockelsby got a start in 1937 by exhibiting fearsome rattlesnakes and selling trinkets. Today the attraction is still fresh and fun. Sporting the world's largest collection of reptiles, including snakes, lizards, and crocodiles, it also features an array of birds, orchids, and other tropical and desert plants, under a massive walk-through skydome. The trained animal act is a bit corny, but three other shows—Birds of Prey, Alligators, and Snakes—are intriguing and worth the admission price.

Other nearby attractions include **Bear Country U.S.A.** (605-343-2290), home to the largest captive collection of black bears, as well as deer, elk, bison, bighorn sheep, timber wolves, and a giant grizzly bear. **Rushmore Waterslide Park** (605-348-8962) has nine slides, some of them 400 feet long. The diversions at **Ranch Amusement Park** (877-302-3321) include go-cart races, bumper boats, and miniature golf.

Carnivals have always played a part in the rural life of South Dakota. Here a horse race through town draws sponsors and crowds. (Center for Western Studies)

■ HILL CITY   *map page 189, B/C-4*

A century after it was founded, Hill City resembles numerous Black Hills communities that were settled by gold miners, faltered when the strike waned, then figured out a way to stay around. The tiny town of 780 residents continues to cater to traffic on U.S. 385: tourists in the summer months, and hunters, fishermen, snowmobilers, and cross-country skiers in the off-season. Historic Main Street is so rustic that it's hard to believe horses aren't tied to the posts in front of the buildings. Nonetheless, some delicious food and interesting shops can be found here. The **Alpine Inn** (225 Main Street; 605-574-2749) in the Harney Peak Hotel has a pleasant Bavarian atmosphere and serves some of the best beef in the region. The bartenders at the **Mt. Rushmore Brewing Company** (349 Main Street; 605-574-2400) pour microbrews and dish up pub fare in a 1902 brick building. Try the buffalo or the walleye entreé for something unique and tasty.

Railroad buffs can get their fill aboard the **Black Hills Central Railroad,** whose **1880 Train,** a vintage steam locomotive and passenger cars makes relaxing two-hour excursions through the Black Hills backcountry, past creeks, pines, canyons, and trestles. Boarding can be done in either Hill City or Keystone, but the Hill City stop offers great food in the High Liner Restaurant car, and the gift shop is the only place in the region with railroad memorabilia. *605-574-2222.*

■ KEYSTONE   *map page 189, C-4*

The only town closer to Mount Rushmore than Hill City is the less-than-scenic Keystone. After you've traveled quiet country byways, smelling fresh pines and listening to streams babble past granite outcroppings, the town at the base of Mount Rushmore turns out to be filled with T-shirt shops, jewelry stores, fast-food outlets, neon-lined blocks of blacktop, and false storefronts. For a dollar, a rumpled, stubbly-chinned "miner" and his pack mule will pose for placement in your photo album.

Keystone's hundreds of motel rooms, dozens of gift shops, and proximity to Mount Rushmore make it one of the busiest towns in the Black Hills for about five months of the year. A former gold mining community that went from boom to bust, then boom again with the carving of America's largest rock group, Keystone seems content to make a buck during the tourist season, then cover its lone traffic light and wait out the winter.

One establishment that provides historical insight is the **Rushmore-Borglum Story** (324 Winter Street; 605-666-4448), a museum dedicated to exploring the life story and work of sculptor Gutzon Borglum prior to his arrival in the Black Hills. The Rushmore-Borglum Story also displays models used by the sculptor in carving the mountain memorial. Another attraction, the **National Presidential Wax Museum** (609 Highway 16A; 605-666-4455), where detailed life-size wax figures of every U.S. president are placed in historical settings, provides an intriguing look at the history of the nation's chief executives. The museum includes a gift shop, grill, and historical artifacts including President Clinton's red, white, and blue saxophone and one of Florida's controversial ballot boxes from the 2000 presidential election. Five miles east of Keystone on State Highway 40 is **Beautiful Rushmore Cave** (605-255-4384), discovered by gold seekers. Tours are conducted of colorful "dripstone" formations, including stalactites, stalagmites, ribbons, columns, and helectites.

Immediately southwest of Keystone on U.S. 16A is the **Iron Mountain Road,** a brainchild of the former South Dakota governor and U.S. senator Peter Norbeck. Norbeck personally laid out the entire course of this scenic highway—much to the disappointment of the engineers and contractors who then had to build it. "This is not a commercial highway," Norbeck snorted when objections were raised. "It's a

scenic road. To do the scenery half-justice, people should drive 20 mph or under; to do it full justice, they should get out and walk!" What Norbeck wrought in the 1930s is still visible today in a roadway that is both a wonder of engineering and a motor-home driver's nightmare.

Iron Mountain Road is well known for its "pigtail" bridges— three consecutive loops over rustic timber trestles that avoid the standard switchbacks commonly used in mountain road construction. As you

Gutzon Borglum inspecting some face rock during the carving of Mount Rushmore in the 1930s. (National Park Service)

drive through three of the narrow tunnels on the roadway, you'll have perfectly framed views of the four faces of Mount Rushmore. Scenic turnouts along the route provide far-off views of Mount Rushmore, vast landscapes of jagged peaks jutting up from the surrounding forests, and hillscapes so large that visitors can watch the dark shadows of clouds race across the treetops from windswept mountain tops to quiet valleys.

■ MOUNT RUSHMORE NATIONAL MEMORIAL *map page 189, C-4*

In 1924, the South Dakota historian Doane Robinson envisioned an enormous sculpture of some of the Old West's legendary heroes—Lewis and Clark, Buffalo Bill Cody, and the great Sioux warriors—carved on the Needles in the Black Hills. After enlisting the support of South Dakota's senator Peter Norbeck, Robinson wrote a letter of invitation to sculptor Gutzon Borglum, then involved with a massive Confederate memorial being carved at Stone Mountain, Georgia.

When Borglum arrived in the Black Hills in the summer of 1925, he decided that the Needles, a grouping of finger-like granite spires that rise from the surrounding pine forests, were too brittle for carving, and their shapes not suitable for representing the human body. Instead, Borglum chose Mount Rushmore, for its sound granite and because the mountain's carveable surface faced southeast, allowing direct sunlight for as much of the day as possible. Borglum furthermore surprised Robinson and Norbeck by informing them that the subjects of the South Dakota sculpture would be national, rather than Western, figures.

Together Robinson, Norbeck, and Borglum chose four presidents for the memorial who would represent the birth, growth, preservation, and development of the United States: George Washington, "father of the nation"; Thomas Jefferson, facilitator of the Louisiana Purchase; Abraham Lincoln, preserver of the Union; and Theodore Roosevelt, builder of the Panama Canal and a frequent visitor to the Black Hills.

In 1927, President Calvin Coolidge arrived to help dedicate the beginning of work on the memorial. For the next 14 years, Borglum and his drill-dusty crew of unemployed miners drilled, blasted, and chiseled the gnarled face of the mountain into the visages of the four presidents. Deep fractures in the rock forced Borglum

(following pages) Mount Rushmore National Memorial. (Robert Holmes)

to change the concept of the carving nine times, funds often ran out, and severe weather caused frequent delays. When Borglum died in March 1941, the unfinished work was taken over by his son, Lincoln, who carried the work to its close on October 31.

As you approach the monument on Gutzon Borglum Memorial Highway (State Highway 244), just outside Keystone you'll see the presidents peeking at you through the trees. It's best to go in the early morning hours, when sunlight from the east casts a warm glow on the four faces. On the main viewing terrace, visitors gazing up at Borglum's work often speak in hushed tones, as if the imposing sculptures could hear.

The more than 2.5 million visitors who flock to Mount Rushmore each year make it one of the most popular national parks. It had long since outgrown its original concession building when a $56 million redevelopment, undertaken during the 1990s, resulted in a new parking structure and other new facilities, including a visitor center and museum and the Presidential Trail, a concrete and plank walkway around the base of the memorial that allows visitors to get closer than ever before to the four presidents. Their faces are lit nightly year-round, but from Memorial Day through Labor Day, a special National Park Service evening program is given, consisting of a 10-minute talk, a 20-minute film, and, the highlight, the slow exposure of light to the monument until it is fully illuminated. A small information center is at the park's entrtance. *605-574-2523.*

■ CUSTER STATE PARK   *map page 189, C-4/5*

Iron Mountain Road enters Custer State Park at its extreme northeastern edge and proceeds south to connect with its lone east-west roadway. The park, established by Sen. Peter Norbeck in 1919, is a 73,000-acre preserve where more than 1,500 bison roam free. "Buffalo jams" are more common here than bumper-to-bumper traffic, and burros often interrupt motorists to beg for something to munch. They'll eat almost anything they're given, and if they're not given anything, these wild donkeys will leave slippery saliva on car windows as an expression of their annoyance.

Custer State Park lays claim to the largest and most diverse population of wildlife, the best accommodations and facilities, and the most spectacular natural

A prairie dog surfaces in Custer State Park. (Robert Holmes)

resources of any park in South Dakota. Its 114 square miles of land alternate between rolling foothills, pine forests, and the fingerlike granite spires of the Needles. Tucked in the forests in separate corners of the park are four resorts owned by the state and operated by the Custer State Park Resort Company (800-658-3530). They're distinctly different, with facilities ranging from comfortable lodge rooms to rustic lakeside cabins.

The **State Game Lodge Resort** served as the summer White House for President Calvin Coolidge in 1927 and was visited by President Dwight Eisenhower in 1953. The historic stone and wood lodge has only seven guest rooms, but 40 nearby motel rooms and 20 cottages supplement the supply. The dining room is known for its excellent pheasant and buffalo dishes. From the lodge, visitors can embark on a four-wheel-drive excursion into the bison herds and hiking trails and trout fishing spots are nearby. **Legion Lake Resort** is centrally located in the park, close to buffalo herds, a golf course, hiking and horse trails, and summer theater at the **Black Hills Playhouse** (605-255-4141). The **Blue Bell**

By 1900, American bison had been hunted to near extinction, but through the efforts of conservationists and cattlemen, freely roaming bison herds, like this one in Custer State Park, now graze in protected areas of the Great Plains.

Lodge and Resort, State Highway 87 South, provides a guest-ranch setting for secluded cabins, camping, hayrides, chuck wagon cook-outs, trail rides, hiking, and fishing.

The most incredible setting, however, is reserved for the **Sylvan Lake Lodge and Resort.** High atop the Black Hills, overlooking a small but stunning lake, the lodge is rustic and comfortable. There may be no better place in the state to settle down with a cocktail and ponder the events of a day than the veranda, which has a splendid view of the Harney Range. Some cabins, set apart on the rugged, wooded hills near the lodge, have fireplaces and waterbeds. Paddleboats, canoes, and mountain bikes are available for rent near the lake. From the lodge, the **Needles Highway** takes motorists and mountain bikers on a 14-mile adventure through pine forests and past the eponymous granite spires to the highest reaches of the park. Vehicles zigzagging among the towering pillars and squeezing through skinny tunnels seldom exceed 30 mph. Among the special spots on the route are the **Needle's Eye,** a slit in a spire about 4 feet wide and 40 feet long, and the **Cathedral Spires,** unique formations of granite towers that rise from the forest floor heavenward. The spires are a Registered National Landmark.

Other attractions within Custer include the 18-mile **Wildlife Loop Road,** the observation deck of the **Mount Coolidge Fire Lookout,** and the **Gordon Stockade,** the site of the first—albeit brief—white settlement in western South Dakota. In 1874, a small group of miners defied agreements between the U.S. government and the Sioux and sneaked into the Hills, remaining in this spot for 90 days before being arrested by the army for violating the Laramie Treaty of 1868. There's also the log cabin of South Dakota's first poet laureate, Badger Clark, best known for his "Cowboy's Prayer." The **Badger Hole,** as it has come to be known, is constructed of native stone and wooden shingles. Its porch extends around a large pine tree that Clark just couldn't cut down. The writer scorned electricity and carried water by hand from a nearby spring. The cabin remains just as it was when Clark sat by the light of a kerosene lantern and penned his short stories, novels, poems, and lyrics.

Hikers will find an extensive network of trails. Among the most popular are the **Cathedral Spires Trail,** the **Sunday Gulch Trail,** and the **Harney Peak Summit Trail,** the last one a 22-mile segment of the 111-mile Centennial Trail. The Resort Company conducts trail rides into the backcountry, and the park provides a horse camp and riding trails. In addition to helping visitors locate bison herds and hot fishing spots, Custer State Park staff lead guided nature walks, gold panning demonstrations, junior naturalist programs, and patio talks throughout the summer months. *Custer State Park Headquarters; 605-255-4515.*

Just east of Custer State Park at the intersection of State Highway 89, U.S. 16, and U.S. 385 stands the city of **Custer,** a thriving community of 1,860 residents whose friendly nature makes it the ideal headquarters for exploring the Black Hills. All told, the town's not much to look at. The main business district has expanded until it now stretches in a "T" far along U.S. 16 and northward up U.S. 385. But the city has several things going for it: proximity to the natural attractions of nearby parks and monuments, snowmobile and hiking trails, numerous scenic byways, and the glad-you-came atmosphere created by residents who are as gracious at the local chamber of commerce as they are at the service station down the street.

In 1874, Lt. Col. George Custer jotted down glowing accounts of the beauty of this site in his journals. Confirmation of gold in the Black Hills was made just east of Custer, in French Creek, when a member of Custer's expedition named Horatio Ross found "colors" in his pan. But the 1,200-man expedition also discovered the region's enduring beauty, and it wasn't long before Custer became the first city to be founded in the Hills. Residents re-create the memorable moments in their history with the **Pageant of Paha Sapa** during the **Gold Discovery Days** (605-673-2244) celebration each July.

Fans of TV cartoon characters Fred, Barney, Wilma, Betty, and Dino won't want to miss the **Flintstones Bedrock City** (605-673-4079) west of town on U.S. 16. The Stone Age theme park has train rides, play areas, and Brontoburger stands. For wood-carving enthusiasts, there's the **National Museum of Woodcarving** (U.S. 16 West; 605-673-4404), which displays hundreds of works by Dr. Harley Niblack, one of the original animators of Disneyland. From June through August, **Dakota Badland Outfitters** (605-574-2525) can put you in the saddle for a one-hour or one-day backcountry trail ride; less strenuous outings include the chuck-wagon dinner ride. For those who want to rise above the smell of saddle blankets, campfire smoke, and baked beans, **Black Hills Balloons** (800-568-5320) provides flights past Mount Rushmore, Crazy Horse, herds of grazing bison, elk, and deer, and scenic lakes and granite peaks. Though it's expensive, there may be no other experience quite like a sunrise or sunset hot-air balloon ride over the Hills, away from the switchbacks, gas gauges, and hot tires of earth-bound travelers.

CRAZY HORSE MEMORIAL *map page 189, B-4*

The Sioux called Crazy Horse their "strange one," believing he had mystical powers, and the white soldiers he engaged in combat may have held those same beliefs. As a leader, Crazy Horse is partially credited with Lt. Col. George Custer's spectacular defeat at the Battle at Little Bighorn and has inspired a great deal of curiosity, controversy, and respect. Today, the legend of Crazy Horse is the inspiration behind a massive mountain memorial being carved in the Black Hills: Crazy Horse Memorial.

The idea for the memorial began in 1939, when Korczak Ziolkowski (pronounced "Core-jock Jewel-CUFF-ski"), an assistant to Gutzon Borglum at Mount Rushmore, received a letter from Chief Henry Standing Bear stating that the Sioux "would like the white man to know the red man has great heroes, too." Seven years later, Ziolkowski agreed to sculpt a memorial for the great Sioux warrior Crazy Horse. He and his wife, Ruth, decided that the sculpture would be the largest ever undertaken—a colossal 563-foot statue of Crazy Horse pointing over his stallion's head to the sacred Black Hills.

The first few decades of work on the mountain were long and arduous. Ziolkowski most often worked alone, wielding a jackhammer and setting his own dynamite charges. In the early days, he had to climb 741 steps up to his workplace on

The Crazy Horse Memorial gradually takes shape in the Black Hills. (Robert Holmes)

top of the mountain, and every time his pneumatic drill stalled he had to descend the stairs again to fiddle with the generator. In 1982, when he realized he was dying, he said to his wife, "I cannot carve Crazy Horse from the grave. There are some decisions you have to make."

In the early 1990s, Ruth Ziolkowski began carving the face of Crazy Horse, rather than the head of the stallion, which her husband had envisioned for the first detail work. The nine-story-high face was finished in 1998, after which attention turned to the 219-foot-high horse's head. By 2003, the upper third had been blocked out.

Drivers passing through the area often hear dynamite blasts on the mountain, a sign that work is progressing. When night blasts are set, they tend to be among the most spectacular events in the Black Hills. Visitors to the memorial may also wish to spend some time at the **Indian Museum of North America**, which houses one of the most extensive collections of Plains Indian artifacts in the country. The museum is in a large complex of structures that also includes the Native American Educational and Cultural Center, where Native American artists display their work during the summer, a restaurant, and a gift shop selling authentic Indian-made items.

Crazy Horse Memorial, 5 miles north of Custer on U.S. 385; 605-673-4681.

■ WIND CAVE NATIONAL PARK   *map page 189, C-5*

Sharing the southern boundary of Custer State Park, Wind Cave National Park consists of 28,300 acres of wildlife preserve aboveground and one long cave below. Bison, elk, deer, and antelope roam the woodlands and high prairies—only humans crawl through the dark. More than 100 miles of mapped passageways rank Wind Cave as the sixth-longest cave in the world. Within its interconnecting corridors are fragile gypsum beard (which will sway gently from the warmth of a spelunker's carbide lamp); tangled mineral-laden bushes resembling small, intricate crystal Christmas trees; and delicate helicite balloons on the cavern walls that will burst at the touch of a finger. On the surface of Windy City Lake, 500 feet below the earth's surface, float tiny calcite rafts.

A few years back, the author of this book accompanied a group of veteran spelunkers into Wind Cave. We wound our way through a maze of passageways best suited for contortionists. While squeezing through holes narrower than my shoulders and dragging myself through an 18-inch-high passage, my battery

Up close and personal with the "strange one" at the Crazy Horse Memorial. (Robert Holmes)

pack fell off my belt and I was left in blackness. After 2.5 hours of slithering, the underground world opened up, revealing a giant ballroom (known as the Club Room) two football fields long (200 yards) and eight stories high. On the floor of the cave sat giant boulders the size of houses. We stopped there to rest and drink our water, hearing only our own labored breathing.

Wind Cave is part of a great cave system that lies beneath the Black Hills—a system some scientists believe has been only five percent mapped. At Wind Cave and at **Jewel Cave National Monument**—the world's third-longest cave, west of Custer on U.S. 16—a maze of rare and unusual boxwork, frostwork, and popcorn formations, as well as of more common stalactites, stalagmites, and calcite crystals, awaits those with enough nerve (and a heavy sweater) to travel underground. Park rangers conduct regular tours of both caves that range from standard sightseeing excursions to genuine spelunking and candlelight expeditions. *Wind Cave National Park; 605-745-4600. Jewel Cave National Monument; 605-673-2288.*

■ HOT SPRINGS *map page 189, C-6*

Years before settlers entered the Black Hills in search of gold, the Sioux and Cheyenne Indian tribes battled for control over the natural warm-water springs of present-day Hot Springs. According to legend, a skirmish raged in the hills high above the springs, on a peak now called Battle Mountain.

Farmers and ranchers followed miners into the area and settled Hot Springs, but in 1890 a group of ambitious entrepreneurs decided to turn the town into a health spa. Leading the pack was Fred Evans, who built Evans Plunge over a number of small sparkling springs and one massive thermal spring of warm mineral water. After the railroad arrived in 1891, and for some 20 years thereafter, trainloads of prosperous visitors disembarked at the Hot Springs depot intent on wallowing in the "healing water" of those therapeutic springs. Families combined mineral bath cures with vacations, enjoying picnic outings in the Hills and stagecoach rides to nearby Wind Cave. Liberal statutes and lax residency requirements turned the community into a divorce center, increasing business for hoteliers, restaurants, and attorneys. By World War I, however, most of that had changed. Doctors were less likely to recommend mineral baths as a cure for ailments, and changes in state law rendered quickie divorces a thing of the past.

The remains of more than 50 mammoths have been uncovered at the Mammoth Site in Hot Springs.

Despite these changes, a visit to present-day Hot Springs is still enjoyable. More than a century after its construction, **Evans Plunge** still accommodates 87-degree F water in its 50-by-200-foot pool, the world's largest natural warm-water swimming pool. It's probably a lot more fun now than it was in the days of swimming caps and modest bathing suits. Three water slides, exercise facilities and Jacuzzis, a children's pool, and water volleyball and basketball supply options beyond leisurely bathing in sun and water. *1145 North River Street; 605-745-5165.*

The same warm waters that gave Hot Springs its name helped fund construction of some beautiful buildings. Intricate carvings and ornamental designs decorate the facades of many sandstone buildings, which blend perfectly with the surrounding sandstone cliffs and evergreen forests of Fall River Canyon. The city's **Historic District**, which includes homes, resort hotels, sanatoriums, and commercial buildings constructed between 1890 and 1915, comprises a large section of the old town, especially along River Street and Chicago Avenue.

As impressive as this city's history and architecture are, nothing is as unusual as the trove uncovered in 1974 during the construction of a new housing project. In June of that year, a heavy-equipment operator named George Hanson was leveling a hilltop when the blade of his grader struck an object that shone white in the sunlight. Hanson stepped down for closer inspection and found a tusk, about 7 feet long, that had been sliced in half. Further examination revealed smaller bones. To his credit and that of landowner Phil Anderson, site preparation was stopped while scientists were contacted to determine exactly what had been uncovered. Professor Larry Agenbroad arrived from Arizona about a week later and determined that mammoth bones had been uncovered. He also realized that there must be more beneath the surface.

In 1975, Agenbroad and his foreman, Jim Mead (both of them professors of geology and quaternary studies at the Northern Arizona University in Flagstaff), led a team of students who began excavating the site. Over the next few years, as the number of mammoths uncovered at the site increased, the scientists began piecing together evidence that a giant sinkhole had literally swallowed the giant beasts. They theorized that the pond was created by a collapsed cavern, and that water rising under pressure from an artesian well partially filled the sinkhole. About 26,000 years ago, when giant Columbian and woolly mammoths roamed the territory, the sinkhole's warm waters acted as a magnet for the large animals. Once in the water, however, they were trapped by the steep, slippery sides of the sinkhole and died. Eventually, the water source became plugged and layers of reworked sand served as a hardened, protective shroud around the animal remains. The mausoleum of mammoths went unnoticed for the next 260 centuries.

The fossilized remains of more than 50 mammoths have now been uncovered at the **Mammoth Site**—the largest paleontological find of its kind in the world. In addition to the mammoth remains, a variety of other species have been unearthed, including the giant short-faced bear, gray wolf, mink, black-tailed prairie dog, western harvest mouse, meadow vole, frog, and minnow, giving scientists vital pieces to the puzzle of what the ancient environment and climate were like when mammoths roamed the grasslands so long ago.

A superb 20,000-square-foot building and educational center was constructed over the site by a nonprofit foundation that oversees the project. Guided tours, junior paleontological digs, and one of the finest scientific bookstores in the region are all available here. Due to its uniqueness, the Mammoth Site experience ranks with Mount Rushmore, the Crazy Horse Memorial, and Deadwood as one of the four most exciting destinations in South Dakota. *1800 West U.S. 18; 605-745-6017.*

Two other attractions in the southern Black Hills are worth mentioning. At a remote location west of Hot Springs—on a gravel road that runs west off State Highway 71—hundreds of mustangs, unclaimed through the Bureau of Land Management's Adopt-a-Horse program, run wild across open range. The **Black Hills Wild Horse Sanctuary,** also known as the **Institute of Range Management and the American Mustang** (605-745-5955), is the first privately owned wild horse preserve in the United States. South of Hot Springs and immediately west of U.S. 385 lies **Angostura Reservoir.** On any given summer weekend, a convoy of vehicles pulling all sorts of watercraft leads through the Hills on its way to the calm waters of this shallow lake. For those in need of a swim, it's well worth a visit.

THE NORTHWEST

It may be more livable now than it was a century ago, but northwestern South Dakota is still the state's least-inhabited region. Interrupted only occasionally by randomly placed buttes, the northwest's flatlands are filled with gumbo, a clay soil that becomes incredibly sticky when wet. During the Indian Wars in the 1870s, half of Gen. George Crook's cavalry horses died of exhaustion trying to cross the gumbo flats in a rainstorm on the way to Slim Buttes. Today, that mud can be found in the wheel-wells of every pickup truck that travels this unforgiving terrain.

The wooded draws of these rolling grasslands are filled with the fossils of dinosaurs who rumbled here 65 million years ago. Tepee rings, buffalo jumps, stone tools, spear points, stylized rock carvings, and other clues prove that people inhabited the **Cave Hills** and **Slim Buttes** of northwestern South Dakota as far back as 9,000 years ago. Indians, and later whites, stalked buffalo, wolves, and grizzly bears through the narrow ravines and across the boundless prairie of the northwest. The history of the region is as sparse as the landscape. The most famous story northwestern South Dakotans tell about this region is the tale of Hugh Glass, which, they assert, proves the hardiness of the first pioneers.

■ LEGEND OF HUGH GLASS

In 1823, the Rocky Mountain Fur Company acquired a license to trade on the upper Missouri under the leadership of Maj. Andrew Henry and Gen. William Ashley. That year, Hugh Glass, a brawny and bearded Pennsylvanian was asked to join Ashley's trading party on an expedition into the territory. Hugh was hunting alone one day that summer when he came upon the fork of the Grand River southwest of present-day Lemmon. As he neared the stream of water, a female grizzly and her cubs appeared in a thicket. From his startled horse, Hugh fired his rifle. The bear charged and the frontiersman was forced to fight at close quarters armed with a knife barely longer than the bear's claws. When his comrades found him the following day, Hugh was broken, badly mauled, bleeding from gashes all over his body, and near death. The bear lay dead nearby. After digging Hugh's grave and waiting two days, General Ashley's party moved eastward, leaving two members behind to tend to what seemed to be the imminent burial of the unlucky man.

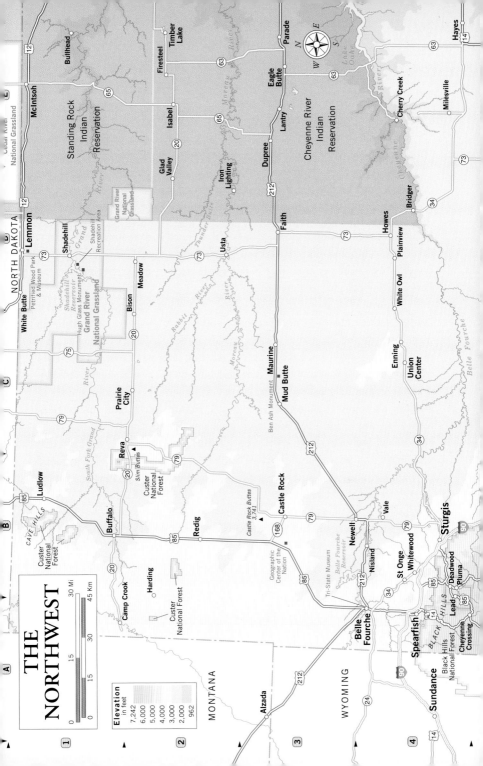

In spite of his broken bones, deep lacerations, and smashed face, Glass continued to cling to life for six more days as the two men watched his chest rise and fall with each labored breath. In between glances, they gazed at the nearby hillsides for sign of Arikara warriors. With no improvement in the big man's condition, the pair decided that Hugh was as good as dead. They gathered up his gun, ammunition, and knife, saddled their horses and left him there on the banks of the Grand.

No one knows how long he remained unconscious. It may have been hours or days. But finally he awoke, in great pain. He drank from the river and was horrified at the bloodied and mangled face that stared back at him. After he surveyed the camp and noticed the yawning, shallow grave and the long-dead campfire, he became enraged that he'd been deserted in the wilderness, with no horse, no food, no gun, and no tools.

In his poem, *The Song of Hugh Glass*, John G. Neihardt contends that it was the burning desire to face those who had abandoned him that led the injured mountain man to survive and become one of the legends of the Old West. (The heroic story of Hugh Glass also formed the basis for Frederick Manfred's novel *Lord Grizzly*.)

Dragging his broken leg behind him, Hugh began to crawl across the territory, drinking from mud puddles and creeks, and eating roots, berries, bugs, and about anything else within his grasp. To avoid hostile Indians, he slithered through tumbleweeds, grass, and sun-parched prairie at night. Weakened by his wounds and a lack of food and water, Hugh spotted the glow of a campfire and steered his course up a hillside to investigate. Instead of finding fellow frontiersmen, Hugh found only a campsite, abandoned except for a pack of wild dogs. Scavenging by the ashes, he found an old buck knife, which he used to kill one of the dogs.

After eating his fill and resting, Hugh spent the next several weeks crawling and hobbling more than 100 miles to the Missouri River, then fashioned a crude raft and drifted another 100 miles to Fort Kiowa near present-day Chamberlain. When he eventually caught up with the men who had left him behind, as well as the rest of the Ashley party, Hugh forgave each of them. Ten years later, as he crossed the ice of the Yellowstone River near the mouth of the Bighorn, a band of Arikara braves killed him.

■ BATTLE OF SLIM BUTTES

After Custer's disastrous defeat at Little Bighorn in June 1876, Sioux leaders Gall and Sitting Bull fled to Canada with 400 lodges (families or small tiyospayes), and

SONG OF HUGH GLASS

           . . . the lean dogs ran
And barked about him, for the love of man
Wistful, yet fearing. Surely he could find
Some trifle in the hurry left behind —
Or haply hidden in the trampled sand —

                 Long he sought
Without avail; and, crawling back, he thought
Of how the dogs were growing less afraid,
And how one might be skinned without a blade.
A flake of flint might do it: he would try.
And then he saw — or did the servile eye
Trick out a mental image like the real?
He saw a glimmering of whetted steel
Beside a heap now washed with morning light. . . .

'Twixt urging hunger and restraining fear
The gaunt dogs hovered round the man; while he
Cajoled them in the language of the Ree
And simulated feeding them with sand,
Until the boldest dared to sniff his hand,
Bare-fanged and with conciliative whine. . . .

                   —John G. Neihardt, 1915

the Sioux bands gradually returned to their agencies, burning grass as they went to reduce the rations for any cavalry mounts that might be in pursuit. Generals Crook, Terry, and Miles began to hunt Indians and by September 7, Crook's ragged and weary column dispatched Capt. Anson Mills with 150 men to travel to Deadwood for supplies.

The next day Mills and his men discovered a village of 37 lodges on the eastern slope of the Slim Buttes, near present-day Reva. On September 9, the soldiers attacked. Within one of the tepees, buttoned up against the rain, was the Oglala chief American Horse and his family. During the cavalry charge, American Horse and his wife and children fled to a nearby ravine with six other warriors. In the six-hour siege of the village and ravine, four of the warriors with American Horse and three of the soldiers died. American Horse, seriously wounded, surrendered with the survivors. Shortly before noon, the balance of Crook's army joined Captain Mills. It was none too soon. That afternoon, Crazy Horse and his 2,000-member band made a show of force and attacked the column of soldiers. With Crook's reinforcements, Crazy Horse could not gain the upper hand and the Battle of Slim Buttes ended in a draw. The next day, Crook's troops moved on toward Deadwood on a diet of horse meat, marking the end of a long and arduous summer campaign. Today, historical markers pinpoint the site of the battle east of Reva on State Highway 20.

Even though the Indians dealt a powerful blow to white encroachment with Custer's defeat and the stand-off at Slim Buttes in 1876, the U.S. government's long-term commitment of men and material to the Indian Wars and its precise and merciless strategy of cutting the enemy's food supply inevitably took their toll.

■ END OF THE HUNT

It is estimated that in the seventeenth century, 60 million bison, often called buffalo, darkened the grasslands of the Great Plains. The adult bull stands about 6.5 feet tall, and weighs more than 2,000 pounds. Apart from eating its flesh, the Plains Indians relied on the shaggy bison's hide for clothing and shelter, its bones for weapons, toys, and utensils, and its droppings for fuel. In addition to the Ashley fur party, numerous other groups of men traveled to the area to hunt on the open prairie,

A buffalo-skin tambourine drum used in Sioux dances. (South Dakota State Historical Society, Pierre)

(opposite) Movie set of an Indian encampment near Sturgis.

trap along the rivers, and trade with the remaining Indians. They discovered a vast expanse of plains where thousands of bison lived. With the arrival of non-Indian hide-hunters and settlement of the plains came the depletion of the species, and by the early 1880s the last great northern herd of bison perished near the Little Missouri River in extreme northwestern South Dakota. As the number of bison dwindled, the last free-roaming bands of Plains Indians were forced to acquiesce to the will of the whites and live on federal reservations.

With the threat of tribal retaliation gone, cattle ranges opened up, cowboys came, and thousands of Texas longhorns were herded to feed on the belly-high grass of South Dakota. Each year, cattlemen from the upper range along the Belle Fourche River would meet to plan two roundups of the giant herds—one in the spring to cut calves for branding, and one in the fall to ready animals for shipment to market. The unified South Dakota Stock Growers Association organized the last major roundup in 1904, just before homesteaders entered the open range.

Fast on the boot heels of cowboys came sheep herders and, later, farmers. Some of the farming communities became small towns, but few survived. Those that did watched their economy rise and fall with the market price for beef, mutton, wheat, and wool.

Although the twentieth century brought improvements in transportation and electrical service for residents of northwestern South Dakota, life in this land of barren buttes and mud flats is much as it was a century ago. Great distances separate ranch from ranch, town from town. Cars and pickup trucks make life somewhat more tolerable, but the region is still prone to severe winter weather and each family must be self-sustaining, able to wait out the plows for days after a blizzard.

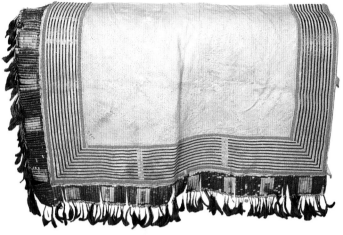

A quilled Sioux saddle blanket. (South Dakota State Historical Society, Pierre)

■ CUSTER NATIONAL FOREST *map page 235, A/B-1/2*

The timbered hills of northwestern South Dakota were rare enough even by the dawn of the twentieth century to motivate the federal government to preserve them. Twenty years before he became president, Theodore Roosevelt hunted bear in this region, and in 1904, he established forest reserves by presidential proclamation in the Cave Hills and Slim Buttes areas. President Roosevelt appointed his good friend and fellow Rough Rider, Capt. Seth Bullock, to serve as the forest's first supervisor. When farmers tilling marginal cropland went bankrupt during the 1930s, the federal government acquired additional land and added it to the forest preserve.

All told, the lands of the Custer National Forest lie within 20 counties in South Dakota, North Dakota, and Montana. South Dakota's contribution to the whole are four areas in the northwestern part of the state administered by the Sioux Ranger District. With ponderosa pine–covered hills and mesas rising above the surrounding plains, these areas are filled with deer, antelopes, coyotes, foxes, raccoons, minks, weasels, skunks, badgers, turkeys, opossums, muskrats, and a variety of falcons, hawks, and eagles. One of the largest merlin (a small falcon) populations in North America calls the district home.

Roundup of the longhorns in the northwestern part of the state photographed by John Grabill in 1887. The following winter, great blizzards wiped out most of the longhorn herds. (South Dakota State Historical Society, Pierre)

Although these hills are not as user-friendly as the Black Hills—there are no designated hiking trails, even though ample hiking and riding opportunities exist—most of the ridges are open and afford spectacular views of the surrounding lowlands.

■ BELLE FOURCHE   *map page 235, A-4*

Thirty miles southwest of the geographic center of the United States stands Belle Fourche, an aging former railroad town that serves as the center of the sheep and cattle industries for northwestern South Dakota, as well as parts of Wyoming and Montana. Though it's also the northern gateway to the Black Hills, its roots are in ranching, and Belle Fourche doesn't show the same flair for tourism as its southerly neighbors. A string of shops, taverns, and offices lines a narrow downtown business district that bustles while the sun's up but slows to a crawl at night. The **Tri-State Museum** (831 State Street; 605-892-3705) explores the history of the town with exhibits and period paraphernalia.

Owl Creek feeds the waters of **Belle Fourche Reservoir,** a few miles east of town on U.S. 212. A popular boating and fishing lake backed up by Orman Dam, the reservoir also is the site of one of the state's most impressive fireworks displays each July Fourth. The pyrotechnics follow the three-day **Black Hills Roundup** (605-892-2676), one of the nation's oldest and best rodeos. About 10 miles east of town, ranchers and paleontologists in 1981 extracted a Tyrannosaurus rex skeleton from Haystack Butte. Only the world's sixth T-rex skull or skeleton find, the dig ultimately yielded about 50 percent of the 65-million-year-old dinosaur's bones.

North of town, motorists head for Wyoming, Montana, or North Dakota. U.S. 212 veers northwest following the Belle Fourche River through a corner of Wyoming and past the Little Bighorn battle site in Montana before connecting with I-90 on its northerly run to Billings. Meanwhile, travelers on U.S. 85 leave the Black Hills and drop to the plains on a straight-line road that runs due north, then northeasterly for 21 miles before reaching the exact geographic center of the nation near Castle Rock Butte.

For generations, the accepted **Center of the Nation** was near Smith Center, Kansas. When Alaska joined the Union on January 3, 1959, mathematical calculations shifted it into Butte County, South Dakota. Seven months later, when Hawaii became the fiftieth state, the center point was again relocated a few miles southwest at the approximate intersection of 44° 58' North with 103° 46' West. The point is designated by a modest marker along the highway.

■ BUFFALO AND BISON *map page 235, B-1 and C/D-1/2*

The old controversy over the name of the shaggy beasts that once roamed the prairie is reflected in the northwest by two towns. "Bison" is the correct appellation, while "buffalo"—actually the term for African and Eurasian species similar to the American bison—is more popular. The town of **Buffalo**, at the junction of U.S. 85 and State Highway 20, has a short business district, a school, and 380 residents who cater to area ranchers and work in the natural gas and oil industry, which has wells operating throughout Harding County. Similar in size and sophistication, **Bison** is located 55 miles east of Buffalo on State Highway 20. Besides its bar, café, and store, Bison's main attraction is the **Anna Carr Homestead,** a sod house built in 1907 that also served as the town's post office.

West of Buffalo on State Highway 20, near the South Dakota–Montana border, is **Camp Crook.** An isolated town of 56 friendly residents, the place had a larger population when its namesake, General Crook, stopped with his troops in the 1870s. It hardly looks any more permanent today. But with no crime, and stark beauty in the surrounding landscape, its inhabitants seem content to hang out at the **Corner Cafe,** where the prime rib is excellent. With no theater, bowling alley, or other form of entertainment, video movie rentals do a brisk business. On special occasions, some residents drive more than an hour south to Belle Fourche or north to Bowman, North Dakota, to take in a movie or do some shopping.

■ TIPPERARY

Arguably the most famous bucking horse ever to grace a rodeo ring was born and raised in Perkins County. Tipperary, a bronc buster's worst nightmare, was foaled in 1905 on a horse ranch near Camp Crook, and as a colt was thought by his owner to have the makings of a good saddle horse. That was, at least, until a ranchhand tried to break him. Tipperary was a pacer, or as a cowboy from the Southwest would term it, a sidewinder. His legs moved in lateral pairs and his body would be alternately balanced on his right and then his left legs. That is unusual in a horse. Measuring 15 hands 3 inches tall and weighing in at half a ton, the blood bay gelding was not large—but he was tricky. Nearly 90 riders attempted to calm Tipperary between 1909 and 1926. Only two were successful in that 17-year career. In 1932, the fabled bronc was one of several horses stolen and trailed into Montana by thieves. With the law in hot pursuit, the horse thieves

(following pages) Rocky buttes dot the plains near the town of Buffalo.

abandoned the herd in a deserted barn. By the time he was discovered there, Tipperary was in poor condition. After being returned to his home range, the horse died in October 1932, at age 27, while standing in a snowstorm.

■ LEMMON   *map page 235, D-1*

As close to the North Dakota border as any town in the state, Lemmon provides a large area of the northwest with medical, shopping, and recreational opportunities. The town's namesake, G.E. "Ed" Lemmon, is credited by the National Livestock Association with handling the largest number of cattle in a lifetime—one million—and for cutting, roping, and bringing to the branding iron the largest number of cattle in one day—more than 900 head. A successful rancher, Lemmon also helped found one of the last towns established in South Dakota. In November 1907, the Chicago, Milwaukee & St. Paul Railroad reached the newly founded town of Lemmon. The rancher sold 163 acres to the railroad on the condition that he be allowed first choice on a homesite. A year later, after selling all his cattle, Lemmon moved to town and built a house, which today is still a private residence. Most of the other buildings constructed during the town's birth were formed of embossed concrete blocks, which provided a convenient and low-cost building material in an area that is virtually treeless.

In addition to one motel, one hotel, and five restaurants, Lemmon is the site of the world's largest park dedicated solely to petrified wood and fossils. The **Petrified Wood Park and Museum** (500 Main Avenue; 605-374-3964) contains more than 400 unusual structures made from specimens found within a 25-mile radius of Lemmon. Nearly all the items displayed form spires, castles, pyramids, or other whimsical shapes. From 1930 to 1932, the park was the pet project of O.S. Quammen, who hoped to learn more about petrified wood and at the same time create a public display of the fossils and provide work to men unemployed during the Depression.

The **Shadehill Recreation Area,** 12 miles south of Lemmon off State Highway 73, is the only area for water sports in northwestern South Dakota. Fishing, hiking, boating, camping, and golfing are popular activities at the site during the summer. Significant populations of deer, small game, and birds keep hunters busy in the fall. In winter, outdoor enthusiasts prefer speedier sports. When the snow flies, so do the snowmobilers.

(above) In South Dakota, hailstones can be as big as softballs. (following pages) A woman and two girls commemorate settler life at the Laura Ingalls Wilder Pageant in De Smet.

PRACTICAL INFORMATION

■ AREA CODE AND TIME ZONES

The area code for all of South Dakota is 605. South Dakota is in the Central Time Zone and the Mountain Time Zone. Sioux Falls, in the Central Time Zone, falls in the same zone as Minneapolis, Chicago, and Omaha with the dividing line generally running along the Missouri River. Rapid City and the Black Hills, which are in the Mountain Time Zone, fall in the same zone as Denver, Salt Lake City, and Phoenix.

■ TRANSPORTATION

For most visitors, South Dakota's appeal lies in its detachment from urban America. The population of its largest towns equals only that of suburbs of most metropolitan areas. Reaching South Dakota often requires more money and time than getting to more centrally located destinations, but the high cost of transportation is generally offset by a significantly lower cost of living. By most U.S. standards, touring South Dakota is a travel bargain.

■ BY CAR

The vast majority of visitors to the state arrive by car on interstate highways. The primary roadway, I-90, slices east-west through South Dakota from Minnesota to Wyoming. A second interstate, I-29, creeps up the state's eastern edge from Sioux City, Iowa, to North Dakota. State highways and secondary roads provide access to many of South Dakota's smaller communities and hidden treasures, and gravel roads and primitive logging tracks reach still deeper into the backcountry. No matter where you travel in the state, it's a good idea to check on weather and road conditions before leaving the pavement. Some parts of the state are known for a soil condition that allows even the slightest rain to turn clay into an impossibly sticky adhesive known as gumbo. The concoction can make vehicle travel and walking extremely difficult.

Highway rest stops and information centers appear infrequently along the interstates. The rest stops are always open, but the information centers close for the winter. The South Dakota Highway Department does a superb job of maintaining roads in drivable condition year-round, but residents often quip that the state has only two seasons: winter and construction. Ground blizzards and heavy snows close down the interstates several times each year, and storms can strike anytime between October and mid-May. Smart motorists travel prepared for the worst. Natives know that a candle in a tin can will heat the interior of a car. Although few people carry items for every eventuality, the ultimate winter survival kit would include snow tires or chains; extra socks and warm clothing; insulated boots; a blanket or sleeping bag; a first-aid kit; nonperishable foods; a flashlight with extra batteries; a shovel, sand, gravel, or traction mats; matches or a lighter; and a window scraper.

South Dakotans are notoriously fast drivers, primarily because of the great distances between points, and state highway patrol officers generally will tolerate minor excesses in speed. The interstates, with the exception of small sections of roadway near Sioux Falls and Rapid City, are posted at 75 mph; motorists on all other highways are officially limited to 65 mph. Patrolmen are somewhat tolerant of speeds exceeding those limits, but they have little patience with nighttime speeders, and none with drunk drivers.

When traveling the Black Hills, commanders of motor homes, buses, and trucks with trailers should examine maps of scenic highways for tunnel heights and restrictions. A fore-check can prevent wedging a perfectly good recreational vehicle between two slabs of granite.

■ BLACK HILLS TUNNELS

ROUTE	LOCATION	WIDTH	HEIGHT
U.S. 16A	6 mi (9.7 km) SE of Keystone	13'6" (4.1 m)	12'6" (3.8 m)
U.S. 16A	4 mi (6.4 km) SE of Keystone	13'6" (4.1 m)	12'6" (3.8 m)
U.S. 16A	3 mi (4.8 km) SE of Keystone	13'6" (4.1 m)	12'6" (3.8 m)
U.S. 16A	1 mi (1.6 km) N of Keystone	20'0" (6.1 m)	10'3" (3.1 m)
S.D. 87	6 mi (9.7 km) SE of Sylvan Lake	9'0" (2.7 m)	12'0" (3.6 m)
S.D. 87	2 mi (3.2 km) SE of Sylvan Lake	8'7" (2.6 m)	11'5" (3.5 m)

■ BY AIR

South Dakota enjoys fairly good air service primarily due to its proximity to regional airline hubs in Minneapolis and Denver. Several major airlines serve South Dakota, although flights are often limited to the extreme eastern and western parts of the state, with passengers boarding and departing at Sioux Falls and Rapid City. Commuter flights link the cities of Pierre, Huron, Aberdeen, Mitchell, Yankton, Watertown, and Brookings. Other travelers charter flights from the many private aviators and flying services in the state.

Denver International Airport (DIA) provides thousands of flights each day to and from most places in the country. The airport's runway is designed to handle inclement weather, which allows travelers to come and go even in the nastiest conditions. It is about a six-hour drive from DIA north to Rapid City, South Dakota. *8400 Peña Boulevard, Denver, CO; 303-342-2000; www.flydenver.com.*

Minneapolis–St. Paul International Airport (MSP) is another major gateway for travel to South Dakota. The airport is only 4 hours from Sioux Falls, South Dakota, along I-35 and I-90. *Lindbergh Terminal, 4300 Glumack Drive, St. Paul, MN; 612-726-5555. Humphrey Terminal, 7150 Humphrey Drive, Minneapolis, MN; 612-726-5800. www.mspairport.com.*

■ MOTORCOACH CARRIERS

Greyhound and Jefferson Lines. Serving eastern South Dakota. *301 North Dakota Avenue, Sioux Falls; 605-336-0885. www.greyhound.com, www.jeffersonlines.com.*

Powder River Lines/Coach USA and Jefferson Lines. Serving western South Dakota. *333 Sixth Street, Rapid City; 605-348-3300. www.coachusa.com, www.jeffersonlines.com.*

Balloons float serenely over the prairies of eastern South Dakota.

■ CLIMATE

South Dakota possesses one of the most extreme climates in the world. Positioned in the center of the North American continent and lacking any natural barriers to the Arctic Circle or the Gulf of Mexico, South Dakota sees virtually every type of weather except hurricanes. Over the past century, recorded temperatures have ranged from -58 degrees F (-50°C) to 120 degrees F (49°C). Yet in many respects the climate is pleasant. Low humidity, brilliant sunshine, and crystal clear skies are the rule rather than the exception.

CITY	FAHRENHEIT TEMPERATURE			ANNUAL PRECIPITATION	
	Jan. Avg. High/Low	July Avg. High/Low	Record High/Low	Average Rain	Average Snow
Sioux Falls	23 2	86 62	110 -42	26.43"	39"
Rapid City	32 9	87 59	110 -34	18.09"	46"
Pierre	28 8	88 64	115 -40	16.21"	28"
Aberdeen	20 -2	83 61	115 -46	23.96"	30"
Deadwood	30 8	79 52	101 -34	29.99"	70"

SOUTH DAKOTA'S SUNNY SEASONS

From a brochure for Sisseton, South Dakota, 1893:

Nothing is more misunderstood or misrepresented than the climate of South Dakota. This state is not a land of frosts and blizzards. On the contrary, it lacks little of being a land of almost perpetual sunshine. During eleven years' residence in South Dakota, but one blizzard has been seen which corresponds with the popular eastern conception of a blizzard. During almost any winter the East has storms which in all respects are worse than the much defamed blizzard of the Dakotas.

The atmosphere of this state is dry and invigorating, and one does not feel the cold as he does in a locality where the air is moist. . . . Spring is a particularly delightful season in this county, all of the seeding being done before the 20th of April. The summer months are pleasant and sunny, and while the mercury is not ashamed to spend a good deal of time "cavorting" around among the nineties, the heat is not of a close, suffocating nature. Breezes are always blowing, and cases of sunstroke or heat prostration are very unusual. The nights are cool, and one always awakens with a feeling of refreshment. The fall months bring the pleasantest weather of the whole year. The sun, dropping southward, sends his rays less directly, and the heat of summer subsides. Almost every day is bright and fair, and the air is laden with healthfulness. Cold weather sometimes occurs before the end of November, but for the most part winter weather is not looked for until the middle or latter part of December.

In New England much of the winter is rainy, cloudy and generally disagreeable, while frequently the heavy fall of snow makes traveling difficult. In South Dakota, at least every five days out of six are bright and cheery. There is seldom a heavy fall of snow, it rarely rains in winter, traveling is nearly always good, and the winter is generally unattended by the discomforts and disagreeable features which characterize that season in the East.

For health and long life, South Dakota beats the world. From the United States census report of 1880, the following death rate in proportion to the population is given for different localities:

Minnesota	1 in 86	All of the U.S.	1 in 66
Pennsylvania	1 in 67	Great Britain	1 in 46
Texas	1 in 64	Dakota	1 in 166

A tornado swirls across the landscape near Spearfish in August 1954. Fortunately, little damage was done to the town. (South Dakota State Historical Society, Pierre)

(following pages) A tremendous electrical storm crackles over the Badlands.

■ FOOD AND LODGING

Eating is one of the least expensive pastimes in South Dakota, and dress is usually casual. Except for private country clubs, you'd be hard-pressed to find a restaurant in the state where ties are required.

By and large, lodging costs change with the season, but they rarely exceed those of other U.S. tourism destinations. Except in peak periods—from June through August and during motorcycle rallies, rodeos, and county fairs—rooms at low to moderate rates are readily available. Summer travelers should call ahead. The best rooms, the most exquisite mountain cabins, and lakeside cottages fill up first.

For reservations call the **South Dakota Innkeepers Association** (2703 West Seventh Street, Sioux Falls; 605-331-4194. www.sdinnkeepers.com). **Black Hills Central Reservations** (68 Sherman Street, Deadwood; 800-529-0105) is a reservation service for western South Dakota, including package vacations.

■ CHAIN HOTELS AND MOTELS

Baymont Inns & Suites. *877-299-6668; www.baymontinns.com.*
Best Western. *800-528-1234; www.bestwestern.com.*
Comfort Inn. *800-228-5150; www.comfortinn.com.*
Courtyard. *800-321-2211; www.courtyard.com.*
Days Inn. *800-325-2525; www.daysinn.com.*
Doubletree. *800-222-8733; www.doubletree.com.*
Econo Lodge. *800-553-2666; www.choicehotels.com.*
Embassy Suites. *800-362-2779; www.embassysuites.com.*
Hampton Inn. *800-426-7866; www.hamptoninn.com.*
Hilton. *800-445-8667; www.hilton.com.*
Holiday Inn. *800-465-4329; www.6c.com.*
La Quinta. *800-531-5900; www.laquinta.com.*
Marriott. *800-228-9290; www.marriott.com.*
Motel 6. *800-466-8356; www.motel6.com.*
Quality. *800-228-5151; www.choicehotels.com.*
Radisson. *800-333-3333; www.radisson.com.*
Ramada. *800-272-6232; www.ramada.com.*
Sheraton. *800-325-3535; www.sheraton.com.*
Super 8 Motels. *800-800-8000; www.super8.com.*
Travelodge. *800-255-3050; www.travelodge.com.*
Westin. *800-228-3000; www.westin.com.*

■ MUSEUMS AND GALLERIES

■ ABERDEEN

Dacotah Prairie Museum. Local east South Dakota history. *21 South Main Street; 605-626-7117.*

■ BADLANDS

Ben Reifel Visitor Center Museum. *Cedar Pass, State Highway 240; 605-433-5361.*

White River Visitor Center Museum. *Off BIA Highway 27; 605-433-2878.*

■ BELLE FOURCHE

Tri-State Museum. Historical exhibits and paraphernalia. *831 State Street; 605-892-3705.*

■ BROOKINGS

South Dakota Art Museum. Extensive collections of Sioux artist Oscar Howe and prairie painter Harvey Dunn, as well as Sioux craftwork and embroidery from the island of Madeira. *South Dakota State University, Medary Avenue at Harvey Dunn Street; 605-688-5423.*

State Agricultural Heritage Museum. Exhibits depict technology, crops, and livestock. *South Dakota State University, Medary Avenue and 11th Street; 605-688-6226.*

■ CHAMBERLAIN

Akta Lakota Museum and the Lakota Visitors Center. A historic look at Sioux life on the Great Plains before the arrival of European settlers. *St. Joseph's Indian School, 1301 North Main Street; 605-734-3452.*

South Dakota Hall of Fame. Exhibits of South Dakota writers and artists. *100 West Lawler Street; 605-734-4216.*

■ CUSTER

Crazy Horse Memorial Studio and the Indian Museum of North America. One of the most extensive collections of Plains Indian artifacts in the country. *U.S. 385; 605-673-4681.*

Jewel Cave National Monument Visitors Center Museum. Large scale map of the cave; touch-screen interactive computer with information on cave minerals, spelunking. *U.S. 16 west of Custer; 605-673-2288.*

■ CUSTER STATE PARK

Peter Norbeck Visitor Center Museum. *U.S. 16A east of Custer; 605-255-4464.*

■ D E A D W O O D

Adams Museum and House. The museum is home to the Thoen Stone, while the historic house reveals the posh side of life on the frontier. *Museum: 54 Sherman Street; 605-578-1714. House: 22 Van Buren Street; 605-578-3751.*

■ F L A N D R E A U

Moody County Museum Complex. Antiques and collectibles from the pioneer past. *706 East Pipestone Avenue; 605-997-3191.*

■ G E T T Y S B U R G

Dakota Sunset Museum. Artifacts from Mandan and Arikara campsites. *205 West Commercial Avenue; 605-765-9480.*

■ H O T   S P R I N G S

Mammoth Site. Fossils of nearly 50 mammoths; educational programs. *U.S. 16 west of Custer; 605-673-2288.*

■ K E Y S T O N E

Mount Rushmore National Memorial Visitor Center and Museum. Video about the memorial's construction; other historic exhibits. *605-574-2523.*

■ L E A D

Black Hills Mining Museum. Displays on the history of the mining industry. *323 West Main Street; 605-584-1605.*

■ L E M M O N

Lemmon Petrified Wood Park. Over 400 unusual structures built from specimens found within 25 miles of Lemmon. *500 Main Avenue; 605-374-3964.*

■ M A D I S O N

Smith-Zimmerman Heritage Museum. Farm implements and household items from nineteenth-century settlements. *Dakota State College, 221 Northeast Eighth Street; 605-256-5308.*

■ M I T C H E L L

Enchanted World Doll Museum. 4,000 dolls displayed in an English-style castle. *615 North Main Street; 605-996-9896.*

Middle Border Museum–Oscar Howe Art Center. Native American exhibits, large collection of works by South Dakotan artists, including Harvey Dunn and Charles Hargens Jr. The Oscar Howe Gallery offers an in-depth look at the life and work of the Sioux artist. *1300 East University Avenue; 605-996-4111.*

Mitchell Prehistoric Indian Village. The site of a town dating back to 900 B.C. Recreated buildings, visitors center, and museum. *Shores of Lake Mitchell; 605-996-5473.*

■ M O B R I D G E

Klein Museum. Local pioneer and Sioux artifacts; restored schoolhouse. Changing art exhibits. *1820 West Grand Crossing; 605-845-7243.*

Scherr-Howe Arena. Murals by artist Oscar Howe. *City Auditorium, 212 Main Street; 605-845-3700.*

■ P I E R R E

Cultural Heritage Center. The South
Dakota State Historical Society's
museum here has exhibits regarding
pioneer and American Indian history.
900 Governor's Drive; 605-773-3458.

Discovery Center and Aquarium. Hands-
on science and technology exhibits. *805
West Sioux Avenue; 605-224-8295.*

■ P I N E   R I D G E

**Red Cloud Indian Mission School
Heritage Center.** Works by artists representing 30 tribes; exquisite star quilts.
*4 miles north of Pine Ridge on U.S. 18;
605-867-5491.*

*Some fine examples of Indian bead and quill work. The vest at the top is a museum piece
at the Cultural Heritage Center in Pierre.*

■ R A P I D   C I T Y

Dahl Fine Arts Center. Rotating exhibits of sculptures and paintings by area artists; 180-foot cyclorama of American history on permanent display. *713 Seventh Street; 605-394-4101.*

Journey Museum. Exhibits of Black Hills history and culture. *222 New York Street; 605-394-6923.*

Museum of Geology. "Talking" dioramas of Badlands geologic and dinosaur history. Fossil, gems, agates, and other minerals. *South Dakota School of Mines & Technology, 501 East St. Joseph Street; 605-394-2467.*

South Dakota Air and Space Museum. Static aircraft and scaled-back versions of bombers and fighters. *Ellsworth Air Force Base, Exit 66 off I-90, 2.5 miles north of Rapid City; 605-385-5188.*

Stavkirke Chapel. Replica of 850-year-old Borgund church in Norway. Open seasonally. *Chapel Lane off State Highway 44 W; 605-342-8281.*

■ S T .   F R A N C I S

Buechel Memorial Lakota Museum. Variety of Teton Sioux artifacts including photographs of Spotted Tail. Herbarium. *350 South Oak Street; 605-747-2745.*

■ S I O U X   F A L L S

Center for Western Studies. Norwegian rosemaled furniture, prairie art, and Sioux Indian artifacts, plus the workshop of the wood sculptor Jim Savage and some of his works. *Mikkelsen Library at Augustana College, 2111 South Summit Avenue; 605-367-4007.*

EROS Data Center (Earth Resources Observation Systems). Data center of Department of Interior. Visitors center contains audiovisual exhibits, including photographs of Earth taken from satellites and aircraft. *10 miles north of Exit 402 on I-90; 800-252-4547.*

Great Plains Zoo and Delbridge Museum of Natural History. Reptiles, birds, and mammals from all over the world. Museum houses hands-on exhibits and dioramas of different climactic zones. *805 South Kiwanis Avenue in Sherman Park; 605-367-7059.*

Old Courthouse Museum. An 1890 quartzite courthouse with three floors of regional history exhibits. *200 West Sixth Street; 605-367-4210.*

Rehfeld's Dakota Galleries. Upper Midwestern, largely South Dakotan original art; prints and sculptures. *210 South Phillips Street; 605-336-9737.*

USS *South Dakota* Memorial Museum. World War II mementos; memorial honoring the highly decorated ship and the 42 men who died serving on board. Open in summer. *Kiwanis Avenue and 12th Street; 605-367-7060.*

Washington Pavilion of Arts and Science. The Pavilion's Visual Arts Center has six art galleries featuring changing exhibits, and the Kirby Science Discovery Center houses more than 80 hands-on science exhibits. *301 South Main Avenue; 605-367-7397 or 877-927-4728.*

■ SISSETON

Fort Sisseton State Park. There are 17 original and reconstructed buildings at this Civil War–era fort. *20 miles west of Sisseton on State Highway 10 then south on State Highway 25; 605-448-5701.*

Joseph N. Nicollet Tower and Interpretive Center. The 75-foot tower here provides views of the great valley carved by a glacier 40,000 years ago. The tower gets its name from the famous French mapmaker. *State Highway 10 and Golf Course Road; 605-698-7672.*

Stavig House Museum. The 1916 three-story Victorian houses a museum highlighting the history of the settlement and the development of Sisseton. *112 First Avenue West; 605-698-4561.*

■ SPEARFISH

D.C. Booth Historic Fish Hatchery and National Fish Culture Hall of Fame. One of the first in the West. *423 Hatchery Circle; 605-642-7730.*

High Plains Heritage Center. Western art, sculpture, cultural festivals. *825 Heritage Drive; 605-642-9378.*

■ STURGIS AREA

Bear Butte State Park Visitors Center. Displays of American Indian history and culture. *Six miles northeast of Sturgis off State Highway 79; 605-347-5240.*

Fort Meade Museum. Old cavalry quarters, historic documents, including photographs of the all-black 25th Cavalry, and the all-Sioux Troop L, Third Cavalry. *Two miles east of Sturgis on State Highway 34; 605-347-9822.*

■ VERMILLION

Austin-Whittemore House. Filled with Victorian displays and settings. *15 Austin Street; 605-624-8266.*

National Music Museum. Over 10,000 musical instruments from all over the world. *University of South Dakota, 414 East Clark Street; 605-677-5306.*

W.H. Over State Museum. Life-size diorama of Teton village; state history exhibits. *University of South Dakota, 1110 Ratingen Street; 605-677-5228.*

■ WATERTOWN

Codington County Heritage Museum. Pioneer and American Indian history. *27 First Avenue Southeast; 605-886-7335.*

Mellette House Museum. Family heirlooms, portraits. Open in summer. *421 Fifth Avenue Northwest; 605-886-4730.*

Redlin Art Center. The center houses original works by artist Terry Redlin, a widely collected painter of wildlife and Americana, as well as a planetarium. *1200 33rd Street Southeast; 605-882-3877 or 877-873-3546.*

■ YANKTON AREA

Dakota Territorial Museum. Sioux artifacts, steamboat displays. *Westside Park, 610 Summit Street; 605-665-3898.*

■ FESTIVALS, EVENTS, AND RODEOS

■ M A R C H

Deadwood: St. Patrick's Day Celebration.
A chance to play in the past in historic
Deadwood, with green beer, corned
beef, and cabbage. *605-578-1876.*

Sioux Falls: St. Patrick's Day Parade. A
good Irish frolic through the central
business district. *605-336-1620.*

■ A P R I L

Brookings: Jackrabbit Stampede Rodeo.
Brahma bulls and saddle broncs.
605-692-6125.

Freeman: Schmeckfest. A celebration of
German heritage, with colorful costumes, crafts demonstrations, and serving tables piled with bratwurst, cheese
buttons, and kuchen. *605-925-7033.*

■ M A Y

Clark: "Little Fellow's" Memorial Service.
A celebration of the friendship between
"Big Bill" Chambers and the "Little Fel-
low" he waved to from the train (see
"Little Fellow of Clark," p. 114).
605-532-5772.

**Crazy Horse Memorial: Crazy Horse
Memorial Open House.** A free weekend
for visitors from South Dakota, North
Dakota, Montana, Wyoming, and Nebraska to come watch the carving in
progress. *605-673-4681.*

■ J U N E

Clear Lake: Crystal Springs Ranch Rodeo.
Saddle broncs, barrel racing, and beer.
888-277-6336.

**Crazy Horse Memorial: Gift from the
Mother Earth Celebration.** Native
American and non-native arts and crafts.
605-673-4681.

Deadwood: Wild Bill Hickok Days. Get
into the spirit of the West with fast-draw
and gun-slinging competitions, a historic parade, and free concerts on Main
Street. *605-578-1876.*

Dell Rapids: Cootie Days. A wild small-
town celebration. *605-428-4167.*

De Smet: Laura Ingalls Wilder Pageant.
The premiere pioneer celebration in
South Dakota, complete with butter
churns, bonnets, square dances, and an
outdoor pageant depicting stories from
the *Little House on the Prairie* series.
605-692-2108.

**Fort Sisseton State Park: Fort Sisseton
Historical Festival.** Blue coats and bayo-
nets gather for military exercises, muzzle-
loading contests, and formal balls.
605-448-5701.

**Lower Brule: Native American Day Cele-
bration.** Recalling the way of life of the
Plains Indian. *605-473-5561.*

Mitchell: Summer Solstice. Arts and crafts
fair in Hitchcock Park. *605-996-5567.*

Rapid City: Black Hills Bluegrass Festival.
Hosted by the Dahl Fine Arts Center. A
western hoe-down worth attending.
605-394-4101.

Rapid City: West Boulevard Arts Festival.
One of the state's finest among many.
605-348-9439.

Wheat fields, azure skies, and brown buttes are the essence of the South Dakota landscape.

Tabor: Czech Days. Tiny Tabor remembers its rich Czech heritage with polka music and plenty of *zelí* (sauerkraut), *koláce* (tarts), and *knedlíky* (potato dumplings). *605-463-2476.*

Webster: Sodbuster Fest. A celebration of pioneer heritage. *605-345-4751.*

Yankton: Riverboat Days Professional Rodeo Cowboys Association (PRCA) **Rodeo.** *605-665-3636.*

■ J U L Y

Belle Fourche: Black Hills Roundup. One of the longest running rodeos in the nation. *605-892-2676.*

Brookings: Summer Arts Festival. Regional art, historic, antique, and Old West booths. *605-692-6125.*

Custer: Gold Discovery Days. The oldest town in the Black Hills recalls its past. *800-992-9818.*

Fort Pierre: Fourth of July Rodeo. Parade and afternoon and evening PRCA Rodeo. *605-224-7361.*

Gettysburg: Civil War Re-enactment & Rendezvous. Recalling the trials of those who settled the region. *605-765-2731.*

Lead: Gold Camp Jubilee. Another reason to celebrate in the northern Black Hills. *605-584-1100.*

Mitchell: Corn Palace Stampede Rodeo. *605-996-5567.*

Mobridge: Sitting Bull Stampede Rodeo. PRCA action, entertainment, and enough refreshments to settle the dust in your throat. *605-845-2387.*

Rapid City: Black Hills Heritage Festival. Fine art, crafts, country bands, and a colorful powwow. *605-341-5940.*

Spearfish: National Impala Convention. The largest gathering of Chevy Impalas and their owners. *605-642-5868.*

Winner: Elks Rodeo. Not the largest rodeo, but townspeople make it one of the best. *605-842-2141.*

■ A U G U S T

Aberdeen: Brown County Fair and Dacotah Stampede Rodeo; *605-225-2414.*

Deadwood: Days of '76. Wild West rodeo performances, parades, and genuine blackjack, poker, slots. *605-578-1876.*

Deadwood: Kool Deadwood Nites. The 1950s and 1960s redux, with more than 500 classic cars on hand, parades, barbecues, and free concerts. *605-578-1876.*

Garretson: Jesse James Days. Fun times and a play recounting the day outlaws Frank and Jesse James outran a posse. *605-594-6721.*

Huron: South Dakota State Fair. Week-long rodeo and nightly entertainment. *605-352-8775 or 800-529-0900.*

Madison: Prairie Village Steam Threshing Jamboree. Weaving looms, belching steam engines, and old-time handmade everything. *800-693-3644.*

Mitchell: Corn Palace Festival. Musical talent such as Willie Nelson and international dance performances. *605-995-8430.*

Mobridge: Lewis & Clark Rediscovery Festival. Triathalon, games, and a barbecue. *605-845-2387.*

Pine Ridge: Oglala Nation Rodeo. *605-867-5491.*

Rapid City: Central States Fair. Top-name entertainers, rodeo and stock car action, plus one of the best U.S. fairs. *605-355-3861.*

Sioux Falls: Sioux Empire Fair. A large fair with a distinctly agrarian slant. *605-336-1620.*

Sturgis: Black Hills Threshing Bee. Old-time machinery and friendly folk who'll tell you how it used to be done. *605-347-2556.*

Sturgis: Sturgis Rally and Races. The largest motorcycle rally in the world. Rock bands, hill climbs, and drag races. *605-720-0800.*

Yankton: Yankton Riverboat Days. Celebrating the era when everything came by water. *605-665-3636.*

■ **S E P T E M B E R**

Crazy Horse Memorial: Crazy Horse Memorial Night Blast. An opportunity to witness history in the making and an impressive dynamite explosion. *605-673-4681.*

Custer State Park: Buffalo Roundup. The roar of 6,000 hooves pounding the prairie in one of the largest buffalo roundups in the world. *605-255-4515.*

Deadwood: Deadwood Jam. Classic entertainment from high-caliber bands. *605-578-1876.*

Eureka: German Schmeckfest. Hearty fare and beer steins. *605-284-2130.*

Mitchell: Corn Palace Polka Festival. Polka bands and dancing. Run by the Corn Palace. *605-995-8430.*

Pierre: Bad River Gathering. Local pageant produced by Native Americans to commemorate their meeting with Lewis and Clark. *605-224-7361.*

Pierre: Lewis & Clark Goosefest. Three days of arts and crafts, local and statewide entertainment, kid's activities, and an array of food. *605-224-7361.*

Sioux Falls: Northern Plains Tribal Arts Festival. Annual show displays works by more than 100 artists from the 33 Northern Plains tribes. Two-day affair is enlivened by Indian dance, music, and storytelling. *605-334-4060.*

Sturgis: Black Hills Highland Festival and Scottish Games. Original Scottish games, Irish dancers, and Parade of Tartans, held simultaneously with the National Sheep Dog Trials. *605-347-2556.*

Yankton: Great Plains Fiddlers Contest. Pickers and grinners rosin up the bow. *605-665-3636.*

■ **O C T O B E R**

Sioux Falls: South Dakota Rodeo Association (SDRA) Championship Finals Rodeo. *605-336-1620.*

■ **N O V E M B E R**

Custer State Park: Buffalo Auction. Buy a buffalo for less. *605-255-4515.*

■ **D E C E M B E R**

Oakwood Lakes State Park: Frozen Foot Rendezvous. Hardy souls re-create a winter encampment. "Mountain men" don leather and furs, and dwell in tents and tepees. *605-627-5441.*

■ POWWOWS

Be sure to call ahead to find out dates and locations. Keep in mind that starting and ending hours for special dances are rarely precise, since performance times depend upon dancers' and musicians' readiness, not the hour on the clock.

■ BLACK HILLS
Black Hills Powwow and Indian Art Market. *Rapid City; 605-341-0925.*

■ CENTRAL
Cheyenne River Labor Day Fair and Rodeo. *Early Butte; 605-964-4155.*

Crow Creek Sioux Tribe Annual Powwow. *Fort Thompson; 605-747-2381.*

Gathering of the Wakanyeja. *St. Joseph's School, Chamberlain; 605-743-3485.*

Lower Brule Powwow & Rodeo. *Lower Brule; 605-473-5561.*

■ NORTHEAST
Flandreau Santee Sioux Powwow. *Flandreau; 605-997-3891.*

Mother's Day Powwow. *Aberdeen; 605-226-7527.*

Sisseton-Wahpeton Agency Village. *Several throughout the year; 605-698-3911.*

■ NORTHWEST
Takini School Wacipi. *Howes; 605-538-4399.*

■ SOUTH-CENTRAL
Annual Rosebud Fair & All-Indian Powwow. *Rosebud; 605-747-2381.*

Fort Randall Powwow. *Lake Andes; 605-384-3641.*

Oglala Lakota College Wacipi. *Kyle; 605-455-6000.*

Oglala Nation Powwow. *Pine Ridge; 605-867-5821.*

■ SOUTHEAST
Northern Plains Tribal Arts Show and Powwow. *Sioux Falls; 605-334-4060.*

■ VOLKSMARCHES

On certain Saturdays and Sundays in the warm summer months, some South Dakotans band together in large groups and embark on day-long hikes known as "volksmarches." Following are some of the more popular ones:

■ BLACK HILLS
Bear Butte Seasonal Volksmarch. *605-347-5240.*

Crazy Horse Memorial Volksmarch. *605-673-4681.*

Custer State Park Seasonal Volksmarch. *605-255-4515.*

Spearfish Volksmarch. *605-642-7310.*

■ NORTHEAST
Lake Herman Seasonal Volksmarch. *605-256-5003.*

Sica Hollow Volksmarch. *605-448-5701.*

■ AERIAL TOURS

■ BADLANDS

Badger Helicopters, Inc. Badlands from the air, from mid-May to mid-September. *East entrance, Badlands National Park, I-90, Exit 130; 605-433-5322.*

■ BLACK HILLS

Black Hills Balloons. Hot-air flights over the Black Hills, plus Badlands, Devils Tower, and Mount Rushmore. From May through September. *Custer; 605-673-2520 or 800-568-2350.*

Rushmore Helicopters, Inc. Three tours from mid-May to mid-September. *Keystone; 605-666-4461.*

■ MOTORCOACH TOURS

A number of motorcoach tour companies take visitors on historic tours through specific regions of the state. Following is a list of companies that operate in South Dakota:

Affordable Adventures. *Rapid City; 605-342-7691.*

Alkali Ike Tours. *Deadwood; 605-578-3147.*

America Tours West. *Keystone; 605-666-4545.*

Boot Hill Tours. *Deadwood; 605-578-3758.*

Dakota Bus Service, Inc. *Spearfish; 605-642-2353.*

Golden Circle Tours. *Custer; 605-673-4349.*

Gray Line of the Black Hills. *Rapid City; 605-342-4461 or 800-456-4461.*

Jack Rabbit Tours. *Sioux Falls; 605-336-3339 or 800-678-6543.*

Old West Tours. *Gillette, WY; 800-868-7777.*

Shebby Lee Tours, Inc. *Rapid City; 605-343-4852.*

Stagecoach West Bus Service. *Rapid City; 605-343-3113.*

■ BLACK HILLS CAVES

Some of the largest caves in the world are found in the limestone formations beneath the Black Hills. Walking tours take visitors on less-strenuous routes, while spelunking tours put cavers on their bellies, pinching through the darkness. Although the preeminent caves—Wind and Jewel—have already been discussed in this book, there are also private cave attractions, listed below.

Beautiful Rushmore Cave. The hour long guided tour of this limestone cavern passes by a large number of cave formations. *Six miles east of Keystone on State Highway 40; 605-255-4467.*

Black Hills Caverns. A variety of tour options. Museum features specimens of cave and geological formations. *Four miles west of Rapid City on State Highway 44; 605-343-0542 or 800-837-9358.*

Jewel Cave National Monument. *13 miles west of Custer on U.S. 16; 605-673-2288.*

Sitting Bull Crystal Caverns. Guided tours offered. *State Highway 16, Rapid City; 605-342-2777.*

Stagebarn Crystal Cave. Guided tours available. *10 miles north of Rapid City on I-90, Exit 48, Piedmont; 605-787-4505.*

Wind Cave National Park. *Hot Springs; 605-745-4600.*

Wonderland Cave. Two-level living cavern 300 million years old. *Nemo; 605-578-1728.*

■ ARCHAEOLOGY AND PALEONTOLOGY

■ BADLANDS

Badlands National Park. Fossils from 23 to 35 million years old erode out of buttes and gullies while pronghorns, bison, and bighorn sheep drift across old homesteads and hunting grounds of the Sioux Indians. The park has marked trails and is open to hiking. Park rangers conduct interpretive programs and give special presentations in the summer. *Nine miles south of I-90 on State Highway 240, Interior; 605-433-5361.*

■ BLACK HILLS

Mammoth Site. Huge Columbian and woolly mammoths came here to drink, but they got trapped in this prehistoric sinkhole and perished. This is where the big boys are buried. The fossils of more than 50 mammoths have been discovered so far, and digging continues. *One block north of U.S. 18 Bypass, Hot Springs; 605-745-6017.*

■ SOUTHEAST

Mitchell Prehistoric Indian Village. Guided tours, artifacts, walk-through lodge reproduction, audio-visual show, walking tour stations, complete buffalo skeleton, gift shop. *Indian Village Road, on the shores of Lake Mitchell, Mitchell; 605-996-5473.*

■ MOUNTAIN BIKING

With more than 6,000 miles of fire trails, logging roads, and abandoned railroad grades, the Black Hills region is the top spot for pleasure biking in South Dakota. Trails crisscross the backcountry and provide exciting opportunities for mountain biking. In addition, many cities and parks throughout the state have bike trails and paths, especially Sioux Falls and Rapid City.

Spearfish Canyon Lodge. Mountain bike rentals and trail maps are available for unguided tours during spring, summer, and fall in beautiful Spearfish Canyon, a National Scenic Byway. *U.S. 14A, Spearfish; 605-584-3435.*

Trailside Bikes. Visit the backcountry of the Black Hills on a mountain bike tour or on a self-guided trip with up-to-date maps and trail descriptions of more than 5,000 square miles of national forest. *Custer; 888-673-2453.*

■ TRAIL RIDES

Blue Bell Lodge and Resort. *State Highway 87 South, Custer State Park; 605-255-4531.*

Canyon Ranch. *11050 Canyon Ranch Road, Veblen; 605-738-2480.*

Crazy Horse Heritage Village. *Three miles north of Custer; 605-673-2999.*

Dakota Badland Outfitters. *Custer; 605-673-5363.*

Gunsel Horse Adventures. *Rapid City; 605-343-7608.*

Palmer Gulch Stables. *Five miles west of Mount Rushmore on State Highway 244; 605-574-2525 or 800-233-4331.*

■ WATER SPORTS OUTFITTERS

Far West River Boat. *Riverside Park, Yankton; 605-665-9760.*

Oahe Windsurfing. *1909 Kennedy Drive, off U.S. 12 west of Mobridge; 605-845-7921.*

Pactola Pines Marina. *23060 Custer Gulch Road, Rapid City; 605-343-4283.*

Seagull's Sailboards. *Brookings; 605-693-4441.*

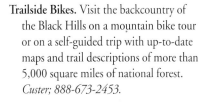 ROCK CLIMBING

Granite Sports. *Hill City; 605-574-2121.*

Sylvan Rocks Climbing School and Guide Service. *Hill City; 605-574-2425.*

■ WINTER RECREATION

■ B L A C K   H I L L S

Deer Mountain Ski Area. *Three miles south of Lead on U.S. 85, Deadwood; 605-584-3230 or 888-410-3337.*

Latchstring Winter Sports Center. *U.S. 14A, Spearfish; 877-975-6343.*

Mount Meadow Resort. *Deerfield Lake, 14 miles northwest of Hill City; 605-574-2636.*

Terry Peak Ski Area. *Off U.S. 85, Lead; 605-584-2165 or 800-456-0524.*

Trailshead Lodge. Snowmobile rentals. *21 miles southwest of Lead on U.S. 85 South; 605-584-3464.*

■ N O R T H E A S T

Interlakes Sports Center. *702 Southwest 10th Street, Madison; 605-256-3556.*

Pleasant Valley Lodge & Ski Area. *12 miles east of Clear Lake on State Highway 22, Gary; 605-272-5614.*

■ S O U T H E A S T

Great Bear Ski Area. *Three miles east of Sioux Falls on I-29 at Rice Street, Sioux Falls; 605-367-4309.*

The ring-necked pheasant is a trophy sought after by hunters throughout the state.

■ NATIONAL FORESTS, PARKS, GRASSLANDS, MONUMENTS, AND MEMORIALS

Badlands National Park. *605-433-5361.*

Black Hills National Forest. *25041 North Highway 16, Custer; 605-673-9200.*

Buffalo Gap National Grassland. *708 Main Street, Wall; 605-279-2125.*

Custer National Forest. *1310 Main Street, Billings, MT; 406-657-6200.*

Fort Pierre National Grassland. *124 South Euclid Avenue, Pierre; 605-224-5517.*

Grand River National Grassland. *Lemmon; 605-347-3592.*

Jewel Cave National Monument. *13 miles west of Custer on U.S. 16; 605-673-2288.*

Mount Rushmore National Memorial. *Keystone; 605-574-2523.*

Wind Cave National Park. *Hot Springs; 605-745-4600.*

■ IMPORTANT ADDRESSES

■ STATE AGENCIES

Department of Game, Fish and Parks. *523 East Capitol Avenue, Pierre; Hunting & Fishing: 605-773-3485. Parks: 605-773-3391.*

Department of Tourism. *711 East Wells Avenue, Pierre; 800-732-5682.*

Department of Transportation. *700 East Broadway Avenue, Pierre; 605-773-3265 (511 or 866-697-3511 for road and weather conditions).*

South Dakota Arts Council. *800 Governors Drive, Pierre; 605-773-3131.*

South Dakota State Historical Society. *900 Governors Drive, Pierre; 605-773-3458.*

Tribal Government Relations. *118 West Capitol Avenue, Pierre; 605-773-3415.*

■ REGIONAL TOURISM

Black Hills, Badlands & Lakes Association. *1851 Discovery Circle, Rapid City; 605-355-3600.*

Glacial Lakes & Prairies Tourism Association. *U.S. 212 West and 33rd Street Southwest, Watertown; 800-244-8860.*

Great Lakes of South Dakota Association. *210 East Capitol Avenue, Pierre; 888-386-4617.*

Southeast South Dakota Tourism Association. *800 Mariners Lane, Suite 104, Yankton; 888-353-7382.*

RECOMMENDED READING

■ HISTORY

Black Hills, White Justice (1991), Edward Lazarus. A history of the Sioux Nation from 1775 to the present, focusing on its interactions and conflicts with the United States.

The Carving of Mount Rushmore (1985), Rex Alan Smith. Definitive history of the carving of the world's largest work of art.

Crazy Horse: The Strange Man of the Oglalas (1961), Mari Sandoz. A vivid portrayal of one of the legendary Sioux leaders.

Exploring with Custer: The 1874 Black Hills Expedition (2002), Ernest Grafe and Paul Horsted. A guide to the Custer expedition, with exceptional photographs from the 1874 trek side-by-side with photographs of the same locations today.

Great Plains (1989), Ian Frazier. A journey through the Great Plains with accounts of the famous (and infamous) folks who've visited there.

Great White Fathers (2002), John Taliaferro. An account of Gutzon Borglum's obsessive quest to create Mount Rushmore that examines the memorial in the context of America's growth and status as a world power.

An Illustrated History of South Dakota (1991), Arthur R. Huseboe. Nearly 400 pages, highly illustrated, with coverage of Hamlin Garland, Oscar Howe, Laura Ingalls Wilder, Gutzon Borglum, and Lawrence Welk.

Lakota Woman (1990), Mary Crow Dog with Richard Erdoes. An irreverent, lively account of the American Indian Movement in the 1970s as told by a feisty Sioux resident of the Rosebud Reservation.

Moon of Popping Trees (1975), Rex Alan Smith. The plight of the Sioux tribes leading up to the tragedy at Wounded Knee and the hardships that followed.

The Native Americans: An Illustrated History (1993), Betty and Ian Ballantine, editors. A large-format, highly illustrated history of America's indigenous peoples. Beautiful archival photographs and paintings.

South Dakota Historical Markers (1974), Jane N. Hunt. Everything you wanted to know about roadside stops but were afraid to ask.

■ LITERATURE

American Indian Myths and Legends (1984), Richard Erdoes and Alfonso Ortiz, editors. A master storyteller and an eminent anthropologist's collection of 160 American Indian myths from 80 tribal groups.

Black Elk Speaks (1932), John G. Neihardt. The powerful recollections of a Lakota holy man.

Bury My Heart at Wounded Knee (1970), Dee Brown. The story of the last massacre of Native Americans.

Confessions of an S.O.B. (1989), Allen H. Neuharth. After picking up cowpies on the Dakota plains, this multimillionaire headed one of the largest media chains in the world.

Deadwood (1986), Pete Dexter. A look at the colorful characters and wild and woolly past of a Black Hills gold mining town.

Giants in the Earth (1929), Ole Edvart Rölvaag. A nineteenth-century immigrant family strives to eke out a living on the prairie.

Land of the Burnt Thigh (1986), Edith Eudora Kohl. Two sisters battle the elements to "prove up" their South Dakota homestead.

Little House on the Prairie series, including *On the Shores of Silver Lake* (1939), *The Long Winter* (1940), and *Little Town on the Prairie* (1941), Laura Ingalls Wilder. A young girl recounts growing up on the prairie.

A Son of the Middle Border (1979), Hamlin Garland. Frontier and pioneer life from a Pulitzer Prize winner.

The Song of Hugh Glass (1915), John G. Neihardt. An incredible tale of courage and tragedy told in poetry.

Sun and Saddle Leather (1915), Badger Clark. South Dakota's poet laureate writes of pines and prairies and the settler's way of life.

Wokini (1994), Billy Mills. A self-help guide written within the context of traditional Plains Indian mythology. The Sioux author is an Olympic gold medalist.

 GUIDES

Birds of the Black Hills (1965), Olin Sewall Pettingill and Nathaniel R. Whitney. A guide to the winged species of western South Dakota.

Jewelry made from Black Hills gold.

I N D E X

COMPASS AMERICAN GUIDES

Alaska	Kentucky	Pennsylvania
American Southwest	Las Vegas	Santa Fe
Arizona	Maine	South Carolina
Boston	Manhattan	South Dakota
California Wine Country	Massachusetts	Tennessee
Cape Cod	Michigan	Texas
Chicago	Minnesota	Utah
Coastal California	Montana	Vermont
Colorado	New Hampshire	Virginia
Connecticut & Rhode Island	New Mexico	Washington
Florida	New Orleans	Washington Wine Country
Georgia	North Carolina	Wisconsin
Gulf South	Oregon	Wyoming
Hawaii	Oregon Wine Country	
Idaho	Pacific Northwest	

Compass American Guides are available at special discounts for bulk purchases for sales promotions or premiums. Special editions, including personalized covers, excerpts of existing guides, and corporate imprints, can be created in large quantities for special needs. For more information, contact your local bookseller or write to Special Markets, Fodor's Travel Publications, 1745 Broadway, New York, NY 10019. Inquiries from Canada should be directed to your local Canadian bookseller or sent to Random House of Canada, Ltd., Marketing Department, 2775 Matheson Boulevard East, Mississauga, Ontario L4W 4P7. Inquiries from the United Kingdom should be sent to Fodor's Travel Publications, 20 Vauxhall Bridge Road, London, England SW1V 2SA.

ACKNOWLEDGMENTS

The photographs in this book are by Paul Horsted unless otherwise noted below. Compass American Guides gratefully acknowledges the following institutions and individuals for the use of their photographs or illustrations on the following pages: **Adams Museum, Deadwood,** pp. 53, 211; **Buffalo Bill Historical Center, Cody, Wyoming,** pp. 156 (Gift of Paul Mellon; 27.86), 206 (Gift of the Coe Foundation; 1.69.172); **Center for Western Studies at Augustana College, Sioux Falls,** pp. 21, 29, 41, 45, 48, 51, 54, 178, 179, 187, 205, 216; **Denver Public Library, Western History Department** (call number X-22154), p. 88; **Georgia State University Foundation, Pullen Library,** p. 115; **Robert Holmes,** pp. 18–19, 170–171, 193, 194–195, 220–221, 222, 227, 229; **Paul Jones,** pp. 145, 184, 190; **Greg Latza/Peoplescapes,** pp. 93, 140, 141, 199; **Library of Congress,** pp. 24–25, 49, 55, 208; **Marquette University Archives, Milwaukee,** pp. 162, 164, 183; **National Archives,** p. 144; **National Park Service,** p. 218; **Smithsonian American Art Museum/Art Resources,** pp. 23, 34, 35, 38–39; **South Dakota Art Museum, Brookings,** p. 105; **South Dakota State Historical Society-State Archives** pp. 26, 31, 36, 42, 43, 46, 47, 57, 63, 67, 74, 76, 81, 83, 94, 111, 123, 124, 139, 146, 147, 154, 163, 238, 240, 241, 255, 261 (top); **Tatanka: Story of the Bison,** p. 210; **Underwood Photo Archives,** p. 59.

We also wish to thank the following individuals for their contributions to this book: Ruth Johnston for her buffalo recipe; Rex Alan Smith for his expert reading; Claudia Nicholson and Marvene Riis of the South Dakota State Historical Society in Pierre; Harry Thompson from the Center for Western Studies; Candace Compton-Pappas for illustrations; John Morrone for copyediting the manuscript; and Ellen Klages for proofreading it.

Thanks also to the South Dakota Department of Tourism for permission to use images by Paul Horsted from their collection and to the South Dakota State Historical Society-State Archives, custodian of the Robert Lusk Papers, 1935–1945, accession number H75-131, for permission to quote from the Frank Lloyd Wright letter on page 169.

The extract from *Giants in the Earth,* by Ole Edvart Rölvaag (on p. 71), is reprinted by permission of HarperCollins Publishers Inc. (Copyright © 1927 by Harper & Row, Publishers, Inc.; renewed 1955 by Jennie Marie Berdahl Rölvaag.)

■ ABOUT THE AUTHOR

A fourth-generation South Dakotan, Tom Griffith brings to this guide a native's first-hand perspective of the state. An award-winning journalist and photographer, Griffith attended the University of London and graduated from the University of Wisconsin before pursuing a career in the newspaper business that took him to Montana and Arizona. He is a former Director of Communications for the Mount Rushmore Preservation Fund and is the author of three books about the memorial: *America's Shrine of Democracy, The Four Faces of Freedom,* and *A Sculptor's Son,* as well as of dozens of history- and travel-related magazine articles. Griffith and his wife, Nyla, live in the Black Hills, where they operate an advertising, marketing, and public relations firm. In their spare time, they enjoy trout fishing, motorcycling, and travel.

■ ABOUT THE PHOTOGRAPHER

Paul Horsted is a Black Hills–based photographer whose roots in South Dakota reach to the late 1800s, when his great grandparents farmed in the east-central part of the state. He first picked up a camera while in high school and has now been a photographer of South Dakota's people and places for more than 20 years. His pictures have appeared in publications such as *LIFE, American History*, and the *New York Times,* as well as in several books about Mount Rushmore, the Badlands, and the Black Hills, including the award-winning *Exploring with Custer: The Black Hills Expedition.* Paul and his wife and daughter reside in the woods near Custer, South Dakota.